"History Is Bunk"

To Jeff
Enjoy the reading!

Brusser

A VOLUME IN THE SERIES

Public History in Historical Perspective

Edited by Marla R. Miller

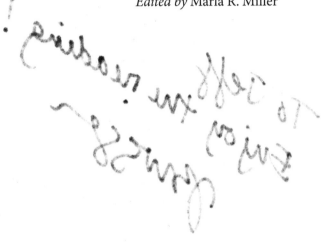

"History Is Bunk"

ASSEMBLING THE PAST
AT HENRY FORD'S
GREENFIELD VILLAGE

Jessie Swigger

University of Massachusetts Press
Amherst & Boston

Copyright © 2014 by University of Massachusetts Press
All rights reserved
Printed in the United States of America

ISBN 978-1-62534-078-8 (paper); 077-1 (hardcover)

Designed by Jack Harrison
Set in Adobe Minion Pro
Printed and Bound by Sheridan Books, Inc.

Library of Congress Cataloging-in-Publication Data

Swigger, Jessie.
"History is bunk" : assembling the past at Henry Ford's Greenfield Village / Jessie Swigger.
pages cm. — (Public history in historical perspective)
Includes bibliographical references and index.
ISBN 978-1-62534-077-1 (hardcover : alk. paper) —
ISBN 978-1-62534-078-8 (pbk. : alk. paper)
1. Henry Ford Museum and Greenfield Village. 2. Ford, Henry, 1863–1947.
3. Americana—Private collections—Michigan—Dearborn.
4. Inventions—Private collections—Michigan—Dearborn.
5. Technology—United States—History. I. Title.
E161.S95 2014
338.76292092—dc23
2014006035

British Library Cataloguing-in-Publication Data
A catalogue record for this book is available from the British Library.

Publication of this book and other titles in the series Public History in Historical Perspective
is supported by the Office of the Dean, College of Humanities and Fine Arts,
University of Massachusetts Amherst.

For Chris and Jack

Contents

Acknowledgments

My name may be the only one on the cover (well, except for Henry Ford's) but scores of people contributed to this project. I do my best to list them here, knowing that I likely forgot a few and hoping that those few will forgive me.

For guidance and support in the early stages of this project, I thank Steven Hoelscher at the University of Texas at Austin, along with Robert Abzug, Janet Davis, Elizabeth Engelhardt, and John Hartigan.

Writing *"History Is Bunk"* was a challenge, but it would have been impossible without the fantastic archivists at the Benson Ford Research Center, who have been enormously helpful over the course of my research. I am forever indebted to them. I am especially grateful to Stephanie Lucas, Linda Skolarus, Jim Orr, and Kathy L. Steiner.

I was honored that former administrators Harold K. Skramstad and Steven K. Hamp agreed to talk with me about their impressions of Greenfield Village. Their perspectives were an invaluable resource. I am also thankful to Anan Ameri for speaking with me about the relationship between The Henry Ford and the Arab American National Museum.

I am indebted and grateful to Marla Miller, editor of the Public History in Historical Perspective series, for her big ideas, provocative questions, and thorough edits. Howard P. Segal and a second reviewer also helped me think more clearly and precisely about the vexing landscape that is Greenfield Village. Clark Dougan did amazing work steering the project through the review process, and he and the editing and production staff at University of Massachusetts Press—Carol Betsch, Mary Bellino, Jack Harrison, and Sally Nichols—have made this work better at every stage of the process.

I am fortunate to work with colleagues at Western Carolina University who make me a better researcher and writer every day. Richard Starnes and Alexander Macaulay helped me find time (and money) to work on this project.

I also benefited from Richard Starnes's insightful comments and Vicki Szabo's inspiring questions. Andrew Denson offered his fresh perspective and encouragement throughout the writing process. Elizabeth McRae's brilliant comments, conversation, and culinary skills have made this book, and my life, much better.

I am also indebted to my family and friends. Keith Swigger introduced me to the joy of studying American history and gave me sage advice from beginning to end. Kathleen Swigger, Bob Brazile, Nathaniel Swigger, and Cindy Potter provided endless support and encouragement. Elena Past was a marvelous reader and the ideal hostess during my research trips.

Christopher Cooper's curiosity, kindness, and general enthusiasm for life were a constant source of inspiration. Chris read countless drafts and indulged me in thousands of conversations about Greenfield Village. He is my partner in the fullest sense of that word. As this work neared completion, our son, Jack Miller Cooper, was born. I wonder what museums will make an indelible impression on him, and look forward to seeing my favorite ones again through his eyes.

"History Is Bunk"

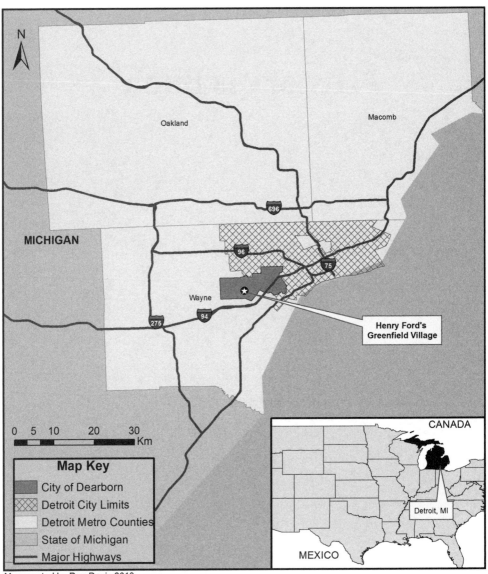

N

Oakland

Macomb

696

MICHIGAN

96

75

Wayne

275

94

Henry Ford's
Greenfield Village

0 5 10   20   30
Km

Map Key

City of Dearborn
Detroit City Limits
Detroit Metro Counties
State of Michigan
Major Highways

Map created by Ron Davis 2013

CANADA

Detroit, MI

MEXICO

Introduction

History is more or less bunk. It's tradition. We don't want tradition.
We want to live in the present, and the only history that is worth a
tinker's damn is the history that we make today.

— Henry Ford, 1916

Henry Ford's outdoor history museum, Greenfield Village, opened in Dearborn, Michigan, on a rainy October 21, 1929, just eight days before the stock
market crashed and plunged the nation into the Great Depression. Ford
scheduled the dedication to coincide with the fiftieth anniversary of Thomas
Edison's invention of the incandescent light bulb, and he named the ceremony
"Light's Golden Jubilee." The connection to Edison was apparent not only in
the choice of date, but also in the layout and focus of the village itself. In fact,
the centerpiece of the village was a replica of the laboratory in Menlo Park,
New Jersey, where Edison—Ford's mentor and friend—invented his famous
light bulb.[1]

On that October day, the almost five hundred guests who toured the village's twenty-eight buildings would have noticed that the landscape mirrored
that of a small town. Greenfield Village was, however, an imagined place.
Named after Michigan's Greenfield Township, where his wife, Clara, was born,
Ford's village was constructed in Dearborn, just a few miles from the farmhouse where he grew up and a short drive from downtown Detroit. Only a few
of the buildings represented local history, however; several were moved to the
village from across the country or, like the Menlo Park buildings, built on the
premises. The homes, artisan and industrial shops, and businesses were not
linked by geography or time period but, as the replica of Menlo Park suggests,
by Ford's personal interests. Guests might have also noticed that there were no
automobiles in the village. Ford excluded them to capture the period before

1

the arrival of his Model T and to indicate that there were aspects of modern life of which he was wary. He imagined a small town where his friends, mentors, and those he admired lived in harmony in a preindustrial age.[2]

The opening of Greenfield Village was widely covered by the national media and attended by a number of notable Americans, including President Herbert Hoover. The attention was unsurprising, given that by 1929 Ford was a celebrity himself. Born in 1863, Ford began his rise to fame when he opened the Ford Motor Company in 1903. In 1908 he revolutionized American life when he produced the Model T, a car affordable enough for the masses. In 1914, when Ford announced his Five Dollar Day, which doubled the average pay for autoworkers, he was heralded for his progressive labor policies. Two years later he solidified his reputation as a man of the modern age in the wake of public controversy over his declaration that history was "bunk." Curiously, a mere thirteen years later Ford opened a museum that paid homage to the past.[3]

The "Light's Golden Jubilee" ceremony was broadcast over 140 National Broadcasting Company radio stations. After speeches by President Hoover and the guest of honor, Edison, announcers Graham McNamee and Phillips Carlin told their audience that Edison, Hoover, and Ford were taking a carriage to the replica of the Menlo Park laboratory. Once inside, Edison reenacted the lighting of his first experimental lamp. Afterward, Hoover, Edison, and Ford joined the other guests in the banquet hall of the Edison Institute Museum, which was still under construction. Adjacent to his ideal small town Ford was building an indoor museum that would use more traditional display methods to chronicle the material culture that mattered to him. Once it was completed, visitors would find objects representing industry, agriculture, and the domestic arts.[4]

Even after it officially opened in 1929, Ford was not finished with Greenfield Village. For the first four years tours were given only upon request, but soon the demand was so high that he opened the village to the general public. On June 22, 1933, adults paid twenty-five cents and children ten cents to see Ford's "animated textbook." Ford continued to relocate and replicate buildings on the 260-acre property until 1945. When he died in 1947, the village encompassed eighty-six structures depicting America from the seventeenth through the twentieth centuries. Ford's construction of the site—from his decision to use the New England village as a model, to his exclusion of automobiles, to his mix of preserved and replicated buildings from across the country—spoke to both his critique of traditional written history and his reservations about the modern world. Greenfield Village used physical objects and buildings rather than written texts to communicate historical information, and in contrast to most written histories, which focused on the nation's political and military past, it privileged stories of invention and entrepreneurialism. Finally, the material culture on display celebrated the values and customs Ford feared the modern world was erasing, while touting the technological achievements and business practices he supported.[5]

When I first visited Greenfield Village and Detroit in 2005, I arrived knowing that the auto industry in general, and Henry Ford in particular, had brought thousands to the city with the promise of high wages. I also knew that Detroit was in the midst of a crisis brought about in part by changes to the same industry that once gave its residents unprecedented economic prosperity. I was prepared to see a city that, beginning in the 1940s, Michigan's white middle class had largely abandoned.[6]

A drive through the Motor City confirmed my preconceptions. Well before the 2008 stock-market crash, housing crisis, and government bailout, Detroit struggled. Abandoned stores, homes, and factories dominated the landscape. While there were some signs of urban rehabilitation—a community garden, some new restaurants, and Comerica Park (the new baseball stadium, completed in 2000)—it was clear that many former residents had used the vast network of local and interstate highways to escape to other parts of Wayne County or to the nearby counties of Macomb and Oakland. Here residents lived in what appeared to be economically prosperous suburban communities. Many of them had their own commercial centers, making it possible to avoid a trip to the urban core altogether.

Another prominent feature of the metro area was the ubiquity of Henry Ford's name. Residents drove on Ford Road, checked into Henry Ford Hospital when they were sick, and were educated at Henry Ford Community College. Despite the obvious failures of Ford Motor Company to deliver its promise of sustained economic growth, metropolitan Detroit continued to venerate the company and the man.

The city of Dearborn is just twenty minutes southwest of Detroit's center, on I-94. In 1917, Ford began construction of the Rouge Factory near what was then called Dearborn Township.[7] By 1927, when Dearborn, with approximately fifty thousand residents, reincorporated as a city, Ford Motor Company had relocated most of its operations from a plant in nearby Highland Park to the Rouge. Dearborn's residents had benefited, at least economically, from Ford's decision to build one of the largest industrial factories in the world. At Dearborn's center was a thriving commercial district bounded by corporate offices bearing the Ford Motor Company name and Ford's museums.[8]

What is today called The Henry Ford has been given a variety of titles over the years. Between 1929 and 1951 it was known as the Edison Institute. The indoor museum was initially called the Industrial Museum; the outdoor museum was the Early-American Village. Soon, however, the museum was renamed the Edison Institute Museum and Ford christened the village Greenfield Village. From 1952 to 1973, and again from 1981 to 2002, marketing materials referred to the complex as The Henry Ford Museum and Greenfield Village; in between it was the Greenfield Village and Henry Ford Museum. Finally, in 2003, the museum and village were collectively named The Henry Ford: America's Greatest History Attraction.[9]

After entering Greenfield Village, visitors can take several paths, but they might begin by walking through the preserved Wright Brothers' Cycle Shop, moved to Michigan in 1938, or the replica of Edison's Menlo Park laboratory completed in 1929. At the village's center, visitors find a large green space flanked by a general store built in 1857 in Waterford, Michigan, a courthouse from Postville (now Lincoln), Illinois, where Abraham Lincoln worked in the 1840s, and Martha-Mary Chapel, constructed for the village in 1929 and named after Henry's and Clara's mothers. To the west stand artisan shops, such as a cooper shop moved from Kingston, New Hampshire, in 1932, and a sawmill from Tipton, Michigan, built around 1850. And to the east are homes celebrating inventors, educators, and cultural innovators. For example, Noah Webster's home was moved from New Haven, Connecticut, in 1937, and the birthplace of textbook author William Holmes McGuffey was relocated from Washington County, Pennsylvania, and re-erected in the village in 1934.[10]

Despite the clear connection to Ford, only a few of the buildings have direct ties to Detroit: the Grimm Jewelry Store, which had been located on the city's Michigan Avenue from 1885 to 1931; the Owl Night Lunch Wagon, which served Detroit customers during the 1890s; a replica of the Bagley Avenue shop where Ford completed his first car, the Quadricycle, in 1896; a replica of Detroit's Edison Illuminating Company, where Ford worked from 1891 to 1899; and a replica of the Ford Motor Company building on Mack Avenue, which opened in 1903. The grounds convey little, if any, sense that Ford's fame and fortune originated in an urban setting. As an imagined small town, Greenfield Village encourages visitors to forget the metropolitan area in which it resides.[11]

Yet for me, the city haunted the village. I could not help but compare the past depicted on the landscape to the one beyond its gates. Inside, small-town life was celebrated as an ideal. Guides and placards intimated an interpretive theme that connected America's industrial innovation to economic progress, but if one began a journey to the village in Detroit, the premise was difficult to accept. Although Detroit was one of the poorest cities in the country, and the urban crisis was clearly linked to the local automotive industry's decline, in 2005 over a million people attended a museum that celebrated Ford and his company (fig. 1).[12] I found myself wondering what drew so many visitors

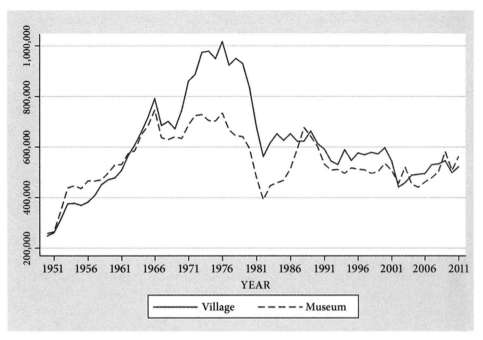

FIGURE 1. Visitor attendance at Greenfield Village, 1950–2011. Graph created by Christopher Cooper from data supplied by The Henry Ford.

to Greenfield Village, what they experienced when they arrived, and whether the obvious divisions between Detroit's urban core and its surrounding suburbs shaped their visit.

"History Is Bunk" explores Greenfield Village's long history, from Ford's initial conception in 1919, to the period following his death in 1947, to its most recent moniker, "America's Greatest History Attraction." The extensive history of the village illuminates the fascinating dialogue that occurs between audiences and those who build and administer representations of the past.

Greenfield Village originated in the mind of Henry Ford, and it was clearly his worldview that determined its design. Ford was also, however, both an innovator and a participant in a broader movement among preservationists, museum builders, and academics interested in venerating vernacular architecture, domestic arts, and technology to achieve a wide range of political and educational goals. Ultimately, Ford and others hoped to shape the present with their depictions of the past. But when Ford opened the gates of his village to the public and charged a fee, he invited audiences to participate in the construction of its interpretation. The fact that Ford chose to build a celebration of small-town life in a suburban community on the outskirts of a city made successful by the automobile industry said much about his worldview. But the location also shaped administrative decisions and visitor encounters in ways that Ford could not imagine. The history of Greenfield Village cannot be disentangled from the racial politics of Dearborn's city government and the urban crisis of Detroit. A consideration of Greenfield Village both in the context of and beyond Henry Ford demonstrates that its interpretation of the past evolved as a dialogue between a number of players including Ford, subsequent administrators, public historians, and visitors.

The longer history of Greenfield Village is found in the rich but largely understudied resources available at the Benson Ford Research Center. Documents such as oral reminiscences of former employees, annual reports, internal memoranda, marketing and education reports, and visitor surveys chronicle the site's history from the perspective of administrators, guides, and visitors in astounding detail.

Most scholarly treatments of Greenfield Village begin in 1929 and end with Ford's death in 1947, identifying it as exemplary of the movement among several of America's wealthy industrialists, beginning in the 1920s, to build outdoor history museums. Geoffrey Upward's *A Home for Our Heritage: The Building and Growth of Greenfield Village and Henry Ford Museum, 1929–1979* (1979), an institutional rather than an analytical study, is still an excellent starting point for those interested in a more complete history of the village. For most public historians, however, the site's relevance is linked to the early preservation and museum movements in the United States, although they disagree on its place in those movements. For example, in his essential *Preservation Comes of Age: From Williamsburg to the National Trust, 1926–1949* (1981), Charles Hosmer argues that while Greenfield Village was one of the first outdoor history museums in the United States, it is best studied on its own terms. It differed from other early examples, such as John D. Rockefeller Jr.'s Colonial Williamsburg and Albert Wells's Old Sturbridge Village, because Ford mixed replicas with preserved buildings to depict a "way of life" rather than to re-create a real time and place from the past.[13]

Mike Wallace has written most critically about Greenfield Village. Like Hosmer, he discusses it in the context of other outdoor history museums built in the late 1920s. He notes, however, that Ford's goals differed widely from those of Rockefeller, who sought to accurately preserve Williamsburg's colonial buildings at the moment before the Revolution, to encourage patriotism, and to celebrate the nation's planter elite. In contrast, Ford used Greenfield Village to celebrate his particular brand of corporate capitalism. While companies like General Motors and Chrysler adopted "newer forms of organization" that relied heavily on investors, and marketed to customers by offering cars in different models and colors, Ford clung to his original business practices. He believed that Ford Motor was successful because it remained a "family firm" and was reluctant to replace the Model T with newer designs. Wallace maintains that Ford included buildings like the replica of Menlo Park and artisan shops from the eighteenth century to demonstrate the connections between "his business approaches and traditional ways."[14]

In her history of historic preservation, Diane Barthel concurs with Wallace, arguing that Greenfield Village was "designed to communicate mythic truths concerning America's greatness and the inexorable path of progress." Greenfield Village and other outdoor history museums were staged symbolic utopias created by wealthy industrialists who "felt the subjective need to create the village that would complement their new 'lord of the manor' status." Ford made a case for celebrating himself and the nation's inevitable improvement, Barthel suggests, when he decided to show change over time by mixing preserved and replicated buildings from the seventeenth through the twentieth centuries.[15]

Historians of the Ford Motor Company and biographers of Henry Ford have argued that Ford used Greenfield Village to promote himself and his business and to present the public with his worldview. David L. Lewis, for example, notes that like Ford's interest in collecting antiques and in old-fashioned dancing, Greenfield Village was an example of his efforts to keep himself and his company in the public eye year-round. In his history of Ford's village industries (nineteen small-scale factories in rural communities less than sixty miles from the Rouge), Howard P. Segal contends that Greenfield Village embodied its founder's commitment to both agriculture and industry. Ford's biographer Vincent Curcio has linked Ford's pacifism and the village, writing that "Ford started his museum to counteract the notion that history was only an accounting of violent confrontation and conflict." For another biographer, Steven Watts, the village and Ford's general interest in the past were evidence of his confliction about the modern industrial world. "The village and the museum," Watts observes, "helped assuage his personal sense of loss by locating the past and present in a single, upward trajectory in which ordinary people created extraordinary advances," while the village simultaneously provided a "*temporary* escape from the intensity of modern life." Ford could play with the past at Greenfield Village, knowing that he could always return to the "material comforts made possible by the River Rouge."[16]

In this study I build on the work of these scholars and others by connecting Ford's personal trajectories more specifically to his construction of Greenfield Village. Ford's xenophobia, his particular sense of the ideal relationship between business owners and employees, his disdain for the city, and his faith in hard work and the inventor-entrepreneur, for example, often informed not only his business practices but also his activities outside of the Ford Motor Company. Ford's decision to build Greenfield Village was the culmination of a long-standing interest in the past, one driven by his complex view of the present. I also tie Ford's personal views and experiences more firmly to individual buildings within the village and consider the degree to which Ford's original vision continued to influence administrators and visitors after his death.

Closer inspection of Ford's interest in the past, and an examination of Greenfield Village after 1947, also helps settle debates about its place in broader histories of the preservation movement and history museums. Greenfield Village both shaped and was shaped by prevailing trends in public history. Although its landscape was clearly influenced by his personal interests and views, Ford used display methods mirroring those used by Americans and Europeans since the late nineteenth century. Further, during the early twentieth century many preservationists, curators, and academics argued for the value of industrial history and the material culture of everyday life. Ford was both part of and a leader in this broader movement. Those who administered Greenfield Village after Ford's death in 1947 reacted to changes in the field during their own careers. From the 1950s to the 1970s, the site's administrators—like their counterparts elsewhere—hired more professionally trained staff and instituted interpretive programs aligned with America's Cold War politics. And during the 1980s, administrators answered calls from the academy, social activists, and public historians to include more histories of women, people of color, and the poor at museums. Scholars have long argued that representations of the past are heavily shaped by the needs of the present. Greenfield Village was no different; the trends that shaped other public history sites also influenced Ford and those who followed him.[17]

"History Is Bunk" also examines how the village's location in the Detroit metropolitan area affected administrators and audiences. Since the mid-1990s, historians such as Thomas Sugrue, Lisa McGirr, Matthew Lassiter, and Kevin Kruse have argued that cities are best understood not only through an investigation of the urban core, but also through an examination of their suburbs. By the same token, suburban institutions are also shaped by their urban centers. Greenfield Village's history, then, has been informed by the history of the greater Detroit area.[18]

I also consider how the national reputation of Detroit and the local reputation of Dearborn influenced the dialogue between administrators and their audiences. Studies of changing race and class relationships in the metropolitan area provide the backdrop for my discussion of how administrators responded to changes in both cities. For example, Kevin Boyle's *Arc of Justice: A Saga of Race, Civil Rights, and Murder in the Jazz Age* (2005) shows that many of Detroit's white residents worked to maintain the color line in housing and labor as early as the 1920s. These tensions solidified during the 1940s. In 1943, racial tensions, a housing crisis, and the challenges of wartime working conditions led to a riot lasting three days. The 1943 riot was, as Thomas Sugrue argues in *The Origins of the Urban Crisis: Race and Inequality in Postwar Detroit* (1996), a harbinger of events to come. By 1967, frustrations created by the departure of the auto industry and the white middle class to suburban enclaves, problems with the city's infrastructure, and "limited housing, racial animosity, and reduced economic opportunity for a segment of the black population" were entrenched. The public image of Detroit as a center of racial conflict solidified on July 23, 1967, when the city's residents rebelled against urban inequality. Over the course of the next five days, the insurrection resulted in 43 deaths, 467 injuries, over 7,200 arrests, and the destruction of more than 2,000 buildings.[19]

The history of Dearborn captures the divisions between the urban core and the suburbs. By 1927, when the Rouge Factory was largely complete, Ford Motor Company managers, the white working class, and immigrants from the Arab world had settled in Dearborn. African Americans working at the Rouge, however, often lived in Detroit's predominantly black neighborhood, Paradise Valley, or moved to Inkster, a small community adjacent to Dearborn. Beginning in the 1940s, the color line in Dearborn was maintained by an openly racist mayor, Orville Hubbard, and his political machine. From 1941 to 1977, "Orvie" mounted a successful crusade to keep African Americans from purchasing homes. Greenfield Village administrators, however, did not see Dearborn's local image as an impediment to attracting visitors. In fact, it was only after 1967 that administrators began to consider the relationship between their visitor population and their location. Declines in visitation were often blamed on the negative publicity generated by the events of 1967 in Detroit, and marketing and public relations campaigns now specified the village's location as Dearborn or Michigan. Beginning in the 1980s, however, a new administration worked to build relationships with other Detroit-area tourist attractions and to embrace the site's location in the metro area. And by the late 1990s, a politically active and expanding Arab American population defined Dearborn as ethnically diverse. Audiences, too, were affected by the public image of both Dearborn and Detroit. Depending on the visitor, and the time, the reputation of either city might have discouraged a visit to Greenfield Village.[20]

Finally, this book contributes to broader conversations about the role museum-goers play in constructing the past. Historians have long been interested in how Americans use history. In 1931, Carl Becker warned historians that "Mr. Everyman is stronger than we are, and sooner or later we must adapt our knowledge to his necessities." At the urging of Becker and others, historians expanded their research to include histories beyond studies of politicians and military heroes. By the 1970s, many historians were practicing what Eric Foner and others have referred to as the "new histories," which emphasized the "experience of ordinary Americans" and "quantification and cultural analysis." These historians often pitted themselves against "consensus" historians of the past and traced their conceptual origins to the social movements of the 1950s and 1960s. As Ellen Fitzpatrick has effectively shown, however, these histories in fact had clear links to scholarship produced in the Progressive era.[21]

More recent historians have dedicated their research to understanding how Americans use the past in their everyday lives in more concrete ways than their predecessors. For example, in their landmark study, *The Presence of the Past: Popular Uses of History in American Life* (1998), Roy Rosenzweig and David Thelen interviewed over fifteen hundred people and asked them how they used and conceived of history. They found that the "most powerful meanings of the past come out of the dialogue between past and present," and that Americans were more likely to respond to representations that appealed to their individual experiences and knowledge. David Glassberg has also considered the various forces that connect Americans with the past in *Sense of History: The Place of the Past in American Life* (2001), contending that Americans care deeply about history "because it addresses fundamental, emotionally compelling questions about their past that they need to authenticate and confirm." Rosenzweig, Thelen, and Glassberg offer useful frameworks for thinking about how audiences constructed the past at Greenfield Village. Visitors often reacted to their encounters with buildings and objects by making connections to their own pasts, their present needs, or their sense of how the past *should* appear.[22]

"*History Is Bunk*" also joins studies conducted by anthropologists who have evaluated the success of new history programs initiated at museums in the 1970s and 1980s. For example, Richard Handler and Eric Gable, in *The New History in an Old Museum: Creating the Past at Colonial Williamsburg* (1997), claim that despite efforts to include the stories of enslaved African Americans, interpreters' obsession with presenting the facts meant that audiences were left without a sense of the social, cultural, and economic forces that shaped history. Cathy Stanton's ethnography of public historians working to revitalize postindustrial Lowell, Massachusetts, using "culture-led redevelopment" draws on encounters with guides, local residents, and visitors. Stanton finds that public historians were most successful at implementing progressive interpretations of the past when they recognized their own socioeconomic position in Lowell and the contemporary problems facing the city. Similarly, in "*History Is Bunk*" I examine the efficacy of the new history programming instituted at Greenfield Village and the degree to which administrators were influenced by local politics as they developed those initiatives.[23]

This book also contributes to the emergent field of museum visitor studies. As George E. Hein has noted, the first known scholarly examination of visitors occurred in 1881, when Henry Hugh Higgins, a founder of the British Museums Association, reported his observations of visitors at the Liverpool Museum (a natural history and art museum) with the goal of furthering the educational mission of the museum. But Higgins's research was anomalous; Hein also points out that between 1900 and 1950 fewer than three dozen articles on visitors were published in education and psychology journals. Most scholars recognize Harris H. Shettel and his colleagues' 1968 study of the United States Office of Education exhibit "The Vision of Man" as the turning point in visitor studies, because they were the first to outline methodologies for studying visitors with the goal of improving exhibits' educational value. Beginning in the 1970s, scholars in education and psychology expanded their research on visitors' engagement with museum exhibits, yet studies of how visitors experienced museums before the 1970s remain limited.[24]

In this book I explore the complex processes through which visitors constructed their encounters with the site's landscape and narrative. Drawing on the unique resources available at the Benson Ford Research Center, "History Is Bunk" adds a historical dimension to the study of museum visitors. Henry Ford and other administrators presented their various versions of the past, but the way these messages were consumed changed over the course of seven decades. During Ford's lifetime, guides at Greenfield Village kept daily records of visitors; after his death, administrators recognized the essential role that visitors played in the site's continued success. Consequently, beginning in the late 1960s they hired marketing firms to conduct visitor surveys, and these surveys expose the experience of people who came to see Greenfield Village.

I have chosen to concentrate on the history of Greenfield Village, as opposed to the indoor Henry Ford Museum, because it better focuses the fascinating process by which the past is constructed. The interpretive approach used in the museum followed more traditional models of display by placing objects behind ropes and glass cases. When it opened in 1933, visitors moved among, for example, rows and rows of farming equipment to see how incremental changes improved the machinery.[25] In contrast, Greenfield Village constructed an alternative past in which the twentieth century's most famous inventors lived side by side. Visitors were encouraged to immerse themselves in the past and to think thematically; in the village, the personal memories, historical information, and expectations that visitors brought with them often played a central role in shaping their experience. Administrators either maintained or altered the village as they pursued both educational and financial goals. Consequently, staff consistently sought feedback from their visitors with the aim of understanding what they desired from their encounters at the village. Over time, messages sent and received changed as visitors and administrators negotiated the past.

Any history of Greenfield Village must begin, of course, with Henry Ford. The chapters in Part I examine the village during Ford's lifetime. In chapter 1 I consider how Ford's nostalgia for his youth, his abhorrence for urban life, and his views on ethnicity and education shaped his business practices, his philanthropies, and his other efforts to preserve the past. This chapter also demonstrates that, despite Ford's claims to the contrary, Greenfield Village was a typical history museum. By the time Ford began building the village in 1926, designers of period rooms and historic house museums had long been using interior decoration and historic preservation to promote various political agendas. Among museum builders, academics, and preservationists, industrial history and the material culture of everyday life were already being lauded as important sources for understanding the nation's history. Ford was just one of many interested in preserving objects and buildings to communicate both nostalgia for the past and concerns about the present.

In chapter 2 I examine the construction and operation of Greenfield Village from 1926 until Ford's death in 1947, arguing that Ford's personal views were reflected on the village's landscape. While a small staff assisted him in the construction and daily maintenance, Ford was the primary decision maker; he determined everything from the location of each building to what products were made for sale as souvenirs. Consequently, the landscape embodied his complicated and at times contradictory worldview. By 1947, the village articulated Ford's beliefs and values concerning the small town, education, the ideal relationship between business owners and their employees, and self-made manhood.

In chapter 3 I argue that between 1929 and 1947 the past was up for grabs at the village. Daily visitors included local residents, schoolchildren, dignitaries, celebrities, and national and international tourists. Although Ford presented visitors with his version of the past, records indicate that encounters with the buildings and objects on display often veered from the industrialist's vision. Visitors consistently saw themselves as authorities on the pasts they encountered and often drew on their own memories to either confirm or challenge the histories with which they were presented. Drawing on tour scripts and journals kept by guides, I describe how visitors experienced Greenfield Village during Ford's lifetime. Ironically, the interpretive emphasis on the power of the individual, the landscape, and the approaches used by guides actually encouraged visitors to consume messages that differed from those communicated in the official narrative.

Part II examines the village after 1947, the year of Ford's death. Chapter 4 chronicles the expansion of the site's administration and staff and their struggle to define the village's purpose and audience. Administrators sought to meet new standards in the field, to build their educational programming, and to attract more visitors. They hired more staff trained in museum work, added new departments, and created clearer lines of authority within the organization. New special events, buildings, and rides aimed both to educate and to entertain. Administrators also began to distance their institution from the Detroit metro area after the summer 1967 riot. Advertising campaigns focused on the Dearborn location, and worked to separate Greenfield Village from Detroit's tourist attractions. Administrators ignored Dearborn's growing reputation as a racist community, which increasingly defined the image of the metro area's suburbs. At the end of the 1970s, alterations to the grounds and the site's narrative reinforced Ford's largely conservative version of the past.

Chapter 5 draws on visitor surveys to demonstrate that by the late 1960s administrators successfully marketed the village to a specific kind of visitor. While guides recorded moments that suggested encounters were diverse during the 1930s, by the late 1960s visitor surveys showed that demographics and comments were strikingly homogeneous. An analysis of 3,837 comments indicates that visitors continued to see themselves as authorities, but instead of grounding that authority in a certainty about the past, they viewed themselves primarily as consumers and focused on the village's ability to meet their needs as a leisure activity. Typical visitors constricted the potential for disparate interpretations. Yet it was during this period that visitor experiences, on the whole, adhered more closely to Ford's vision. Visitors expressed a desire to consume a sanitary and entertaining past, free from the kind of conflict and culture that defined urban spaces such as Detroit.

In chapter 6 I examine efforts to implement interpretive programs influenced by what historians defined as "new histories" beginning in the 1980s. The site's board of trustees responded to shifts in the academy and decreasing attendance by appointing Harold K. Skramstad, who held a doctorate in American civilization, president. Skramstad spearheaded a campaign to change the site. A working historical farm was added, staff wrote a "new curriculum" based on more rigorous historical research, and the African American Family Life and Culture program was instituted. Administrators reconsidered their isolationist approach and sought to integrate Greenfield Village into the Detroit metro area tourist market. Staff felt that the success of programming about African American history was dependent on the participation of local black residents. As Skramstad recounted in an interview, he and his team initially faced challenges from the Dearborn city government, which continued to enact policies aimed at preventing African Americans from using the city's public spaces. By the time he departed in 1996, however, a shift in Dearborn's policies, the political activities of the city's Arab American community, and the village administration's commitment to building relationships with the metro area's black community signaled change.

The final chapter traces the changes at Greenfield Village after Skramstad's departure in 1996. The new president, Steven K. Hamp, spearheaded the addition of special events and material culture highlighting the site's function as a leisure space while maintaining much of the new history programming. By the time Hamp resigned in 2005, the village and the indoor museum were rebranded as "The Henry Ford: America's Greatest History Attraction." That same year, the Arab American National Museum, a Smithsonian Institution affiliate, opened in Dearborn, forever altering the city's reputation as a white enclave and perhaps encouraging a more diverse audience to visit Greenfield Village. In 2006 the Henry Ford appointed its first woman president, Patricia E. Mooradian, who oversaw the addition of more programming celebrating African American history and the continued expansion of the village's options for entertainment.

By the early 2000s, the past depicted at Greenfield Village continued to remain, for the most part, distant from the history of Detroit. In many ways, the village offered an escape from the troubling present of the metropolitan area rather than a framework for understanding its origins. Given the seriousness with which administrators considered the interests and desires of visitors, however, it would seem that this was the version of America that the site's audiences wanted to consume.

Henry Ford once challenged the veracity of history by calling it "tradition." But in many ways Ford worked to popularize his version of tradition by procuring the objects and buildings that were important to him. He hoped Greenfield Village would communicate values he feared were disappearing from American life—in many cases by his own hand. As an employer, Ford was well known for his controlling approach, and he might have hoped that by creating his own museum he could also direct society at large. But once he opened the site to the public, Ford ensured that his tradition would be assembled not only by him but also by the administrators who followed and by those who paid to see it. At Greenfield Village, many different constituents negotiated the meaning of the pasts on display and collectively determined which ones were bunk.

I

"GOODBYE TEXTBOOKS, HELLO AMERICA"

The Ford Years

The Bentley High School of Kansas came to the Village in a bus on the back of which they had painted, "Goodbye Textbooks, Hello America."

— "Greenfield Village Journal," June 4, 1934

1

The Fording of American History

We're going to start something. I'm going to start up a museum and give people a true picture of the development of the country. That's the only history that is worth observing, that you can preserve in itself. We're going to build a museum that's going to show industrial history, and it won't be bunk! We'll show the people what actually existed in years gone by and we'll show the actual development of American history from the early days, from the earliest days that we can recollect up to the present day.

— Henry Ford, 1919

In 1915 Henry Ford began purchasing land along the bottomland of the Rouge River, near the townships where he and his wife, Clara, grew up. By 1926, buildings collectively known as the River Rouge Factory complex covered over one thousand acres. Designed primarily by the renowned architect Albert Kahn, at its height of production the main Rouge Factory employed over a hundred thousand workers, and used vertical integration to mass-produce Ford vehicles at affordable prices. The Rouge was celebrated as a technological triumph and a symbol of the modern consumer society.[1]

In 1926, Ford surveyed 260 acres of empty land sitting a little over a mile from the Rouge Factory. He had very different plans for this tract. In stark contrast to the Rouge, which embodied the possibilities of industrial capitalism, on this bucolic meadow Ford planned to build a museum complex to preserve objects and buildings that would chronicle the American past. An indoor museum would trace the nation's industrial and domestic history through the display of machinery and household objects, while an outdoor museum, which would come to be named Greenfield Village after Clara's birthplace, would use an imagined small-town landscape to show how those objects had once been used in everyday life.[2]

When Ford chose the site for his museum he was sixty-three years old, famous, and wildly wealthy. He had made his fortune by building and selling automobiles, inventions that had come to define the modern age. The Ford Motor Company was incorporated in 1903, and five years later Ford had initiated mass production of the Model T.[3] Accessible and practical, the Model T forever changed daily life. By 1914 he was celebrated not only as an inventor but also for his announcement that Ford Motor Company workers would receive five dollars a day—more than double the average paid to automobile employees at the time. As his biographer Vincent Curcio notes, Ford instituted the new pay scale to decrease turnover at his factories, to prevent his workers from unionizing, and to control his workforce. Not everyone was eligible, however; only married men, single men under twenty-two supporting siblings or widowed mothers, and women supporting families qualified for the new rate. Further, to receive the wage employees were required to adhere to Ford's edicts regarding personal behavior, abstaining from alcohol, making regular deposits into a savings account, and maintaining a clean home. Staff made routine house visits to ensure that eligible employees were following Ford's mandates. Still, international accolades followed Ford's announcement of the new pay scale. Politicians, journalists, and ordinary people from the political left and right praised Ford for his fair labor practices as well as his industrial achievements.[4]

Given the Model T's associations with modernity, Ford's decision to build a history museum may seem strange. But while Ford frequently touted the benefits of technology, by the time he began developing Greenfield Village he had already established himself as a critic of the world he helped make. Not long after launching his Five Dollar Day, he began to denounce many of the social and cultural changes wrought by the industrial revolution. He believed that the modern age was stripping important customs and social structures from American life, ones that he saw as the foundations of his own success. Like many others, Ford thought solutions for the present could be found in the material culture and traditions of the past. To ensure that the objects and values he found relevant were preserved, he began collecting books and antiques and restoring buildings, efforts that set the stage for the construction of Greenfield Village.

The World according to Ford

One of Ford's primary fascinations with the past was his own biography; indeed, he published his autobiography in 1922, at the relatively young age of fifty-nine. Ford saw his own childhood as ideal. It is unsurprising, then, that he eventually populated Greenfield Village with buildings from his early life.[5]

Henry Ford was the first of five children, born in 1863 to William and Mary Ford. By that time, William had a small farm in Springwells Township, near Dearborn. William had immigrated to the Detroit area in 1846 from Ireland, and with hard work and help from family he moved slowly but surely into the middle class. In 1861 he married Mary Litogot, whose parents were Belgian immigrants. By then, William had amassed 120 acres and built a seven-room white clapboard frame house. He grew wheat, corn, and hay, and also raised livestock, smoked meat, and maintained a small fruit orchard. Henry expressed no desire to follow in his father's footsteps. But he viewed his rural upbringing with great nostalgia, and his father's and his own rise up the economic ladder and his pleasant memories of growing up on a farm would be reflected both in his initial interests in collecting the past and his later construction of Greenfield Village.[6]

When he turned seven, Henry began his education at the one-room Scotch Settlement School; the school—a decade old when Ford enrolled in 1871—was named for the Scottish immigrants who initially settled the area in the early nineteenth century. Ford's favorite teacher was a large, intimidating man named John Brainard Chapman; when Chapman took a job at the nearby Miller School in 1873, Ford followed him. Chapman and the other instructors relied on a series of books that Ford would later go to great lengths to collect: the McGuffey Reader series.[7] The author of the series, William Holmes McGuffey, was born in 1800 in Washington County, Pennsylvania, in a small log cabin. He went on to receive a degree in philosophy and language from Washington College (now Washington & Jefferson College) and to work as a university professor and administrator. In 1835, McGuffey signed a contract with the Truman & Smith publishing company in Cincinnati to compile a spelling book and four school readers.[8] The series ultimately included six books; the first four focused on reading instruction, and the last two were literary anthologies. McGuffey's readers used the phonics system. Students sounded out letters first, then encountered one-syllable words alongside pictorial illustrations, and so on. By 1844 the series was so popular that a fifth reader was commissioned. McGuffey died in 1873, and six years later the sixth reader was published. From 1839 to 1920 the McGuffey Reader series was used to teach some 116 million children to read in schools across the country, reaching the height of popularity during the Gilded Age. The readers (and readings) also provided students with moral instruction, which, as one of Ford's biographers, Steven Watts, has observed, shored up the lessons Ford was learning at home from his mother, Mary.[9]

Although she died when he was twelve, Mary Ford remained a central figure in Henry's life. He would go on to speak of her teachings in interviews and to build a chapel at Greenfield Village to honor her memory. Watts has argued that Mary was guided by a Victorian ethos that required emotional self-control, frugality, and hard work with the purpose of contributing to the market economy, values that young Henry adopted. Ford's efforts to collect the past would be driven by a desire to find material symbols of these values.[10]

Armed with a Victorian sensibility, an eighth-grade education, and a distaste for farm work, if not farm life, Henry Ford set out at age sixteen to make his fortune in Detroit, which by 1879 had grown to become an industrial city of over one hundred thousand people. He worked a series of jobs, all taken with the intention of expanding his skills as a mechanic. In 1882 he returned to the family farm, and three years later he met Clara Jane Bryant at a local dance. After a brief courtship they were engaged, and in 1888 they married.[11]

In September 1891, Ford secured a position as an engineer in the Detroit branch of the Edison Illuminating Company, which provided electricity to the city's residential market. He was thrilled to find employment at one of Thomas Edison's companies, not only because it offered the chance for good wages and further training in mechanics but also because Ford was a longtime admirer of the self-made inventor. Henry and Clara moved to an apartment on John R. Street and soon settled into a routine in one of America's fastest-growing cities. Two years later they had their first and only child, a son they named Edsel, after Ford's childhood friend Edsel Ruddiman.[12]

In 1893, Henry Ford was thirty years old and had just been promoted to chief engineer at Edison Illuminating's Detroit facility. That same year Ford—and over twenty-seven million others—attended the Chicago World's Fair. There he saw countless inventions heralding the new industrial age, including a two-cylinder Daimler engine from Germany. The engine inspired Ford with an idea that would make him millions: a horseless carriage.[13]

Amidst the numerous displays of modernity assembled on the fairgrounds in Chicago's Jackson Park, Ford might have also viewed a symbol of America's past: "The New England Log Cabin and Ye Olden Time Restaurant." The colonial-themed restaurant was the latest iteration of the emerging "period room" installation gaining traction in museums, fairs, and expositions. In 1863 the U.S. Sanitary Commission—an organization that raised money to support efforts to aid wounded Union soldiers—had been the first group to re-create a colonial kitchen to inspire Unionist sentiment and raise funds for their cause. Soon, many others were constructing and displaying colonial-themed rooms. A decade later, the "colonial kitchen" was expanded to an exhibit called the New England Home and Modern Kitchen at the Philadelphia Centennial Exposition, and in 1880 George Sheldon and the Pocumtuck Valley Memorial Association in Deerfield, Massachusetts, offered tours of a colonial kitchen, "old time" parlor, and bedroom. The popularity of the period room was propelled by the Colonial Revival, a general enthusiasm for all things colonial that culminated with the Centennial but continued through the end of the nineteenth and into the early twentieth century. The period room became a unique vehicle for communicating patriotism, nostalgia, and nationalism. Years later, when Ford undertook his first preservation projects, perhaps he would recall this. Now, however, upon returning to Detroit, Ford—inspired by his viewing of the combustion engine—began spending his spare time tinkering with a four-cycle engine. In June 1896 he drove his horseless carriage, known as the Quadricycle, through the city.[14]

That August, Ford, together with Alexander Dow, who managed the Detroit branch of Edison Illuminating, traveled to New York City to attend a convention of representatives from Edison electrical companies across the nation, including Thomas Edison himself. Edison was a self-taught inventor and offered many men a model for success in the industrial age, including Ford, who was particularly impressed by Edison's use of scientific theories to create practical machines for the common man. On the third evening of the convention, Ford somehow secured an invitation to an exclusive dinner honoring Edison. During the dinner, Dow mentioned that Ford had built a gas-powered car, and Edison began to ask Ford questions. This first meeting would turn into a friendship that lasted until Edison's death in 1931. Ford was so inspired by Edison that he would eventually name his museum complex the Edison Institute after the venerated inventor.[15]

In 1899, Ford left Edison Illuminating for the Detroit Automobile Company, with a manufacturing plant on Cass Avenue. William H. Murphy, a Detroit lumber baron, along with other investors, agreed to finance Ford's effort to build an automobile for mass production. After two years of work, however, Ford had not succeeded. Many of the stockholders left the company, and in 1901 the Detroit Automobile Company dissolved. Still, Murphy continued to support Ford, and in November he financed the Henry Ford Company. Three months later, Ford was still perfecting his prototype. The delay led Murphy to hire Henry M. Leland, director of Leland & Falconer, a Detroit machine shop, to inspect Ford's work. As Steven Watts maintains, when Leland was hired Ford began to see the company's board as a "hostile, elitist group who wanted to constrain him."[16] Ford's experience at the Henry Ford Company, Watts argues, led to a lifelong resentment of wealthy business investors and a "dogged self-reliance." "On the one hand," Watts observes, Ford was "clearly attuned to the new business world of mass manufacturing and mass marketing, especially in its technological dimension," but "defined himself, in the best traditional terms, as a self-reliant individualist who owned his property, earned his way, and was beholden to no one." Ford's approach to and beliefs about business would find their way into his collecting endeavors.

In 1902, Ford became famous for his "999" race car, which he had been building while working under Murphy. The car featured an eighty-horsepower engine, and when Barney Oldfield drove it to victory in the Manufacturer's Challenge Cup race held in Grosse Pointe, Michigan, Ford received national attention. The celebrity he gained, along with the financial support of a local coal dealer, Alexander Y. Malcolmson, set the stage for what would become one of the most successful automobile companies in American history.[17]

By the spring of 1903, Ford had set up an "assembling plant" on Mack Avenue in Detroit and completed a prototype called the Model A. On June 16, 1903, Ford, Malcolmson, John and Horace Dodge (owners of the Dodge Brothers Machine Shop), and Charles H. Bennett (president of the Daisy Air Rifle Company), along with several of Malcolmson's relatives and business associates, became the original investors in Ford Motor Incorporated. The next year Ford moved operations to a new plant on Detroit's Piquette Avenue. In 1908 the company announced the release of the car that would come to define Ford the company and Ford the man: the Model T.[18]

The Model T was an immediate commercial success. The demand was so high that Ford quickly realized a different manufacturing process would be required, and in 1910 a third new plant, in nearby Highland Park, opened. At the Piquette plant, Ford workers had built each car from the ground up, but at Highland Park each worker was assigned a specific task that he completed while standing in a stationary position on an "assembly line." The new method allowed Ford to produce over twenty thousand Model T's the first year and over eighty thousand by 1912. By 1913, Highland Park's workforce of sixteen thousand produced half of the cars in the United States.[19]

As he garnered more wealth and fame, Ford turned his attention to pursuits beyond the Ford Motor Company, working not only to build his fortune but also to influence the present. Of particular concern to him was the nation's and Detroit's growing immigrant population. Between 1880 and 1900, nine million immigrants from eastern and southern Europe had arrived in the United States looking for work in the expanding manufacturing industry. Their entrance sparked waves of anti-immigrant sentiment that eventually found their way into federal policies. Immigrants initially settled in urban areas, and with the rise of ethnic politicians and cultural shifts, tensions between rural and urban residents increased. Ford's xenophobia, anti-Semitism, and strident belief in the benefits of small-town life reflected these national tensions.[20]

In 1890, the year before Ford found work at Edison Illuminating, the Jewish population in Detroit was relatively small, hovering around one thousand (out of 206,000).[21] But just as he was finding success in Detroit, many residents were increasingly expressing anti-Semitic and xenophobic beliefs. During the 1890s, Irish and Polish residents attacked Jewish peddlers, newspapers often printed ethnic slurs, and the city's Baptist residents launched a conversion campaign.[22]

As the historian Neil Baldwin points out, Ford came of age during a period when many Americans, driven by anxieties about a rapidly changing society, adopted xenophobic beliefs and practices as a salve. Ford was one of those, and by 1914 he was doing his part to Americanize immigrants through his company's Sociological Department. The department was initially created to determine whether Ford Motor employees qualified for the five-dollar pay rate by meeting the standards Henry Ford established for their private lives. Advisers conducted routine domestic inspections to assess and evaluate each employee's level of cleanliness, thriftiness, and general ability to follow the "path of righteousness." Watts argues that Ford was prompted to create this unprecedented department by a "grab bag of early-twentieth-century reform impulses." The department's work certainly drew on the emerging field of social science. (The American Sociological Association was established in 1905.) But Ford also used the department to demand adherence to a moral tradition based on nineteenth-century Victorian values and to teach his workers the "new values of consumer abundance." Although the department's most controversial activities ended by 1921, it continued to operate in some form through 1948.[23]

One of the Sociological Department's tasks was to classify employees by ethnic origin. In 1916, for example, the department categorized the 40,903 employees working at the Highland Park plant. Fifty-eight different nationalities were listed, including 1,437 Jewish employees, 106 "Negro" employees, and 555 Syrian employees. The high number of Syrian workers was the result of successful recruiting efforts in the Middle East by Ford Motor and other automobile companies, and this population would continue to grow and shape the identity of both Detroit and Dearborn in the twentieth century. Of course, the department's method for categorizing immigrants, as Jonathan Schwartz observes, was flawed because staff generally conflated an employee's nationality and his or her ethnicity. The largest number of employees were listed as "Americans" (16,457), but "Americans" often included second- and third-generation immigrants. Thus the categories said more about how Ford Motor staff identified workers than about how workers saw themselves.[24]

The Sociological Department staff was also responsible for administering the Ford English School. As Neil Baldwin notes, the school's graduation ceremony exemplified Ford's belief that education was also a tool for Americanization. In 1917 the ceremony was held in a baseball field near the Highland Park plant. A wood, canvas, and papier-mâché "Melting Pot" was constructed at second base; flights of steps led to the pot's rim. Seated in grandstands, families and coworkers looked on as a brass band played and a procession entered from a gate on the side of the field. Immigrants dressed in their native garb sang songs from their nations of origin and marched forth while a Ford employee, dressed as Uncle Sam, led the group up to a ladder where they descended into the "pot." Soon, these Ford Motor Company workers reemerged as "Americans," wearing the company badge and sporting derby hats, coats, pants, vests, stiff collars, and polka-dot ties.[25]

In 1914, the same year that Ford established the Sociological Department, he engaged in a public battle over the books that he had read in school—the McGuffey Reader series. In the spring of 1914, one of Ford's friends, Rabbi Leo Franklin, led Detroit's B'nai B'rith Anti-Defamation League (ADL) in a campaign to eliminate *The Merchant of Venice* from local public schools, arguing that the character of Shylock supported anti-Semitic beliefs. That fall, the ADL sent circulars to school superintendents explaining why *The Merchant of Venice* was unfit for classroom use, claiming that the play depicted Shylock as a representative of the Jewish people and a conglomerate of negative stereotypes. Ford opposed Franklin because some editions of the McGuffey Reader series included excerpts from the play. Along with the story of Shylock, Ford would have read a number of other stories in McGuffey's readers, such as "Paul's Defense before King Agrippa," that cast Jews as avaricious or dangerous opponents of Christianity. Baldwin argues that Ford's defense of the readers was indicative of his childhood exposure to anti-Semitism in the pages of McGuffey's readers, and linked his prejudices to what would become his first collecting endeavor.[26]

The same year that Rabbi Franklin and the ADL launched their campaign, Clara Ford, who also learned to read using McGuffey's series, was watching some schoolchildren when she suddenly remembered the verse "Hear the children gaily shout / 'Half past four and school is out.'" This memory inspired a search for the edition containing the verse. While the episode with Rabbi Franklin reminded the Fords of their affection for the series, Clara Ford's memory sparked the couple's curiosity about its contents. In tandem, these two events led the Fords to a lifelong interest in collecting copies of the readers that shaped their early educational experiences. By the 1930s, the Fords owned 468 McGuffey's readers in 145 editions.[27]

The Fords left Detroit for Dearborn Township (nine miles away) in the spring of 1915. They lived in the Ten Eyck farmhouse while they waited for construction of their Fair Lane estate to finish. By the spring of 1916 the estate, where Ford would live until his death in 1947, was complete. The move coincided with Ford's ongoing construction of the nearby Rouge Factory. In many ways, the decision to leave Detroit represented Ford's desire to escape the modern city and foreshadowed what would become an obsession with collecting and replicating the past that defined his youth.[28]

Just after Ford began collecting McGuffey's readers and entered into the public tangle over their contents, he sought a more explicit avenue for expressing his opinions, and in 1916 he purchased the *Dearborn Independent.* Part newspaper and part magazine, the weekly *Independent* included articles on national and local events, poetry, and short stories. In each issue, "Mr. Ford's Own Page" expressed the industrialist's views on politics, the economy, society, and culture. Ford did not personally write any of the articles that appeared in the *Independent;* a journalist, William J. Cameron, composed "Mr. Ford's Own Page." As Watts observes, Cameron "displayed a unique talent for interpreting and expanding his boss's cryptic 'intuitions,' as Ford often described them." Vincent Curcio notes that while Ford used a ghostwriter, the ideas communicated were clearly his: the *Independent* "published no opinion except by his instigation and with his approval." That Ford did not personally write any of the articles, Curcio adds, became a useful tool for combating negative publicity. Despite "considerable evidence that each issue was read to him before it was published," Ford could deny authorship when it became "convenient and necessary." Edited by Edwin G. Pipp from the *Detroit News,* the paper soon boasted a wide national audience, which grew to 650,000 by 1924 and then to 900,000 in 1926.[29]

In 1920, Ford told Pipp that he planned to publish a series of articles titled "The International Jew: The World's Foremost Problem," which would run for two years. Pipp soon resigned in protest, but Ford was undeterred. The articles forever altered Ford's public image as friendly and folksy, but they also garnered him new fans; the *Independent's* readership expanded during the era of these anti-Semitic articles. Because nativism and xenophobia pervaded progressive and conservative thought during the early years of the twentieth century, the paper found support from a wide spectrum of readers. Many, however, were outraged. Along with Jewish leaders like Louis Marshall and Herman Bernstein, the Federal Council of Churches condemned the series. After resigning, Pipp made a number of public remarks calling Ford's crusade "unfair, cruel, bigoted, and contrary to the American spirit."[30]

While Ford attacked Jews most directly, his beliefs often reflected a broad-based xenophobia that was tied to a critique of cultural change. In "Mr. Ford's Own Page: Change Is Not Always Progress," he argued that the "trouble with us today is that we have been unfaithful to the White Man's traditions and privileges." He went on to blame immigrants for "sapping" Americans' "courage and demoralizing our ideas."[31] Ford claimed that immigrants were responsible for the decline of America's cultural traditions and proposed that the agrarian economy of the past offered a remedy. In "What Makes Immigration a Problem," he explained that in the past immigrants had settled farmland, which Americanized them by indoctrinating them to the benefits of property ownership, independence, and capitalism. In contrast, contemporary immigrants moved to cities, where ethnic enclaves and political leaders allowed them to preserve their cultural identities. The solution, he proposed, was to force immigrants to move to the West. By farming and working the land, or living in small towns, they would learn how to be true Americans. "Settled on the land," he argued, "the immigrant would more readily imbibe American ideas and would be less amenable to the . . . racial rulers" who already controlled local politics. Ford's obsessions with both rural life and immigration were perhaps drawn from his belief that his biography offered a model for others to follow. The child of immigrant parents, he believed that his own experiences growing up on a farm led him to great success.[32]

Ford's critique of urban life went further. In "Mr. Ford's Own Page: The Small Town," he announced that "every social ailment from which we suffer today originates and centers in the great cities." And in "The Modern City—A Pestiferous Growth," he argued that along with economic disparity, the city also created a false sense of community. It failed to combine the three great arts—"Agriculture, Manufacture, and Transportation"—and aesthetically, it was the most "unlovely sight this planet has to offer." He provided a solution, however, writing that "we shall solve the City Problem by leaving the City."[33]

Ford put his ideas into practice by building many of his own factories in suburbs and small towns. For example, he constructed the Rouge Factory not only to expand production but also because he felt he could exercise more power on the outskirts of Detroit. Beginning in 1918, he built other factories in small towns, which he called his "village industries." Nineteen of these villages were located in southern Michigan. One, named Fordlandia, was located in Brazil. Many of the villages were built along rivers and not more than sixty miles from the Rouge complex, and each contained a factory that produced parts for the Ford Motor Company. Ford hoped to create communities that combined the latest technology with the values and pace of small-town life. They were, as Howard P. Segal has argued, "sophisticated *alternative* forms of emerging technological society, intended as models for others to emulate."[34]

Despite his call for immigrants to become farmers, Ford feared that Jewish leaders were moving to control the agricultural sector. In "Jewish Exploitation of Farmers' Organizations," Ford claimed that Aaron Sapiro, the founder of the National Council of Farmer's Cooperative Marketing Associations, was the leader of a Jewish conspiracy to create one large farming cooperative, thus ruining the independent farmer.[35] Sapiro filed a defamation lawsuit against Ford, and in 1927 the trial began. Ford decided to settle out of court, and at the end of 1927 he stopped publishing the *Independent*. He even issued a public apology, albeit a half-hearted one. He blamed his employees and professed ignorance about the paper's anti-Semitic articles, claiming, "Had I appreciated even the general nature, to say nothing of the details, of these utterances, I would have forbidden their circulation without a moment's hesitation, because I am fully aware of the Jewish people as a whole."[36] Still, in 1938 Ford accepted the Grand Cross of the Order of the German Eagle from Adolph Hitler. He was the first and only American citizen to receive the award, the highest honor the Third Reich could bestow on a non-German citizen.[37]

Ford established his xenophobia, anti-Semitism, and disdain for urban life both through the company policies enforced by his Sociological Department and his hobbies. Increasingly, he turned his attention to the material culture of the past to express his worldview. Just as his village industries were offered as an alternative to urban industrialism, Ford used the past to demonstrate an alternative economic, social, and cultural vision for the present.

Is History Bunk?

Although Ford expressed nostalgia for his own past when he began collecting old McGuffey's readers in 1914, he was openly skeptical and critical of history as a larger scholarly enterprise. In 1916 the *Chicago Tribune* reported Ford's memorable pronouncement that "history is more or less bunk." This assertion was just one of many that the *Tribune* identified as evidence of Ford's ignorance. An editorial titled "Ford Is an Anarchist," which criticized Ford's controversial pacifist stance during World War I as uninformed, unrealistic, and a threat to the nation, led the industrialist to file his most famous lawsuit. The unnamed author condemned Ford's recent announcement that Ford Motor Company employees who joined or were recruited by the National Guard to fight in border disputes with Mexico would lose their place at the company and would be required to reapply if they returned. The author went on to claim that "a man so ignorant as Henry Ford may not understand the fundamentals of the government under which he lives," and that the "proper place for so deluded a human being is a region where no government exists except such as he furnishes." The editorial finally proposed that Ford move to "Chihuahua, Mexico." Ford filed a million-dollar libel lawsuit to prove that he was neither an anarchist nor ignorant.[38]

The trial was still pending two years later when Ford launched a senatorial campaign as a Democrat from Michigan. The *Tribune* continued its criticism, now in an effort to squelch Ford's political ambitions. In an August 1918 editorial, the *Tribune* listed excerpts from "authenticated interviews with Mr. Ford" that exemplified the degree to which his pacifism and ignorance rendered him unprepared for public office. Included among the excerpts was Ford's statement that "the word 'murderer' should be embroidered on the breast of every soldier and every naval sailor."[39]

The following year, the libel case against the *Tribune* finally went to trial in Mount Clemens, Michigan. To show that Ford was indeed ignorant, attorney Elliott G. Stevenson placed him on the stand and spent eight days asking him a variety of questions. Ford failed miserably, particularly when it came to a series of questions testing his knowledge of American history—unsurprising given his admitted disdain for the subject. Some of Ford's most notorious mistakes included his erroneous dating of the Revolutionary War to 1812 and his assertion that Benedict Arnold was a writer. But the jury ultimately sided with Ford. Although the defense provided ample evidence that he was ill informed, they failed to offer convincing proof that he was an anarchist. Still, the jury awarded him only six cents, and in that regard the trial ended in a draw. From a public relations perspective, however, Ford was more successful, as many small-town papers and residents came to his defense.[40]

Still, Ford was bothered by assertions that he was uneducated, and by critiques of his statement about history in particular. He spent the next two decades trying to reframe and clarify his infamous comment about history in various interviews, proclaiming that it was written history that he objected to, which he felt excluded important narratives. The history represented in textbooks, he asserted, was "bunk" because it ignored the histories of technology, invention, and agriculture.[41]

Ford presented his interest in the daily lives and material culture of ordinary people as singular. Yet by the early twentieth century, several historical societies and museum professionals were challenging the traditional conventions of aesthetics, which had long dominated the collections of prominent art and history museums. William Sumner Appleton's Society for the Preservation of New England Antiquities had been working to preserve vernacular colonial architecture since 1910, for example. Even academics, whom Ford claimed were at fault for writing inaccurate and incomplete histories, had long been questioning a disciplinary focus on political and military history. James Harvey Robinson's *New History* (1912), which argued that history should be useful to the present, crystallized a disciplinary shift that Ellen Fitzpatrick contends had been in the works for almost two decades. By the time Ford was calling for his vision of a new history, many professional and lay historians had long been engaged in similar pursuits.[42]

Along with the trial, another event that likely sparked Ford's interest in preservation was the impending destruction of his birthplace. In 1919, when the construction of a new road threatened to destroy his childhood home, he had it moved two hundred feet. He had a replica of a windmill on the property designed, and he excavated the land to search for any remaining traces of material culture. As he refurbished the farmhouse's interior, Ford became obsessed with finding a replica of the woodstove that heated the family dining room, the Starlight No. 25.[43]

Ford's preservation of his own home foreshadowed his interest in replicating and preserving the homes of other inventors, scientists, and educators. His fascination with the home also followed a national trend. In fact, by the late 1910s, many believed that the home was central to the formation of self-made men. One manifestation of that notion had been the nation's historic house movement. Although it began in the antebellum period—perhaps most famously with the establishment of the Mount Vernon Ladies Association in 1853 to preserve George Washington's Mount Vernon—the historic house movement in the United States grew exponentially after the Civil War. The 1876 Centennial raised new interest in the homes of the founding fathers, and between 1870 and 1890 the number of historical societies more than doubled. Societies regularly purchased historic homes for their headquarters, and often turned them into museums as well. By the early 1900s the surge in historic homes was related to progressives' desire to change the domestic culture of eastern European immigrants and to move away from Victorian consumerism. As Patricia West has noted, even popular magazines like the *Ladies' Home Journal* argued that these styles "had the power to uplift character and contribute to civic virtue." Furniture manufacturers tapped into these politics and used catalogs, magazines, and representations of the past to sell furniture in the Arts and Crafts and Colonial Revival styles. The politics of the historic house movement were similar to Ford's, and in just a few years Ford would begin preserving and replicating houses for more pedagogical purposes.[44]

Soon Ford had organized a team of agents not only to locate the Starlight No. 25, but also to develop a broader collection of everyday household furnishings, clothes, machines, and vehicles from the eighteenth and nineteenth centuries. William W. Taylor was a member of the Society for the Preservation of New England Antiquities and had worked as a curator for the Harrison Gray Otis House in Boston before he was hired by Ford to search the Northeast for collectibles. Frank Vivian, who joined the San Francisco branch of the Ford Motor Company in 1918, traveled the western states looking for objects Ford might find interesting. Israel Sack, who owned an antique store in Boston, found furniture for Ford; Charles Newton, one of Ford's lawyers, managed any legal paperwork that was required and accompanied Ford on his quests for farming equipment; and Harold Cordell worked as bookkeeper and coordinator of these reconnaissance missions. Ford charged his staff with combing the country for items that he found emblematic of *his* American past.[45] Initially, he stored the excess items in the tractor plant office on Oakwood Boulevard in Dearborn, and by 1921 the building was filled with plows, player pianos, traction steam engines, hunting rifles, inkwells, and grease lamps.[46]

As Ford would later admit, there were many objects that represented histories that he did not believe to be bunk. These histories had, unsurprisingly perhaps, clear connections to his personal experiences. They reflected the political, social, economic, and cultural views that shaped his professional life and other philanthropies, ones that promoted his vision of self-made manhood, his belief that small towns were ideal landscapes, and his faith in the inventor-entrepreneur and in industrial and technological progress.

Ford's collecting was initially driven, it seems, by sentiment, but soon his efforts took on a more polemical tone. He first experimented with historic preservation on a large and more public scale in 1923 at the Wayside Inn in Sudbury, Massachusetts. The inn had been made famous when Henry Wadsworth Longfellow immortalized it in his *Tales of a Wayside Inn* (1863), in which several friends gather on an autumn evening and recite poems around the fire in the parlor of a venerable hostelry. Readers quickly identified the characters as Longfellow's friends, and the inn as Howe's Tavern in Sudbury. Longfellow's popularity led many to visit the site, and in 1896 a Massachusetts wool merchant, Edward Lemon, purchased the building and renamed it with the intention of creating a "mecca for literary pilgrims." Lemon was largely successful, and throughout the early 1900s many artists and writers were inspired by the inn's literary heritage. When Lemon died the inn passed into the hands of his wife, but she soon found it too difficult to manage, and in 1922 a trust, which included men like B. Loring Young, speaker of the Massachusetts House of Representatives, and politician Charles Francis Adams, was formed to save the property. To save the property in perpetuity, the trustees wrote letters to wealthy Americans well known for their interest in New England heritage, including Henry Ford. When he bought the building in 1923, Ford told reporters that he planned to restore the Wayside and the 140 acres that came with it as a "historical museum."[47]

Beyond the plea from the trustees, Ford's interest in the Wayside Inn was almost surely grounded in his experience at school and his ongoing investment in McGuffey's readers. As Angela Sorby's study of the role of poetry in shaping American education curriculum shows, when Ford began attending his one-room schoolhouse in 1871, the memorization and recitation of poetry was often used to teach reading skills. Longfellow's poetry was a mainstay of the McGuffey series, so Ford likely read and perhaps memorized some of Longfellow's work. Given his interest in preserving pasts associated with his childhood memories, the Wayside Inn was an unsurprising project.[48]

Shortly after restoring the inn, Ford began using it as a place to entertain. On the second floor, a ballroom allowed Ford and his friends to engage in one of their favorite activities: dressing and dancing as colonial Americans. Ford occasionally provided the music by playing the fiddle. He also hired a local resident and dance instructor, Benjamin B. Lovett, to teach him and Clara the quadrille, caprice, and mazurka. And yet, in another indication of Ford's complex relationship with the past, what may seem a harmless hobby was in fact tied to his xenophobia. His colleagues remembered that during his anti-Semitic tirades, Ford often spoke of the importance of preserving colonial music as a tool for combating Jews in the entertainment industry who, he alleged, were using jazz and the film industry to subvert American cultural traditions.[49]

Soon Ford opened the Wayside Inn to the public. For a fee of twenty-five cents adults could tour the historic site, and children could enter for free. But Ford continued to operate the inn as a restaurant and hotel, too. In 1924 guests could eat dinner for $2.50 or have afternoon tea for $1.50. Alternatively, guests could purchase "the American plan" (a phrase Ford coined), which included a room and meals. Prices ranged from six to seven dollars depending on whether guests stayed on the first or second floor. The inn could accommodate up to twenty-two guests.[50]

Ford not only preserved the inn but also added furniture and buildings from the surrounding area he felt were historically significant. For example, in 1924 he decided to move the furniture from Ebenezer Burrill's home in Swampscott, Massachusetts, to the grounds of the Wayside Inn. According to reporters, Ford chose the Burrill home because it was the "social center of the town" during the eighteenth century. That same year he moved two other dwellings from North Kingstown, Rhode Island—the Sanford and Congdon homes—to the Wayside. John Sweet, who was one of the first Europeans to settle in Rhode Island, originally owned the Sanford home. The original owner of the Congdon place, Richard Smith, built the first trading post in North Kingstown.[51]

The Burrill furniture and the Sanford and Congdon homes were not defined by their national fame. Instead, it was local folklore and history that marked them as significant and important, and this was enough for Ford. He was interested in buildings that were typical and that defined vernacular architecture. Ford would repeat this pattern when he chose buildings for inclusion at Greenfield Village. While most of the structures were connected to famous men, a few were simply archetypes of small-town life.

Ford also believed that the one-room schoolhouse was the ideal educational setting. In 1926 he purchased a little schoolhouse in Winchendon, Massachusetts, which he claimed was the one mentioned in one of his favorite boyhood poems, "Mary Had a Little Lamb." Ford had charged his researchers with determining whether the poem was fact or fiction, and he came to believe that they found the real Mary of the poem as well as its author: eleven-year-old Mary Sawyer and twelve-year-old John Roulstone. Although Sarah Josepha Hale, the editor of *Godey's Lady's Book,* had clearly written the poem and was the first to publish it in her 1830 collection *Poems for Our Children,* Ford contended that Roulstone and Sawyer had conceived of the first lines, and that in discovering the poem's actual history he had also located the schoolhouse, which he would reopen on the grounds of the Wayside Inn.[52]

Four years later Ford did open a school in Sudbury, one that included not only the schoolhouse but also the other buildings on the property, which Ford had by then expanded to some three thousand acres. Instruction at the Wayside Inn School for Boys exemplified Ford's signature mix of progressive and traditional pedagogies by offering hands-on instruction in a colonial setting. A *New York Times* reporter, Eunice Fuller Barnard, described the school during a visit, writing that thirty-one boys between ages twelve and seventeen from "different national and racial stocks" were living "in apparent harmony with one another and with the eighteenth century pine, pewter and Puritanism of their surroundings." Barnard observed that the boys learned to sew, to do their own washing, farm, and build radios, motors, and furniture, and the school's superintendent told the *Times* that the students were "given a balanced amount of academic and technical study."[53] These early efforts in Sudbury were harbingers of things to come. Ford's use of the past to celebrate his personal values, his interest in preserving vernacular architecture, and his desire to use historic settings for educational purposes would find fuller fruition at Greenfield Village.

Beginning in 1923 Ford turned his attention to two new projects closer to his Fair Lane estate in Dearborn. First, he purchased the one-room Scotch Settlement School, which he had attended as a young boy, and reopened it. Students from ages three to six were taught using the pedagogical style that was coming to define Ford's approach to education. Students read *McGuffey's First Reader* and engaged in hands-on learning activities. The following year, Ford bought the 1836 Botsford Inn and forty-one acres surrounding it. Located a few miles west of Detroit on Grand River Avenue in Farmington, Michigan, the Botsford Inn was a large, two-story wood-frame structure with a balcony stretching across a broad facade. Ford financed the inn's restoration, intending to turn it into a museum and hotel along the same lines as the Wayside Inn. Plans for development came to a halt when it was discovered that the city's sewer and water lines did not yet reach Grand River Avenue. Consequently, although the Botsford was occasionally used for private parties, the building remained closed to the public until 1934.[54]

Ford's preservation of his childhood home, his antiquing, his addition of buildings to the Wayside Inn property, his re-opening of the Scotch Settlement School, and his preservation of the Botsford Inn set the stage for a much larger project close to home: the construction of a museum complex in Dearborn Township. The site would draw on some of the same approaches he used at the Wayside Inn, and would reflect his interest in social engineering. It would also establish Ford as a participant in two international movements aimed at broadening the definition of what counted as history and at displaying that history in a setting that attempted to re-create the past on the landscape.

The Edison Institute and the Museum Movement

By 1925, Ford was committed to building a museum complex that would expand on his earlier preservation activities. Named after his friend Thomas Edison, the Edison Institute that Ford came to envision would include an indoor museum chronicling the nation's technological history and an outdoor museum that represented how those technologies were used in everyday life. While Ford touted the complex as unique for its time, the museum and the village were, in fact, exemplary of transnational movements to expand the definition of history and to move objects outside of glass cases and into the world.

Ford hoped to display domestic implements in his outdoor history museum to demonstrate the objects that shaped everyday life. In this desire, too, he followed a budding national trend: by 1924, administrators of the Metropolitan Museum of Art—taking cues from the popularity of period rooms and historic houses—had already opened the American Wing, a series of rooms that re-created scenes from American daily life (albeit of a high style) by featuring domestic American furniture from the late seventeenth to the early nineteenth centuries. Though it was partly rooted in contemporary anxieties about immigration and Americanization, the American Wing also elevated everyday material culture to the status of art.[55]

Ford also argued that his decision to show chronological shifts in agriculture and industry by displaying various iterations of farming equipment was unique. But by 1925, the year before he determined the location for the indoor museum and the village, the material culture of the industrial revolution had long been collected and placed in museum settings abroad. That year, the historian Charles H. Richards called for American museum professionals to construct sites like those standard across Europe, presenting case studies of the Conservatoire des Arts et Métiers in Paris, the Science Museum in London, the Deutsches Museum in Munich, and the Technisches Museum in Vienna. Richards argued that similar museums were necessary in the United States because "to attempt to present these things through books is unsatisfactory and tame." Instead, he wrote, the processes of industry must be "revealed to the eye and set forth in the simplest and clearest possible fashion," through the physical display of objects. Only then, he proposed, can we understand the changes wrought by the industrial revolution.[56] While we don't know whether Ford read Richards's work, he was certainly not the first to lament the lack of industrial history museums.

Julius Rosenwald, a philanthropist and the chairman of Sears, Roebuck and Company, was directly inspired by Europe's industrial museums. In 1911, Rosenwald toured the Deutsches Museum in Munich with his son, who was particularly impressed with the hands-on aspects of the exhibits. In 1926, Rosenwald pledged $3 million for the construction of an industrial museum in Chicago, in the Palace of Fine Arts building that had been constructed for the 1893 world's fair. That same year, the city's South Park District passed a $5 million bond to restore the building. The Chicago Museum of Science and Industry, replete with hands-on exhibits, opened in 1933.[57]

Ford, then, was part of a movement of professionals and philanthropists who argued for a historical narrative that included industrial and technological developments. At Greenfield Village he planned to expand on the idea behind the period room and the historic house to re-create an entire small town from the past. He collected not only homes but also shops, public buildings, and schools. Although Ford was the first to open an outdoor history museum in the United States, by 1925 such sites had long been used overseas as tools for displaying the past. Artur Hazelius had opened the first outdoor history museum in 1891 in Stockholm, and by 1928 approximately 150 outdoor museums existed in Sweden alone.[58]

Closer to home, just as Ford was beginning his work on Greenfield Village he was asked to consider another project—returning the architecture of Williamsburg, Virginia, to its eighteenth-century origins. The idea for Colonial Williamsburg had emerged much earlier than Ford's plan for Greenfield Village. In the early 1900s, the Reverend W. A. R. Goodwin, rector of Bruton Parish Church, worried that Williamsburg's colonial architecture was disappearing. In 1905, Goodwin restored his church, and he developed a lifelong interest in preservation. After a brief period in Rochester, New York, Goodwin returned to Williamsburg and found a deteriorating local economy. He believed that heritage tourism would offer a solution to the city's financial problems while preserving its historic architecture. He was also fueled by anxieties similar to Ford's—fears about what he saw as an expanding movement of anarchy and socialism caused in part by immigration.[59]

In 1924, Goodwin approached both Henry Ford and John D. Rockefeller Jr. with his restoration plan. Ford—having already conceived of creating his own site—declined, although Goodwin continued to appeal to him through

1925. For Ford, Greenfield Village was a far more appealing project because it allowed him to reconstruct the past on his own terms, while at Colonial Williamsburg he would be confined by a verifiable history rooted in a specific time period and place. Rockefeller, however, took on the project, believing that the site offered an opportunity to educate Americans about what had been lost due to industrialization most specifically. After a decade of restoration activity, he would open Colonial Williamsburg to the public in 1934.[60]

During construction, and as the two sites began to welcome visitors in the 1930s, Rockefeller and Ford remained interested in each other's projects. The Ford family had a long history with the Rockefellers. Douglas Brinkley notes that Ford was an admirer of John D. Rockefeller Sr., and that Edsel Ford and the younger Rockefeller shared an interest in aviation and philanthropy. The relationship between the two families extended to their historical projects. John D. Rockefeller Jr. was in attendance at the Light's Golden Jubilee ceremony, and in 1935 Kenneth Chorley, Colonial Williamsburg's vice president, wrote to Ford and thanked him for visiting Williamsburg. Chorley reminded Ford that he and other Williamsburg staff planned to visit Greenfield Village soon. It seems, then, that the presidents and staff of the first two outdoor history museums in the United States had a collaborative and collegial relationship.[61]

Rockefeller's and Ford's approaches to architectural preservation differed widely. Like Greenfield Village, Colonial Williamsburg preserved architecture and the interiors of homes and buildings to re-create scenes from the past. What set Williamsburg apart not only from Greenfield Village but also from later outdoor history museums was Rockefeller's decision to employ professional architects to restore the buildings. In contrast, Ford, for the most part, hired men without professional training. Both museums mixed documented information with popular mythologies to create a narrative about the past, but Williamsburg's buildings would meet more rigorous standards of authenticity defined by the emerging profession of historic preservation.[62]

The degree to which Ford influenced other large-scale preservation projects is difficult to ascertain, but the men at the forefront of these projects often moved in the same circles. For example, at around the same time that Goodwin was developing his plan for Williamsburg, Frank Boyden, the headmaster of Deerfield Academy in western Massachusetts, attempted to expand preservation in the town of Deerfield. Inspired by the partnership between Goodwin and Rockefeller, Boyden sought financial contributions from the wealthy parents of one of his students. When Henry N. Flynt, a New York lawyer, enrolled his son in Deerfield Academy in 1936, Boyden quickly cultivated a friendship with him. By the early 1940s, Flynt and his wife, Helen Geier Flynt, were purchasing old homes and consulting with professionals in the decorative arts to restore them to their original state. The result was the museum now known as Historic Deerfield. During the restoration process, the Flynts purchased many of their antiques from Ginsberg & Levy in New York City, the same shop frequented by Ford, Rockefeller, and other wealthy collectors of the period.[63]

Nearby in Southbridge, Massachusetts, Albert B. Wells and his three brothers also consulted with Ford and Rockefeller as they began constructing an outdoor history museum, Old Sturbridge Village. The Wells family had made its fortune from the American Optical Company. In his leisure time, Albert Wells collected machinery from the colonial period, and his large collection soon needed more space than the family home could provide. After conferring with Rockefeller and Ford in 1936, the Wells family decided to build an educational outdoor museum based on an early New England village. The family created reproductions of buildings, but focused more on providing an educational experience than adhering strictly to architectural history. Ten years later, Old Sturbridge Village opened to the public. Visitors saw an ideal New England village that included buildings from a variety of local sites. Its interpretation mixed fact with popular myths, and its goal was to inculcate visitors not only with colonial material culture but also with the values that the Wells family believed a functional American citizenry required.[64]

Throughout the 1940s, many other outdoor museums would be completed, planned, or under construction. In 1944, Stephen Clark opened the Farmer's Museum in Cooperstown, New York. Clark worked with staff from the New York State Historical Society and others to re-create a typical 1800s Otsego County town. While Clark, like Ford, did not try to preserve or re-create an actual place, he focused on collecting buildings from a general county and time period.[65] Mystic Seaport, in Mystic, Connecticut, had been home to the Marine Historical Association since the late 1920s, but after the association acquired a whaling ship in 1941, staff began developing plans to re-create a nineteenth-century seafaring community. Henry Hornblower II, a Boston stockbroker, founded Plimoth Plantation, Inc., in 1947 (the year of Ford's death), and soon construction began on a re-creation of the Pilgrims' first settlement in the New World. Certainly these institution-builders owed some debt to the model pioneered by Ford at Greenfield Village.[66]

When Ford began constructing Greenfield Village and the museum in 1926, he was guided by nostalgia for his rural upbringing and his anxieties about modernity. While he did not want to return to the past, he certainly believed in its value. His worldview, expressed in his policies at the Ford Motor Company and in the *Dearborn Independent,* along with his early forays collecting and representing the past, suggested the village's form, in terms of both the material culture it would display and the messages Ford hoped it would send.

Biographers of Ford and scholars of public history have noted that Greenfield Village was one of several outdoor history museums built during the
1920s, but their studies point more often to the village's singularity rather than
its connection to broader trends among preservationists, museum builders,
and academics. Just as Ford was not the only man who recognized the commercial value of the automobile, he was not alone in his mission to display
America's colonial, industrial, and pastoral pasts. While Ford viewed his
interest in the objects that shaped daily life and technology as innovative, by
the 1920s there had long been calls for similar shifts in what constituted the
historical record. Ford and others mixed reproduced, constructed, and preserved buildings at outdoor history museums. Ford's project was novel in the
sense that it reflected one man's sense of the past and how it should be used in
the present. But it was also, in terms of form, content, and display, an amal-
gam of practices under development since the late nineteenth century. Greenfield Village links several trends: the call for academic histories that treated
the lives of ordinary people seriously; a movement to preserve preindustrial
landscapes, architecture, and material culture; and a push to use objects and
real-world experiences as educational tools. Greenfield Village's history, then,
tells us about much more than Henry Ford.

2

A Permanent Pageant of America

This village is the first step toward the realization of a great project on which Henry Ford has been working for many years—the assembling of a permanent pageant of America. Besides, it is to serve as a part of a technical school illustrating the development of the domestic and industrial arts in America. It is easily, in its fullness, the most tremendous adventure in historical presentation that has ever been undertaken.

— SAMUEL CROWTHER, *Ladies' Home Journal* (1928)

In 1927, the year after Henry Ford determined that Greenfield Village would be built on his land in Dearborn, he began dedicating his energies to its design. One of his intentions was to venerate Thomas Edison, the kind of man Ford felt was ignored in traditional histories. Ford planned to celebrate his friend and mentor by restoring and transplanting Edison's Menlo Park laboratory—where between 1876 and 1886 Edison invented the telephone transmitter, phonograph, and incandescent lamp—from New Jersey to Dearborn. Unfortunately, with the exception of a photographic studio where the bulbs for Edison's first incandescent lamps were blown, the Menlo Park laboratory, carbon shed, carpenter shop, and library had met various fates that made preserving them impossible. Undeterred, Ford decided to create replicas using original drawings and photographs. Edison himself collaborated on the plans, directing Ford to Francis Jehl, a former assistant at the laboratory from 1878 to 1879 and again in the early 1880s. Jehl was still working for the Edison Illuminating Company in Europe, but arrived in Dearborn in 1928 to help supervise construction. He would continue working at Greenfield Village until his death in 1941.[1]

Ford used a variety of techniques to imbue the Menlo Park replicas with a sense of historical authenticity. Most famously, he had seven boxcar-loads of New Jersey clay moved to Dearborn and spread over the planned location for the Menlo Park buildings. When one shutter from the library was found in New Jersey, Ford snapped up that as well, and he placed a single slat from the original shutter in each of the ones on the replica. In many ways, Ford's approach reflected his Victorian sensibilities. The New Jersey clay and the shutter slat were treated as relics whose authenticity would somehow emanate to the rest of the replicated building and infuse it with historical meaning.[2]

The Menlo Park replica set the stage for how the past would be preserved at Greenfield Village. Often, Ford restored buildings in their entirety, but he also asked his staff to build replicas that incorporated what was left of the building, or installed material culture that linked the copy to the original structure. Ford would preserve, replicate, and construct buildings that were associated with his friends, his heroes, and his own life. In many cases, the men he wanted to celebrate were, like Edison, still alive, and he would use their memories to guide how he assembled his pageant of America.

That Ford chose to replicate the Menlo Park laboratory was unsurprising given his friendship with Edison. Other choices, such as his decision to move two brick slave cabins to the site, were unexpected. While the physical construction of the past would follow patterns similar to those used to build the Menlo Park complex, the wide range of his worldview guided Ford's thematic approach. Ultimately his project would include public buildings, artisan and machine shops, homes, and schools that embodied his idealization of small-town life, his view that education should blend traditional and progressive pedagogy, his belief that inventor-entrepreneurs were central to a company's success, and his veneration of self-made men. Ford's "tremendous adventure in historic preservation" was grounded very much in his present.[3]

Ford's Architects

When he began to design and build Greenfield Village, Ford relied primarily on the assistance of Edward Cutler, a glasscutter at Ford Motor Company. Cutler was born in London, Ontario, in 1882; after attending the Cincinnati Art Academy, he found steady employment at various glass companies until the outbreak of World War I. In 1915, at the age of thirty-three, Cutler was hired as a windshield cutter at Ford's Highland Park plant. He requested and eventually received a transfer to the drafting department, and in 1922 he and his drafting group relocated to Dearborn, where they worked on Model T designs in one of the tractor buildings at the Rouge Factory complex. Ford often spent time with Cutler's group because the building was also one of the holding areas for Ford's antiquing projects. The two men struck up a friendship when Cutler was recommended by his drafting boss to design a windmill for Ford's Fair Lane estate in Dearborn. Cutler's ability to sketch quickly and in great detail impressed Ford, and soon he was involved in Ford's other historical projects, most notably sketching several of the buildings that were restored at the Wayside Inn in 1924.[4]

In 1927, after Ford chose the site for his outdoor museum, he asked Cutler to draw a landscape that looked like a "village." Cutler's design mirrored an archetypal nineteenth-century New England village by placing public buildings and businesses around a common green space and populating surrounding streets with homes and shops. Cutler later recalled that "the idea was to have a New England village, as near as I could gather," and that "the idea of a commons was one of the first considerations, and a church, a town hall, and a hotel." Ford approved Cutler's design, and the former windshield cutter moved from relative obscurity to the center of one of Ford's grandest philanthropic endeavors.[5]

As plans for Greenfield Village took shape, Ford and Cutler selected a location for the adjacent indoor museum. As we've seen, the Edison Institute Museum would use objects to demonstrate chronologically the development of American manufactures and domestic arts. Ford hired Robert O. Derrick of Detroit, the only professional architect who would play a significant role in the project, to design the museum. Derrick and Ford had met in 1928, while they were both sailing to Europe on the ocean liner *Majestic*. Unlike Cutler, Derrick had extensive professional training. After obtaining degrees from Yale and Columbia, he joined the New York architectural firm Murphy & Dana. Shortly after World War I, he opened his own firm in Detroit. At the time the two men met, the thirty-eight-year-old Derrick had received acclaim for his design of the Grosse Pointe Club and the Hannan Memorial Y.M.C.A. in Detroit. During their voyage, Ford asked Derrick if he had any design suggestions for his museum, and Derrick proposed that the facade of the building mirror that of Independence Hall in Philadelphia. Ford agreed, and upon returning from Europe Derrick received the commission to build the indoor museum.[6]

Derrick took his new project seriously and began by visiting other industrial and historical museums. He traveled to Chicago's Museum of Science and Industry and then to the Deutsches Museum in Germany. Based on his tours of other museums, his model included a large basement for collections storage, a practice that was common at the time. But Ford was more interested in using the space for exhibits, and Derrick omitted it from the final design plan. Thus while Derrick sought to follow the standards set by others in the field, Ford was not guided by such impulses; final decisions were made based on his personal taste.[7]

The design of the museum's facade went much more smoothly for Derrick. Ford obtained drawings of Independence Hall, and after weeks of study Der-

rick created plans replicating every detail of the original, including the inconsistencies. Pilasters, windows, and doors were off center, for example. When
Derrick mentioned the possibility of correcting the inconsistencies, Ford
declined. He seemed to believe that replicas of buildings were more authentic
if their architectural flaws were included.[8]

Once the locations for the Village Green, Menlo Park, and the indoor
museum were determined, Ford began planning the rest of the landscape. In
many cases Cutler would construct replicas of buildings, but he also supervised the preservation of several historic structures. When he was interviewed
in 1951, Cutler recounted the preservation process that he and his team used:

> The first thing we do to preserve a building that we are going to tear down
> and move is to measure everything up thoroughly. Before you start to tear
> down anything, you make a lot of sketches to show the different details and
> the way things are arranged. You've got to do a thorough measurement
> job so there are no slip-ups, because you can't tear that down, put it all in
> a freight car, bring it in, and dump it off. You have to know what you are
> doing. As you tear it down you ordinarily numbered the pieces and marked
> where it had been, all the main pieces of construction; all the door frames,
> window frames, timbers, trusses, everything that meant construction, it was
> all numbered. Of course you couldn't number siding or stuff like that, or
> bricks. I always followed a job like that right down to the bottom.[9]

After the buildings arrived they were reconstructed and, in many cases, placed
on blocks until Ford determined on which street they would be located. In
1929, for example, Ford moved a small two-story home, built in 1860, from
Dearborn to the village. John Brainard Chapman, Ford's favorite teacher,
had lived there. Eleven years would pass before Ford finally decided on a
permanent location for the building, behind the Scotch Settlement School on
South Dearborn Road. The street names, like the buildings, were indicative of
Ford's interests and biography. For example, Christie Street commemorated
the first street to be lit with Edison's incandescent light bulbs. Bagley Street,
named after the street where Ford lived when he built the Quadricycle, commemorated his personal past. And Ford's fascination with the small town was
embodied in the inclusion of a Main Street.[10]

Cutler and his team quickened their pace when Ford announced that the
dedication ceremonies would be held on October 21, 1929, to commemorate
the fiftieth anniversary of the lighting of Edison's incandescent bulb. When
guests arrived, they saw twenty-eight buildings, but Ford would add over fifty
more between 1929 and 1947 (figs. 2 and 3), representing different time periods and vastly different geographic locations. A few were connected to local
history, but most were not. What linked the buildings to one another was

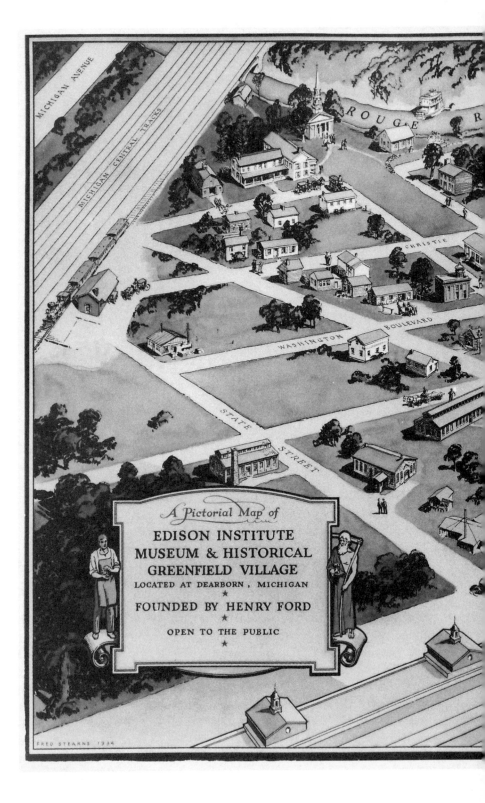

MICHIGAN AVENUE

MICHIGAN CENTRAL TRACKS

ROUGE R

CHRISTIE

BOULEVARD

WASHINGTON

STATE STREET

A *Pictorial* Map of

**EDISON INSTITUTE
MUSEUM & HISTORICAL
GREENFIELD VILLAGE**
LOCATED AT DEARBORN , MICHIGAN
★
FOUNDED BY HENRY FORD
★
OPEN TO THE PUBLIC
★

FRED STEARNS 1934

FIGURE 2. Greenfield Village in 1934, not long after it opened to the public. The landscape looked, as Ford desired, like an ideal New England village. From the collections of The Henry Ford (P.A.8972).

1—Parking Lot
2—The Edison Institute Museum
3—Gate Lodge Entrance
4—Floral Clock
5—Village Barn
6—Chemical Laboratory
7—Village Print Shop
8—Loranger Gristmill
9—Henry Ford Birthplace
10—Edsel Ford Building
11—Armington & Sims Machine Shop
12—Hanks Silk Mill
13—Deluge Fire House
14—Lunch Wagon
15—Plymouth Carding Mill
16—Weaving Shed
17—Blacksmith Shop
18—Kingston Cooper Shop
19—Currier Shoe Shop
20—Toll House
21—Tintype Studio
22—Post Office
23—Plymouth House
24—Riding Stable
25—Pioneer Log Cabin
26—Gardner House
27—Waterford General Store
28—Clinton Inn
29—Herb Garden
30—Martha-Mary Chapel
31—Steamer Suwanee
32—Scotch Settlement School
33—Logan County Courthouse
34—Slave Huts
35—George Washington Carver Memorial
36—Mattox House
37—Chapman House
38—George Matthew Adams Birthplace
39—Steinmetz Camp
40—McGuffey Group
41—Stephen Foster Birthplace

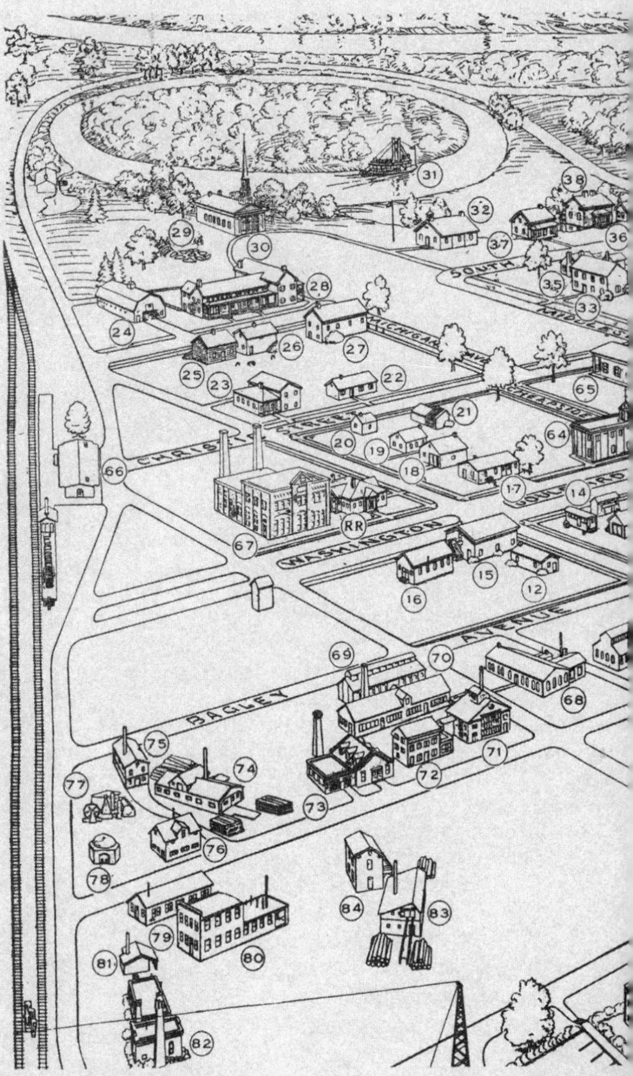

42—Swiss Watchmakers' Chalet
43—Luther Burbank Birthplace
44—Ann Arbor House
45—Noah Webster House
46—Secretary House
47—Cotswold Group
48—Cotswold Forge
49—Cape Cod Windmill

50—Plympton House
51—Susquehanna House
52—Edison Homestead
53—Covered Bridge
54—Fort Myers Laboratory
55—Sarah Jordan Boarding House
56—Menlo Park Group
57—Building Number 11
58—Miller School

AIR VIEW OF GREEN

FIGURE 3. The village in 1947, the year of Ford's death. By this time, Greenfield Village was largely complete; note the addition of numerous other buildings between 1934 and 1947. From the collections of The Henry Ford (EI.21.6).

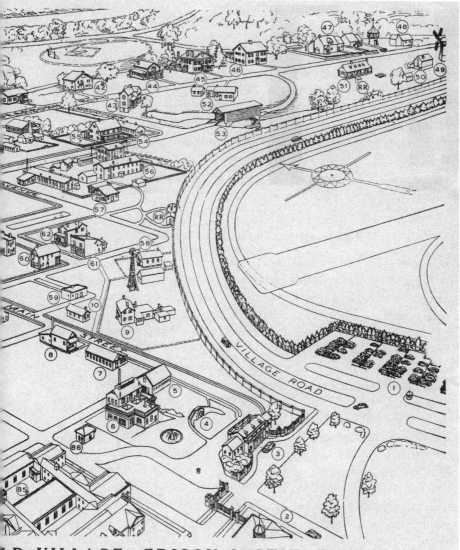

LD VILLAGE, EDISON INSTITUTE

not a specific time or place, but Ford's interest in what they represented. As Samuel Crowther reported in the *Ladies' Home Journal* just as construction began in 1928, Ford's village was "a cross section of a hundred villages rather than a representation of one village." Although many of the buildings dated to "Colonial and post-Colonial America," Crowther noted, the village also contained "some buildings and things which date back much further; as for example, a tenth century cottage from the Cotswolds." This village, he argued, follows "real life, for while antiquarians may make period divisions, real life does not." "Neither," he wrote, "will the village be of any one section of the country, for that again would too greatly restrict its scope."[11]

The Structures of Small-Town Life

When Ford asked Cutler to sketch a landscape modeled after an archetypal New England village, the results were in some ways predictable. The village landscape had long been popularized and mythologized in nineteenth-century Romantic literature and by social reformers and landscape architects of the early nineteenth century. Ford came of age in a world where this space symbolized the politics and ideology that he espoused in other arenas. As the historian Joseph S. Wood has argued, "in popularizing the New England village tradition Romanticists articulated an American settlement ideal of 'having both,' the best of both city and country."[12] Thus Ford's anti-urbanism, faith in technology, and love of rural life could all be reconciled in the landscape of the New England village. There were no bars, no pool halls, no gambling centers, and a very limited government in this world; instead, Ford's small town was populated with inventors, small business owners, and writers and artists who depicted Americans as folksy, traditional, and conservative. Ford made a case for the future as well as the past—he proposed that a community's economic and social health were inextricably linked to the small town, albeit his idealized version of it.

By 1947, when the Greenfield Village landscape reached completion, visitors moved through Ford's vision of the small town. Before entering the village proper, visitors crossed railroad tracks and passed the original Smith's Creek train station (now restored), where Edison had worked as a young boy. The station grounded the village in the moment immediately preceding the arrival of the Model T. In the center was the Village Green, surrounded by buildings representing local businesses and small-town government. Slightly beyond the green were the Menlo Park buildings, as well as the other shops, schools, and homes that Ford believed represented the American past.

As I noted earlier, the design and appearance of the village reflected Ford's personal understanding of what constituted historical authenticity. In some cases it was re-creating original buildings down to the last detail (as with the replica of the Independence Hall facade); in others it was adherence to an idea of the past or historical generalities. Whitney Martinko's work shows that Ford's sense of preservation seems to have followed early nineteenth-century definitions of the practice, which did not distinguish between restoring a building to its original form, partial restoration, or replication; each approach achieved the same goal of keeping the past alive and useful for the present.[13]

On the Village Green, two buildings represented local business. One was the Waterford Country Store, the first building moved to the village in 1927. Built in 1854, the two-story wooden structure was originally located in Waterford, Michigan, thirty miles northwest of Detroit. The second building was the Clinton Inn. The two-story building was purchased before the Waterford store, from a woman named Ella Smith, but it took until the spring of 1929 for Cutler to complete its restoration. The inn featured square white columns, a wide piazza on the first floor, and a veranda on the second floor. Cutler later recalled that while he and other staff members were decorating the interior of the inn's dining room for display, they moved some bottles onto the shelves to make it look more like a tavern. When Ford, an avid supporter of temperance, inspected the building, he demanded their removal. Apparently Clara Ford convinced her husband that the bottles made the inn complete and more authentic, but Ford's initial reaction exemplified how his sense of morality could influence his representation of the past.[14]

The centerpiece of the Village Green was the Martha-Mary Chapel, built in 1929 and named after Clara's and Henry's mothers, respectively, though the resonance with the biblical figures Martha and Mary was surely fortuitous for the Fords and their Christian clientele. Ford asked Edward Cutler to use a church in Bradford, Massachusetts, for inspiration; according to Cutler, the church embodied Ford's "idea of a New England church." Still, the Martha-Mary Chapel was not a "duplicate by any means," because the church in Bradford was much larger. Instead, Cutler "used the pictures" to capture the "character" of the Bradford church. The brick chapel's defining features were its location at the head of the Village Green and its prominent steeple. Along with the name, the chapel included another sentimental autobiographical detail: the bricks and doors came from the building where the Fords were married. Once it was completed, weekly nondenominational services were held at the chapel, and the Fords often attended. The services fit with Ford's somewhat peculiar views on religion. As a young boy he attended an Episcopal church with his family, but as an adult he dabbled in mysticism. Ford's biographer Steven Watts observes that as he aged, Ford "tried to bend Christianity to fit the shape of his mystical convictions," such as a belief in reincarnation.[15] Ford seemed to believe that a moral compass, albeit a somewhat flexible one, was required for one to succeed.

The landscape of Greenfield Village also intimated Ford's views on government. Although he ran as a Democrat from Michigan in his failed campaign for a Senate seat in 1918, Ford was wary of politics and politicians. He had long expressed a belief in limited government, but nothing captured his distaste for the expansion of federal powers better than his reaction to New Deal policies and politics. As he continued to add buildings to the village, he found himself at the center of a standoff with the federal government. In June 1933, Ford refused to support the National Industrial Recovery Act, which included provisions to protect the collective bargaining rights of unions. In response, President Roosevelt encouraged Americans to boycott Ford vehicles, although sales at the Ford Motor Company actually increased between 1933 and 1934.[16]

It is not surprising, then, that the few symbols of government evident on the village's landscape reflected Ford's preference for local rather than federal institutions. In 1929, Cutler completed construction of the Town Hall, a wooden structure in the Greek Revival style, at the foot of the Village Green. Like the church, the Town Hall embodied Ford's view that communities were built by private and local institutions. One structure that seemed to veer from this theme was an 1830s post office from Phoenixville, Connecticut, that was moved to the village in 1928. William W. Taylor, who had obtained antiques for Ford since he began restoring his childhood home in 1919, had secured the post office, which arrived in time for the dedication ceremony and was placed on Christie Street. The postal service may have been indicative of the kind of federal institution that Ford did support. Finally, a courthouse from Potsville, Illinois, where Abraham Lincoln worked when he was a country lawyer during the 1840s arrived in 1929 and was placed on South Dearborn Road near the Village Green. The two-story vernacular-style courthouse provided a small reminder of the presidency and thus of the federal government, but the physical building was clearly a representation of local and state government. It is no coincidence that Ford chose a building that captured Lincoln's humble beginnings rather than his role as president of the United States.[17]

The One-Room Schoolhouse

Ford's educational project at the Wayside Inn was just one of many. In 1911 he had opened the Dearborn Valley Farm School for Orphan Boys, which became the Henry Ford Trade School in 1916. The trade school, which remained open until 1952, offered instruction to young men at various Detroit manufacturing plants. In fact, many of the Greenfield Village guides would be recruited from the school. Other Ford-run schools operated in Georgia, Michigan's Upper Peninsula, and as far away as Fordlandia in Brazil.[18]

At each of these schools Ford instituted his particular mix of traditional instruction and hands-on learning, and at Greenfield Village he created a physical representation of that pedagogy. The village suggested that self-made men were born and raised in humble beginnings and then made their way through small, local schools. But Ford didn't merely celebrate those institutions by adding historic school buildings with blackboards to the imagined village; he provided his version of an idyllic upbringing to real Michigan children by opening a school system at Greenfield Village that mirrored his own experience.

Three one-room schoolhouses stood on the village landscape. The first was Ford's own childhood school, the brick Scotch Settlement School, purchased in 1923 and moved to the village in 1929. Ford also paid homage to William Holmes McGuffey by building a one-room "McGuffey School" in 1934, constructed using logs from an eighteenth-century barn found on the McGuffey property in Washington County, Pennsylvania. Finally, in 1943, a replica of the wooden Miller School, which Ford attended in 1873 and 1874, was built.[19]

The Scotch Settlement became the first building that the Greenfield Village schoolchildren used for classroom exercises. For Ford, the brick one-room school was something not only to be venerated but also emulated in the present. In 1929, twenty-nine students selected from Ford Motor Company employees living on the west end of Dearborn attended grades one through seven at the Scotch Settlement. Over the years, enrollment at the three schools expanded to include children of Ford and Edison Institute employees, as well as families from across Dearborn and the metropolitan area.[20]

Ford hired Benjamin Lovett to administer the school system. Lovett exemplified Ford's appointment of men with professional pedigrees that did not necessarily match their duties. With six dancing schools in Massachusetts, Lovett was well known for his expertise in colonial dance, which led Ford to hire him as an instructor at the Wayside Inn in 1923. Six years later, Lovett and his wife, Charlotte, moved to Dearborn when Ford asked him to direct the Greenfield Village school system. He remained in the position for seven years. Lovett hired instructors, observed teachers and students, and of course administered the Early American dancing program. He shared Ford's philosophy of pragmatic knowledge and hands-on learning. He explained to a *Detroit News* reporter that the benefits of dance instruction far exceeded physical exercise; as children learned colonial dances, he said, "parents could see the growth in social training as well as in habitual graceful carriage, a considerable part of this the result of the constant emphasis on these things in the dancing lessons." "We cling to the old American folk dances," he continued, "because they were typically American and provided much greater opportunity for this social training than the modern dances."[21]

Lovett was also responsible for recruiting teachers. These included E. Lucille Webster, who in 1932 left her position at a public school in southern Wayne County to join the Greenfield Village staff. She and one other instructor were responsible for educating approximately seventy students in grades one through seven at the Scotch Settlement and the Town Hall. Webster explained that Lovett hired her on the condition that she keep her hair long (presumably to make her look like the Victorian schoolteachers of his mind's eye) and work "seven days a week, if needed." Webster received $200 each month and a two-week vacation in the summer.[22]

As the students moved from seventh to eighth grade, additional instructors were hired, teachers expanded their curriculum, and (in time) the Miller and McGuffey schools were used as schoolrooms. Webster noted that many of the rooms in the village's houses were also used for classrooms and that the "schools became campus-type schools where the children left their home school to attend a class in another building."[23] In 1933, for instance, the first through third grades were taught at the Clinton Inn. Village buildings were also used for experiential learning. For example, the 1750 Secretary Pearson House—moved from Exeter, New Hampshire, in 1929 because of Ford's interest in colonial architecture and because it belonged to New Hampshire's first secretary of state, Joseph Pearson—became a prime location for teaching home economics. Once a week, female students went there for sewing lessons, and often "three to six girls were chosen to live at the Secretary House for a week and to actually care for a house and prepare meals."[24]

Inside the village's one-room schoolhouses, teachers adhered to Ford's sense of the ideal education. Following the nineteenth-century one-room school model, each room contained students at several different grade levels, and instructors used McGuffey's readers in the classroom. But Ford insisted on the "learning by doing" approach as well. Consequently, Webster wrote, "if we were studying science, we went outdoors and saw the material such as trees, shrubs, insects, weather, soil, etc." And when studying history, "we used the buildings and collections of the Village and Henry Ford Museum as an integral part of our education." Ford played a significant role in how the school operated. "If Mr. Ford learned that we did not have sufficient material to answer our questions," she wrote, "he often purchased books and came to us with them."[25]

One student writing an essay for the weekly school newspaper explained that the village's schools had taught him to apply what he learned in textbooks to actual problems that he was asked to solve in the machine shop and in the garden. He also pointed to the important foundations provided by the

McGuffey readers. The museum setting offered Ford a particularly useful platform as he worked to make his ideal education a reality.[26]

In 1934 the Edison Institute High School opened in the east wing of the Edison Institute Museum. Soon the high school boasted a music department, a physical education teacher, and horseback riding lessons. By 1937, Webster wrote, the school system provided education to 189 students and employed 18 faculty members.[27]

Representing the Inventor-Entrepreneur

As Mike Wallace has argued, at Greenfield Village Ford sought to link the modern inventor-entrepreneur to "traditional ways." Ford saw eighteenth-century artisans, craftsmen, and farmers as independent and self-reliant; their economic fates were tied, he believed, to their own efforts. Despite the differences between artisans and factory workers, Ford saw clear links between his work and an earlier era.[28] This view was manifested most clearly in his conviction that business owners were primarily responsible for their company's success or failure. For example, Steven Watts notes that when confronted with the Great Depression, Ford blamed speculation in the stock market, but refused to recognize the "larger mosaic of problems" including "pyramid structures of corporations holding one another's stocks, growing poverty in the nation's agricultural sector, serious maldistribution of income, and a destabilization of the international debt structure." Ford claimed that once entrepreneurs identified the problems in their own companies, the global economic crisis would end.[29]

Ford linked the twentieth century inventor-entrepreneur to older business practices by placing smaller-scale replicas of his and Thomas Edison's companies in the same space as shops that dated to as early as the eighteenth century (a cooper shop built in 1785 was moved from Kingston, New Hampshire and erected at the village in 1932). The village did not contain such physical symbols of corporate America as banks, or buildings where stocks were exchanged and board meetings were held. Instead, Ford charged Cutler with building replicas of Edison's Menlo Park laboratory before 1929, and later added replicas of the Edison Illuminating Company in Detroit (a reduced-scale replica of the original built in the village in 1944) and the Ford Motor Company's first factory on Mack Avenue (fig. 4; it was built in 1945 at one-quarter the size of the original building). Ford also included several buildings associated with older histories of artisan work and industry, such as a jewelry shop built in 1885 in Detroit and a gristmill built in 1832 in Monroe, Michigan. The undersized versions of the Edison Illuminating building and the Ford Motor Company slightly misled visitors but made the physical connection between industrialists and the business and manufacturing practices of the eighteenth and nineteenth centuries clearer. At the reduced size, the two replicas bore more physical resemblance to the older, preserved buildings.[30]

The businesses that Ford included reflected his vision of the ideal relationship between the inventor-entrepreneur and his labor force. The small scales of the Edison Illuminating and Ford Motor Company replicas suggested that Edison and Ford, like employers of earlier eras, initially worked in close proximity to their employees. At Menlo Park, the image of the worker was far removed from the monotonous and impersonal assembly line. Instead, the industrial laborer was envisioned as a member of an elite scientific team, working toward the invention of the incandescent light bulb. Even the replica of the Ford Motor Company captured the period before Ford began using moving assembly lines, since at the Mack Avenue plant teams of workers had assembled Ford cars one at a time. Perhaps Ford chose to build a replica of that particular plant because it captured the moment before he became embroiled in controversy with his massive labor force.

Ironically—or perhaps unsurprisingly—at the same moment Ford was romanticizing his company's origins, workers at Ford Motor Company, Chrysler, and General Motors were demanding more rights. In March 1932, a crowd of approximately 2,500 unemployed workers and radicals gathered inside Detroit to participate in a "Ford Hunger March" organized by the Trade Union Unity League, the Communist Party, the Young Communist League, and the recently formed Unemployed Councils. Marchers planned to confront Ford and his managers in Dearborn at the River Rouge plant. When they arrived, three dozen Dearborn police and Ford Motor Company security guards attempted to stop them. Police fired tear gas, and the protesters responded by launching rocks at them. At the end of the battle, four protesters had been killed. While the local and national press castigated the Communist organizers, depicted Ford Security as victims, and defended Henry Ford's private property rights, labor activists and many workers supported the marchers. When a mass funeral march was organized, the *New York Times* reported that there were ten thousand participants.[31]

Ford's most public battle with the labor movement occurred in 1937 when the United Auto Workers and the Committee for Industrial Organization (soon to become the Congress of Industrial Organizations) launched an organizing drive. Formed just two years earlier, the UAW had already led successful sit-down strikes at General Motors and Chrysler. Union leaders then turned their attention to Ford. The UAW's drive began with a leaflet distribution campaign that was to take place on a pedestrian overpass during a scheduled shift change at the Rouge Factory. The organizers included not only UAW members but also teachers, clergymen, and several journal-

FIGURE 4. Ford had a replica of the Ford Motor Company built at a reduced scale. The smaller building suggested that the company had more in common with local businesses than large corporations. Interestingly, the Rouge Factory, which epitomized the impersonal industrial factory, was just a short drive from the village. Photo by author, 2011.

ists. The group was halfway across the bridge when Ford's personal police, the "Ford Service Department," attacked them. Many photographs were taken of the attack, and soon what reporters named the "Battle of the Overpass" was national news. The National Labor Relations Board filed a claim documenting Ford Motor Company's violations of the Wagner Act. As the historian David L. Lewis notes, the company was then ordered to cease its efforts to interfere with employees' organizing rights and to reinstate twenty-three employees fired for their involvement in union activities. Despite negative press coverage that deeply damaged Ford's public image, company officials appealed the case. In 1940 the company was found guilty of unfair labor practices in nine plants. Still, Ford refused to draw up a formal contract with the UAW until 1941.[32]

In a climate marked by gains by organized labor, Greenfield Village offered Ford both a retreat from the present and a tool for promoting his public image. In arguing that the origins of industrial capitalism were familiar, friendly, and accessible, Ford humanized business owners. By representing the spaces where men like himself and Edison worked before their businesses became corporate empires, he depicted inventor-entrepreneurs not as corporate owners unknown to their employees, but as men who understood the challenges of working on the front lines as well as the rewards of success.

Homes and Self-Made Manhood

Although laboratories and factories were an important part of the Greenfield Village landscape, Ford's notions of self-made manhood were most clearly communicated in his preservation and re-creation of homes and schools. By 1947, the site's twenty-two homes included two brick slave cabins, William Holmes McGuffey's log cabin birthplace, and, of course, Ford's own childhood home. Ford principally chose homes associated with famous inventors, scientists, cultural innovators, and his own life to link self-made manhood and domestic life. For example, in 1930 he asked Cutler to restore a small, rustic summer cabin in Schenectady, New York, where Ford's and Edison's friend Charles Proteus Steinmetz, a mathematician and electrical engineer, had stayed in 1896. In 1936, Cutler supervised the movement of the New Haven, Connecticut, federal-style house, built in 1823, where Noah Webster wrote much of his *American Dictionary,* and by 1937 the home was erected in the village. The following year, Ford moved the home of George Matthew Adams from Saline, Michigan. The modest two-story wooden house, built sometime during the 1840s, drew Ford's interest because he was a fan of Adams's popular newspaper column, "Today's Talk."[33]

Ford also included homes that spoke to his other interests. His enthusiasm for western European architecture and heritage led him to move a Cotswolds cottage and forge (both brought from England in 1930) and to construct a Swiss watchmaker's chalet in 1935.[34] The two buildings made little sense in terms of re-creating a history of America, but they did point to Ford's fascination with many Americans' English heritage and his xenophobic notion that Anglo-Saxon culture was superior to that of eastern Europe. There were no homes, from Lithuania, Armenia, or Serbia, countries from which a number of Ford employees had immigrated.[35] The homes that Ford excluded from the landscape were also telling, as he built a narrative of the past that ignored aspects of American history he found irrelevant.

One kind of home that Ford did find relevant was the historic birthplace, which symbolized most explicitly his view of the role that family played in a man's success or failure. Of the twenty-two homes, six were preserved or replicated birthplaces of men whose innovations brought them fame and fortune: the Ford Homestead, the William Holmes McGuffey Birthplace, the

Wright Homestead, the Stephen Foster Birthplace, the George Washington Carver Building, and the Luther Burbank Birthplace. A clear example of Ford's celebration of the self-made inventor was the preserved birthplace of the famous botanist and horticulturist Luther Burbank, which was moved to the site in 1936 and re-erected by 1937. The brick two-story house contained seven rooms and was built around 1800; it was originally located on farmland in Lancaster, Massachusetts. Burbank, who was Ford's good friend, had followed a route to success of which the industrialist approved. He grew up on a farm, was largely self-educated, and first found fortune by selling his own invention, the Burbank potato.[36]

Ford's interest in commemorating birthplaces reflected broader national trends. As Seth Bruggeman notes, Americans' fascination with birthplaces emerged in the late nineteenth century as part of the post–Civil War "modernity crisis" that "owed its intensity to the war's ravages, rampant industrialization, savage class conflict, and a sudden onslaught of new immigrants and shifting domestic populations." By the 1930s, "monument builders celebrated birth en masse."[37] Ford, who preserved his own birthplace with precision, clearly assigned great significance to the role of domestic environments in shaping one's character and future as well. For him, a man's domestic origins determined his ability to contribute to the economy and to make daily life more efficient and comfortable.

Ford's inclusion of preserved and constructed birthplaces of successful inventors, scientists, and educators seem obvious choices given his personal trajectories. The wide range of birthplaces he included on the village grounds, however, also spoke to his views on race. Ford purchased and relocated or constructed several homes between 1935 and 1943 that were connected to African American history. When read in the context of Ford's belief in self-made manhood, his decision to create replicas and preserve homes associated with black Americans suggested that he had a progressive sense of social justice. His labor policies, however, complicated that perspective.

Ford operated in a metropolitan landscape increasingly defined by racial tensions. In the 1910s and 1920s black southerners migrated en masse to the Northeast, Midwest, and West to escape Jim Crow segregation and to take advantage of economic opportunities in other parts of the nation. The Great Migration led to a radical shift in Detroit's demographics. In 1910 there were 5,741 African Americans living in Detroit, just 1 percent of the total population. By 1920 that number had increased seven-fold, to 40,838, or 4.1 percent. By 1930, 120,066, or almost 8 percent, of Detroit's 1,568,662 residents were African American.[38] In the 1910s, many black residents found work in factories, but by the early 1930s most white employers limited blacks to menial and dangerous jobs. The Ford Motor Company was an exception.[39]

Initially, Ford instituted company policies that indicated he believed in racial equality. As Beth Tompkins Bates has argued, "Ford challenged the stereotype of the black man as servant when he put out the welcome mat for African Americans two decades before General Motors and Chrysler hired blacks for any but foundry or janitorial jobs." During the 1910s the company cultivated close relationships with the city's leading black ministers and in this way was able to recruit what Thomas Sugrue has called an "elite corps of black male workers." Further, Ford offered black Americans employment in positions normally confined to white workers. During the 1920s, Bates notes, Ford "placed many in skilled positions, such as crane operator, mechanic, electrician, bricklayer, and tool-and-die maker." Ford Motor Company's treatment of black workers shifted throughout the 1930s, however. Bates writes that "the job security that had been a hallmark for all workers, particularly blacks, at Ford eroded during the Great Depression," and in 1933 Ford initiated a labor policy that transformed the "foundry from an integrated department into one that was virtually all black." Those who publicly criticized the company's treatment of black workers were fired, and by the end of the 1930s, Bates contends, "much of the gratitude the black community had traditionally felt toward Ford had been replaced by fear."[40]

Some of Ford's philanthropic efforts to help the black community suggest that his sense of social justice was rooted in a paternalistic view of the relationship between whites and blacks. While most of Detroit's African Americans lived in the Paradise Valley neighborhood on the city's east side, many of the Rouge plant's African American employees lived in Inkster, a community adjacent to Dearborn. In 1933, Ford launched a project to rehabilitate Inkster, which Bates has argued revealed the power of his public relations skills. By the early 1930s, even Ford Motor was feeling the effects of the Great Depression, and the famous five-dollar-a-day pay had been reduced to four dollars at the Rouge plant. Inkster residents who worked at the Rouge technically received the same amount, but they received only one dollar in cash, while the remaining three were "saved" for the "rehabilitation" of their community. Ford established a public commissary, reopened the public school, and provided men with seeds and garden allotments and women with sewing machines. While Ford offered black residents of Inkster material benefits, he garnished the wages of Inkster's residents and determined what he believed they needed to thrive. In fact, he treated African Americans with the same paternalism that guided his earlier efforts to Americanize eastern European immigrants.[41]

Bates observes that Ford's Inkster experiment received "mixed reviews" throughout the 1930s. At the national level, Ford was "hailed as the savior of black Inksterites in black newspapers." Inside the community, however, many residents felt ambivalent toward Ford and his company, particularly as he assumed more authority over their lives. In 1941, shortly after the Ford Motor Company reached an agreement with the UAW, one that succeeded through support from the company's black workers, the Inkster project was ended. To Hayward S. Ablewhite, a Sociological Department employee who was appointed president of the Edison Institute in 1949, it seemed that Ford closed programs like the Inkster Commissary to punish black workers who supported the union's activities.[42]

Ford also accepted other efforts to maintain the color line outside of his company. Issues shaping daily life for many of the metro area's residents, such as equal opportunity in housing, seemed to escape him. The reason so many of Ford's black workers lived in Inkster was that Dearborn residents used a variety of techniques to ensure that African Americans could not purchase real estate there. Yet Ford did nothing to move black Americans into Dearborn, nor did this kind of segregation seem to register for him as a form of social injustice.[43]

The complexity that defined Ford's views on race found symbolic form at Greenfield Village. Ford's 1935 acquisition of a home in which the popular songwriter Stephen Foster was purportedly born illustrates his interest in the links between home life and the cultural innovator. (In 1953, after it was determined that the building was not Foster's birthplace, it was renamed the Foster Memorial.)[44] Foster, the first American composer to support himself with sales from his sheet music, became famous in 1848, when "Oh! Susanna" was published. Numerous other hits, including "Camptown Races," "Jeanie with the Light Brown Hair," and "My Old Kentucky Home"—songs still known today—followed. Foster's life was shortened by alcoholism, but his music remained a fixture of American life well into the early twentieth century. During the demonstration of his tinfoil phonograph at the Smithsonian Institution, Thomas Edison recorded Foster's "Uncle Ned." Foster's music was also, of course, a favorite of Henry Ford's.[45]

Almost twenty of Foster's popular songs, including "Old Black Joe" and "Old Kentucky Home," were written to be performed in blackface and in an imagined African American dialect as part of minstrel shows. The lyrics offered sentimental versions of the South and enslavement. As the Foster scholar Ken Emerson has argued, "Old Black Joe" "epitomizes Foster's racial condescension." But the song was also praised by men like the influential scholar and activist W. E. B. Du Bois because it was so clearly shaped by the phrases and melodies present in slave songs. Emerson maintains that "despite its demeaning stereotypes, 'Old Black Joe' comes closest of Foster's famous songs to the African-American spiritual, and it approaches that tradition with sympathy and respect."[46] Henry Ford's personal feelings about Foster's use of blackface minstrelsy are unknown. Certainly his interest in preserving

the lyricist's home might have been driven by nostalgia for the "old South"
(perhaps including slavery), or simply by an appreciation for African American musical traditions. But in any case, Ford's interest in Foster's birthplace
suggests that his views on race were complex.

Ford more clearly indicated his view of African American history when
he moved two slave cabins to the village. In 1934 he purchased the Hermitage
Plantation in Ways Station, Georgia, a small town near Savannah. Before tear-
ing down the plantation house to build a newer home for himself and Clara,
Ford decided to relocate two of the brick slave cabins still on the premises
and occupied by black families to his outdoor museum (fig. 5).[47] In moving
the structures, Ford made the case that African American history should be
preserved and taught, a notion that many were only beginning to embrace by
the 1930s. (Carter G. Woodson had founded the *Journal of Negro History* in
1916; Du Bois's groundbreaking *Black Reconstruction* appeared in 1935.) But
Ford restored the cabins to a pristine condition (fig. 6), creating a mislead-
ing view of the institution of slavery. The restoration also erased the fact that
impoverished black Americans were still living in the cabins at the time that
he purchased and moved them, which would have highlighted the degree
to which Jim Crow laws still maintained the color line in twentieth-century
America.

Ford also venerated his friend George Washington Carver at Greenfield
Village. Carver was a botanist, inventor, and educator who shared Ford's
fascination with soybeans. He was born into slavery on a farm owned by his
master, Moses Carver, in southwestern Missouri, in what is now Diamond,
a small town not far from Joplin. The exact date of his birth is unknown,
but biographers speculate that it was sometime in 1865. Carver's father died
before he was born, and when he was an infant, he, his mother, and his sister
were kidnapped by bushwhackers. Moses offered one horse as ransom for his
slaves, but only George was returned. Emancipation freed young George from
slavery, and Moses Carver and his wife raised him until he was ten, when he
struck out to attend a school for black children eight miles away. Carver went
on to become the first black student, and later the first black faculty member,
at Iowa State Agricultural College. In 1896, Booker T. Washington invited him
to direct the agricultural department at the Tuskegee Institute in Tuskegee,
Alabama, where he found fame as both an educator and an inventor through
his experiments with peanuts.[48]

Carver also shared an interest of Henry Ford's. "Chemurgy," or creating
industrial products from agricultural materials, grew increasingly popular
during the 1930s. Ford had long been interested in uniting industry and agriculture. He began donating to the Tuskegee Institute in the early 1900s and
started dabbling in chemurgy in 1929, when he built an agricultural research

Figure 5. The Hermitage slave houses in their original location near Savannah, Georgia, around the 1930s. When the houses were moved to Greenfield Village, they would be restored to near-pristine condition. From the collections of The Henry Ford (P.B.103658).

Figure 6. The Hermitage slave houses around 1935, after restoration. From the collections of The Henry Ford (P.O.6000).

lab in Greenfield Village. Ford began writing to Carver about his chemurgical experiments in 1934, but the two did not meet until 1937, when Carver agreed to attend a chemurgical conference in Dearborn. Ford and Carver were both particularly enthusiastic about the soybean plant, which could be grown as food, used as oil, or converted into plastic. After the conference, the two continued to correspond. In 1940, Ford demonstrated his admiration for Carver by naming a school after him on the property he had purchased in Ways Station, Georgia. [49]

By the 1940s, Carver had become a symbol for such divergent groups as civil rights activists and New South advocates, each touting his accomplishments to promote their distinct agendas. During the 1940s, some whites pointed to his role at the Tuskegee Institute to demonstrate the benefits of segregated education. For others, Carver's achievements in botany were cited as evidence that African Americans possessed intelligence equal to whites'. In many ways, Carver was the ideal representative of Ford's self-made manhood theme. His accomplishments matched or exceeded many of those already represented on the Greenfield Village landscape. [50]

Ford and Carver continued their friendship. In 1942, Ford invited Carver to Dearborn to dedicate the Nutritional Laboratory of the Ford Motor Company on Michigan Avenue in Dearborn. Prior to his arrival, Ford designed a small wooden slave cabin that he said was loosely based on Carver's recollections of his birthplace. Drawing on Carver's memories would perhaps inevitably have led to an inaccurate replica of the cabin, since according to his biographer Gary Kremer, Carver's memories of his childhood were murky at best. In fact, the Carver cabin would look nothing like the twelve-by-twelve cabin, now long vanished, where Carver was actually born. [51] At the village, Carver's cabin only nodded to reality; like the slave cabins, it celebrated African American history, but in a way that largely ignored the painful and traumatic realities of enslavement. Unlike the one-room cabin of Carver's actual birthplace, the reconstructed version, with an exterior made of pine logs from Iron Mountain, Michigan, contained two small rooms. On Ford's request, governors from every state donated representative wood for the interior paneling. Perhaps most remarkable was that southern governors were willing to donate wood for this purpose while Jim Crow laws were in full flower. The cabin struck a chord with Carver; upon viewing the construction on his 1942 visit, he decided to spend a few nights in it. Ford clearly respected and venerated his friend, but it is unclear what he thought about, or even if he recognized, the social injustice Carver faced as an African American. [52]

Ford built the Carver cabin to honor and please his friend, but it only gestured to history. It would be fairly obvious to those who viewed the building that it was a recent construction, because the interior paneling was identified with the names of the states from which it came. For Ford, it seemed important to acknowledge Carver's rise from humble beginnings, but not to create a realistic portrayal of his early life; the horrors of enslavement were not communicated at the Carver building. By 1947, four years after Carver's death, the building had been renamed the Carver Memorial, a title that more clearly reflected its purpose.[53]

Ford added one other site that marked his interest in African American history. In 1943 he moved the home of an African American tenant farming family from Ways Station, Georgia, to Greenfield Village and named it the Mattox House after the family that had owned it.[54] Ford's passion for rural life and the farmer were well known; the inclusion of the Mattox home, however, suggests that he was unsympathetic to critiques of tenant farms and sharecropping, in particular the fact that so many white landowners used the system to maintain the color line in the early twentieth-century South.

By the mid-1940s, then, Greenfield Village contained a significant number of buildings depicting African American history. Ford was clearly part of a broader movement to preserve black history using the built environment. In 1943 the Missouri farm where Carver was born was dedicated as the George Washington Carver National Monument, and six years later the Booker T. Washington National Monument opened in Franklin County, Virginia.[55] The nostalgic messages sent at Greenfield Village and Ford's philanthropic efforts to assist—but at the same time control—African Americans in his own workforce and community complicated readings of these buildings. Even Edward Cutler was unsure of Ford's position when it came to African Americans. He said that he did not "ever remember Mr. Ford expressing an opinion on the Negro question," but that "what he *did* was more outstanding than any opinion." It seems that while Ford did not support a pre–Civil War racial hierarchy, he did ignore more contemporary manifestations of social injustice.[56]

Ford's homes also reflected his understanding of the role that class played in the development of self-made men. He included several homes that suggested the residents were born into or had achieved middle-class status; the Luther Burbank Birthplace and the Wright Homestead were larger and more well appointed, for example. But many of the homes Ford restored or constructed—such as the slave cabins and the Carver Building—supported a rags-to-riches theme.

The McGuffey Birthplace exemplified Ford's desire to demonstrate that those born into modest circumstances could achieve great success. In 1930, Ford's interest in McGuffey Readers extended to the village's landscape when he initiated a search for William Holmes McGuffey's birthplace. Two years later, he traveled to West Finley Township in Pennsylvania and purchased the building—a one-room, almost windowless log cabin with a massive chimney occupying one end—from Mr. and Mrs. Henry V. Blayney, who claimed to be relatives of the McGuffey family. The *New York Times* reported that the house was "now crumbling in ruins, but most of its timbers remain intact, and the place could easily be reconstructed in its original form." After completing some minor repairs Ford had the cabin shipped to Dearborn in November 1932, and during the next two years it was reconstructed and modified. When the cabin opened to the public on September 23, 1934, the 134th anniversary of McGuffey's birth, relatives of McGuffey were in attendance and the ceremony was broadcast by NBC.[57]

The McGuffey Birthplace reiterated Ford's belief that one's original material conditions did not prevent success. His humble origins notwithstanding, McGuffey went on to receive a degree in philosophy and language, worked as a university professor and administrator, and made an indelible impact on education. Like the Carver cabin, McGuffey's birthplace clearly communicated the message that success was not limited to those born into wealth. Since Ford embraced the moral lessons and educational approach advocated by the readers themselves, the home, and of course the replica of the McGuffey school, supported a number of his agendas.

One of the most famous homes at the village that linked a middle-class upbringing to invention and the small business was the Wright Brothers' Home and Cycle Shop, moved from Dayton, Ohio. The house was also where Orville was born in 1871 (Wilbur Wright was born in 1867 in Millville, Indiana). The family stayed in the home until 1877, when they moved to Cedar Rapids, Iowa, and four years later to Richmond, Indiana. The Wrights returned to Dayton and the house on Hawthorne Street in 1884. In 1892, Orville and Wilbur started the Wright Cycle Company, where they sold and repaired bicycles. By 1895 they were building and selling their own bicycles, but soon they began work on the project that would make them famous: in 1903, after three years of experimenting, they flew the first power-driven heavier-than-air machine in Kitty Hawk, North Carolina.[58]

In 1936 the *New York Times* reported that Ford had purchased the Wright brothers' birthplace and their cycle shop in Dayton. Between 1937 and 1938, Cutler and Ford worked with Orville Wright to move and restore his childhood home and one of his first entrepreneurial endeavors. How or when Orville Wright and Henry Ford met is unknown, but Ford and his son, Edsel, were involved in the aviation industry at least as early as 1923, when they invested in the Stout Metal Airplane Company, and Orville Wright was in attendance when the Edison Institute was dedicated in 1929.[59]

Wright, whom Cutler described as a "funny old cuss," was heavily involved in moving and reconstructing both the family home and the cycle shop. The classic but modest Victorian-style home included a wraparound porch. Inside, the dining and living rooms were decorated with furniture and displayed to the public based on Wright's recommendations. Adjacent to the home stood the brick cycle shop, which featured two large storefront windows and the Wright Cycle Company sign.[60]

Ford also wanted to display the Wrights' 1903 Kitty Hawk Flyer, which Orville Wright had loaned to the Science Museum of South Kensington, London, in 1928 after a very public dispute with the Smithsonian Institution. For unknown reasons, however, the restored Kitty Hawk Flyer remained in London.[61] Cutler later said that he thought "there was a promise to bring the first Wright plane to the Village and put it in a building in back of the homestead," adding, "I think Mr. Wright had promised Mr. Ford that the plane would come to the Village, because I made quite a drawing [of] a building to house that Wright plane," but "there was a hitch in there some place because it never materialized."[62] After the restoration of the home and cycle shop was completed, on April 16, 1938, children from the village's school chorus performed before guests and a radio audience at the dedication ceremonies. Ford's ghostwriter, William J. Cameron, who had been appointed public relations manager for Greenfield Village in 1921, described the significance of the buildings at the village to those in attendance and those listening at home and added, "Today we dedicate two other buildings—the boyhood home and the bicycle shop of Wilbur and Orville Wright. They, too, are plain buildings, like a hundred thousand others of their period or of this, and they likewise are given place in this history collection for the one and all-sufficient reason 'the doer's deed that dignifies the place.'"[63]

Finally, Ford moved his own childhood home to his outdoor history museum, enshrining the domestic space that had nurtured an international celebrity and one of the world's wealthiest industrialists. Restoration of the unoccupied and largely empty two-story house had begun in 1919, when highway officials announced that it was in the path of a planned road. Ford and his three surviving siblings decided to move the unoccupied house and outbuildings two hundred feet in order to save them. Shortly afterward, Ford began to restore the home as closely as possible to its condition in 1876, the year his mother died. He began by excavating the ground around the building. Workmen found a rusty pair of Ford's skates, along with dish fragments that were used to reproduce the family china. Fred Black, a staff member of the *Dearborn Independent*, editor of the Ford Motor Company newsletter, advertising manager, and by 1935, secretary-treasurer of the Edison Institute, remembered "workmen bringing him [Ford] some big trays with old rusty materials they had dug up, and he'd go over every piece very carefully to determine what it had been." When original objects were unavailable, Ford assigned Cutler and others the task of locating replicas, such as a piece of worn red carpeting for the stairwell and, of course, the Starlight No. 25 stove. By the early 1920s the restoration was largely complete, and the Fords began to use the home, now replete with furnishings from or reminiscent of Henry's younger days, to host their colonial dances. On July 29, 1944, the day before his eighty-first birthday, Ford at last moved the family homestead to Greenfield Village (although it remained closed for public viewing until after Clara Ford's death in 1953); it was already so close that Cutler and his men simply cut it in two and moved it by truck.[64]

The range of homes Ford chose for the village also explicitly rooted self-made manhood in domestic life and suggested his views on urban life and women's roles. Ford celebrated homes from agricultural, rustic, or small-town settings, or ensured that homes appeared as if they originated in that setting. By including homes at the village, he also implicitly celebrated wives and mothers, who by the 1930s had long been associated with domestic space. Women, too, played an important role in the development of self-made men. As the Martha-Mary Chapel indicates, Ford certainly respected his own mother, and on the whole seems to have respected women as wives and mothers. Although Cutler said that Ford "never discussed his philosophy on the part a woman should have in the home or on the outside," he also noted that Ford often consulted Clara when it came to furnishing the interiors of the structures. In general, Cutler remembered that when Ford dealt with women who worked at the village, "there was never any lack of consideration, on his part, of their ideas."[65]

Operating the Village

As Ford continued to add buildings that supported his worldview to the Greenfield Village landscape, he also developed a loose organizational structure that ensured his control over most of the site's day-to-day activities. Lines of authority and operational models developed slowly over time at both the indoor museum and village, and they fluctuated greatly during Ford's years as president. At the highest level was the Edison Institute board of trustees, created in 1929, which oversaw both facilities. The original members included Ford himself (who also served as president of Greenfield Village) as well as Clara and Edsel. Fred Black was added to the board in 1938. The board's responsibilities were minimal, however, given Ford's interest in dominating the site's operations. The first organizational chart was not written until 1934. That year, Ford was listed as president, Clara as vice president, and Edsel as secretary and treasurer, with Ernest Liebold listed as assistant secretary and treasurer. Beneath the board were forty-three other management positions. According to their titles as they were listed on an organizational chart, only a few of these men wielded significant power: Edward Cutler (Planning and Layout), Ray Dahlinger (Supervision Construction and Grounds), Fred Smith (Superintendent of Museum Building), Frank Campsall (Supervision Personnel and Purchases), and William A. Simonds (Manager of Guides and Public Relations).[66]

By 1934 Ford had recruited a number of other Ford Motor Company employees to maintain Greenfield Village. Ray Dahlinger began his career by working on the assembly line, but soon he was conducting tests on Ford cars in the Highland Park plant's experimental room. There he met Henry Ford and soon found himself serving as his bodyguard and chauffer. In 1917, Ford introduced Dahlinger to Evangeline Côté, a company employee who was rumored to be Ford's mistress. Dahlinger and Côté married, but soon they were sleeping in separate quarters while Ford resumed his relationship with Evangeline. According to Steven Watts, it was his affair with Evangeline that motivated Ford to offer Ray Dahlinger a more prestigious position as supervisor of both the Ford airport and Greenfield Village. Ford also found work for Evangeline in the village's schools. The relationship between Ford and Evangeline may have explained Ray Dahlinger's at times odd behavior and Ford's even stranger responses. For example, Cutler remembered that Dahlinger took many of the furnishings placed in the village's buildings for his personal use, and that Ford responded by saying "Ah, forget it!"[67]

Like Dahlinger and Cutler, most of the men building and administering the village had no training in the kind of work in which they engaged. For example, in 1934 Fred Smith was listed as Superintendent of Museum Building, though he had never been a curator. Ford's personal secretary, Frank Campsall, was responsible for "Supervision [of] Personnel and Purchases," and he played an important role in purchasing buildings, but he had never before worked in a museum.[68]

Some men with significant power possessed experience more closely related to their work at Greenfield Village. In 1934, Francis Jehl (Thomas Edison's former assistant) was identified as "Curator of Menlo Park." Since Jehl had actually worked with Edison, he was able to draw on his personal experience when speaking with visitors and maintaining the laboratory. William Simonds was listed as "Manager of Guides" and "Director of Public Relations."[69] Although he had never managed a staff of museum guides, Simonds had long been writing for a public audience. Fred Black's communication skills likely served him well when he worked as a liaison between Ford and Robert Derrick during construction of the indoor museum and as secretary-treasurer starting in 1935. According to Black, Edsel Ford had asked him to take the position, which required him to manage the corporate records and finances. Black recalled that the "job also involved being nominal director of the Museum, Village and the Institute," but he "found out very soon, of course, that the real director was Henry Ford, who wanted to carry out his own ideas."[70] Ford planned to present *his* version of the American past to the public, and he plainly wanted people around him whom he trusted, more than men who brought special expertise. Consequently, professionals or those with experience concerning best practices when it came to preservation techniques, curatorship, or interpretation, were rarely consulted.

The management of Greenfield Village during this period can be best described as haphazard. Cutler observed that "there was no breakdown between people," and that "the only organization of the Village was my office." He recalled, for example, that the facility "never had a formalized system of accounts." While Cutler often handled finances when it came to purchasing and furnishing buildings, Ford frequently told him not to worry about money. Cutler said that when he told Ford that a building's costs were too high, Ford would respond by saying, "When did I ever say anything to you about money?" Cutler purchased buildings and antiques, but another office handled payments, and Cutler was never exactly sure how or when payments were made. Further, while Cutler was responsible for managing various employees, such as the construction crew, Dahlinger had the power to fire them.[71]

In contrast to John D. Rockefeller's work at Colonial Williamsburg, Ford often hired men without backgrounds in historic preservation or architectural history to manage the daily activities of Greenfield Village, and his employment decisions seemed to stem from his desire to control what happened there. The result was that Ford determined not only the village's landscape and its themes but also the degree to which his staff understood the site's purpose.

The Village Opens

Shortly after the dedication ceremony in 1929, requests to view the village increased to almost five hundred per day. Ford was happy to share his version of the past with an eager public and soon initiated a loosely organized system. Students from the village's schools gave selected visitors a tour in groups of twenty-five, while Ford prepared the site for larger-scale visitation. In 1931 he opened the Dearborn Inn, a few hundred yards from the village and close to the Ford Airport's passenger terminal on Oakwood Boulevard in Dearborn. The inn had two restaurants: the English Coffee Shop was open from seven in the morning until nine in the evening and served lunch and dinner, and also advertised an a la carte service and soda bar; the Early American Dining Room served lunch for $1.25 and dinner for $1.75. Within the village, Ford authorized the construction of a colonial-style waiting room and two public restrooms, which were completed by the summer of 1933. Greenfield Village officially opened to the public on June 22, 1933, and one week later the Edison Institute Museum opened. The museum's initial floor plan included a decorative arts section, a mechanical arts section, and the re-creation of a street of common eighteenth- and nineteenth-century shops. Like the village, however, the museum remained under construction and in a state of flux throughout the 1930s and into the 1940s.[72]

After Greenfield Village opened to the public, guides were recruited from the Henry Ford Trade School, the village's high school, and other local high schools. The guides, who were first managed by William Simonds, could number anywhere from ten in the winter season to 150 during the summer when attendance rates were higher. Simonds was unsure of how best to use the guides. Initially they were assigned to one particular visitor group, later to a set of buildings, and eventually each guide stayed in one specific building. At times, all three approaches were used. Occasionally, older village schoolgirls served as guides, although both Henry and Clara Ford resisted this practice, fearing they might get romantically involved with the male guides.[73]

How visitors traveled through the village also changed over time. At first they boarded horse-drawn carriages at the gatehouse and were taken to the Clinton Inn, which served as another welcome center. Soon, however, the growing number of visitors made this process unfeasible. Shortly after 1933, visitors walked through the village; empty horse-drawn carriages were driven by to maintain the pre-automobile atmosphere.[74]

Ford also recognized that visitors would likely want and be willing to pay for souvenirs. Although it is unclear exactly when souvenirs were first offered, by 1939 a fairly extensive selection of products was available for sale. A number of them presented more extensive details about each building at the village or documented their visit. A sixty-four-page booklet contained a more extensive tour of the village than the free eight-page booklet. The first two volumes of Francis Jehl's reminiscences about his time at Menlo Park were also available in paperback for fifty cents each, or visitors could pay one dollar each for the cloth-covered versions. Guests could also purchase Benjamin Lovett's book of calls and instructions for old-time dances, *Good Mornings*. For those interested in sharing their visit with others, the post office offered a variety of thirty-five different postcards in color and black and white featuring some of the most popular buildings in the village; visitors also could purchase small souvenir packets that contained twenty-four views of village and museum scenes.[75]

Ford also organized the sale of traditional crafts and goods from the past. For example, the Plymouth Carding Mill (moved in 1929) sold a variety of woven goods. The Sandwich Glass Plant—a replica of the 1825 plant on Cape Cod in Massachusetts, completed in 1932—was another popular building that offered souvenirs. Visitors could purchase small glass pitchers in blue, red, yellow, amber, or white. The Tintype Studio, which Ford had asked Cutler to construct before opening day in 1929, made and sold tintypes for ten cents upon request. At the Kinston Cooper Shop (moved in 1932), visitors could purchase wooden barrels, pitchers, churns, and buckets that were built without the use of nails. The Loranger Gristmill (moved in 1928) sold cornmeal, stone-ground flour, and soybean flour. Visitors could also buy items at the Pottery Shop and at the Cotswold Forge, which offered handmade nails and horseshoe paperweights for sale.[76]

Ford took several steps to move Greenfield Village toward a model that reflected the public's interest in the site as both a museum and a tourist attraction. The sale of souvenir items met his secondary goal of keeping the past alive in the present. By hiring craftsmen who not only practiced nineteenth-century crafts but also sold those crafts to the public, Ford (somewhat ironically) embraced consumption as a tool for preserving cultural traditions he feared modernity was erasing.

The End of the Ford Era

Edsel Ford died suddenly in 1943. The following year, Ford had a replica of Edsel's second-floor garage workshop at the Ford home in Detroit built in the village and called it the Edsel Ford Building. Henry Ford II, Edsel's oldest son, replaced his father on the Edison Institute's board of trustees; Edsel's second son, Benson, had joined the board the year before. L. J. Thompson, who managed the financial accounts at Fair Lane, also joined the board.[77]

Edsel's death accelerated the decline of Henry Ford's own deteriorating health, and two years later he suffered a debilitating stroke. Ford's health problems and his son's death initiated debates about who would control the Ford Motor Company and the Edison Institute. Ford had initially planned for Edsel to take charge of both the company and the museum and village. According to Ford's will, when Edsel died the Ford Motor Company would be turned over to a board of trustees. Now, after much debate within the family, Ford agreed to alter the will, and he appointed his grandson, Henry Ford II, president of the Ford Motor Company in 1945, while Henry himself remained president of the Edison Institute Museum and Greenfield Village. For the next two years Clara Ford tended to her husband's needs as family members and employees watched one of the world's most powerful men become, as Ford's physician John G. Mateer wrote, "a pleasant vegetable."[78]

According to Cutler, it was shortly after Edsel's passing that control of Greenfield Village shifted to Clara Ford and Dahlinger, while Smith took charge of the indoor component of the Edison Institute. By 1945, Cutler remembered, "Mrs. Ford was giving the orders, and he [Dahlinger] had, more or less assumed the authority." Cutler was never fond of Dahlinger, and it seemed the feeling was mutual. In 1946, Dahlinger arranged for Cutler's transfer to the Rouge Factory. "I don't know why Dahlinger had made this arrangement for me," Cutler said, but he proposed that Dahlinger was a "very jealous-minded man," and that he was "anxious to get rid of" Cutler.[79]

Before his stroke, Ford planned to continue adding new buildings and expanding the school system. Cutler claimed that Ford planned to add a "harness shop" and "several little shops for little industries and old-time handcraft jobs." After the stroke, however, while day-to-day operations for the most part remained consistent under Dahlinger, plans for improving the village came to a halt.[80]

Ford's last visit to the village occurred on April 7, the day he died. A heavy rainstorm had caused the Rouge River to flood, and the *Suwanee* riverboat was largely submerged in the lagoon at the village, where it was docked. Ford was, according to the historian David Lewis, clearheaded that day and "appeared interested in his surroundings." He asked his driver to take him on a tour of several sites damaged in the flood, including the *Suwanee*. As he viewed the damaged riverboat, he laughed and said, "We'll soon put it back on an even keel again." Ford died at Fair Lane that night. His body lay in state in the museum, and more than a hundred thousand people arrived to pay tribute to the famous industrialist. Three days later he was buried in the family cemetery on Joy Road in Detroit.[81]

As Ford assembled Greenfield Village, it was clear that his decision to preserve or construct a particular building was motivated primarily by the social, political, and cultural currents in his own life. The village served as a vehicle for expressing Ford's views on everything from religion to race. Further, his almost complete control over the indoor museum and the village created a dependent and loosely defined organizational structure, one that ensured that Ford almost single-handedly determined the site's purpose, appearance, and offerings to the public.

By constructing his ideal small town, Ford turned his worldview into a landscape. The choice to model Greenfield Village after an idealized New England village reflected his belief that the small town far exceeded the urban landscape in allowing capitalism and culture to flourish, as well as his concern that the federal government was impeding progress through its interference in the free market. Ford made his vision of an appropriate education a reality by preserving one-room schoolhouses and opening them to Michigan students. His choice to include preserved and replicated shops from the moment before large-scale factories were built communicated his idealized relationship between business owners and their employees. Finally, Ford's selection—and exclusion—of homes represented his views on the proper conditions under which self-made men best thrived.

Ford was also full of contradictions and idiosyncrasies, and these, too, found there way onto the village's terrain. What seemed to be a museum about American history included a cottage from England and a replica of a Swiss chalet. And the buildings representing African American history were suggestive of Ford's complex and inconsistent policies regarding black workers at Ford Motor Company. While the village's construction and narrative was certainly comparable to other museum projects of the time, it was also very much Henry Ford's "pageant of America" that visitors would pay to see.

3

The Public's Village

Welcome to Greenfield Village, ladies and gentlemen. Today we ask you to try to forget the hustle and bustle of the atomic age and return briefly to the simple, rugged life our forefathers knew.

— Greenfield Village tour script, 1945

Henry Ford hoped that Greenfield Village would serve not only as a veneration of pasts he deemed valuable but also as a proposal for how Americans should live in a modern age. Despite Ford's efforts to send specific messages, however, visitors' experiences spanned a broad spectrum. Diverse encounters with the village were related, in large part, to the wide range of visitors who arrived between the village's launch in 1929 and Ford's death in 1947. Shortly after opening day, Ford invited celebrities, politicians, and fellow inventors to tour what many locals referred to as his "dollhouse." Later marketing campaigns targeted vacationers as well as local residents. The interpretation of a past that visitors themselves remembered also laid the groundwork for disparate encounters. Ford chose buildings and objects that reminded him of his own childhood and life experiences; visitors viewed material culture that was familiar to them as well, and their personal memories either reinforced or challenged Ford's intended messages.[1]

A multiplicity of visitor experiences was in some ways expected given the dramatic shifts that occurred between 1929 and 1947. A devastated economy and a war reshaped notions of success, industrial capitalism, and America's place on the global stage. During World War II, attendance at the village reached an all-time low, reflecting the degree to which most Americans were engaged in the war effort, either fighting abroad or working in factories at home. By 1946, however, the Great Depression was over, United Auto Workers had contracts with the Big Three—Ford, General Motors, and Chrysler—and veterans began to use federally insured mortgages to purchase houses at

71

astoundingly low interest rates. African American Detroiters remained optimistic about the prospect of gaining civil rights by working through organizations like the local chapter of the National Association for the Advancement
of Colored People. Many Americans chose to spend their expanding income
and time on leisure pursuits, and as a result attendance at Greenfield Village
rose steadily.[2]

Visitors from Detroit would have been particularly affected by contemporary economic, political, and social shifts. The historian Thomas Sugrue
identifies the Great Depression and war years as a pivotal time in Detroit's
history, one that strengthened or destroyed institutions that worked toward
racial equality and class fairness. As *Life* magazine announced in 1942, Detroit
was simultaneously an arsenal of democracy and dynamite.[3] The same was
true of Greenfield Village, where accounts of visitors demonstrate that the
past, too, was up for grabs. Ford hoped to communicate his values and beliefs,
but visitors often negotiated the past with guides. Their interpretation of the
village's buildings and objects was a mix of the site's official narrative and their
personal views.

Selling the Village

Initially, Ford and his staff did not create a publicity campaign for the village, perhaps because one was unnecessary; Ford's national fame ensured that
many clamored to see his version of the American past. There were plenty of
local visitors to draw on as well. In 1930, the village's location near the River
Rouge plant made the site accessible to over a hundred thousand Ford workers there, as well as to the residents of Detroit, who by then numbered almost
1.6 million.[4]

Potential local visitors during this time period were racially, ethnically, and
economically diverse. By the 1930s, African Americans comprised almost 8
percent of the metro area's population, and Italian, Greek, and Polish immigrants had established enclaves in the urban core. The Detroit area also had a
large population of immigrants from the Middle East. Based at least partially
on the growth of the auto industry, Detroit and its suburbs became a popular
destination for Middle Eastern immigrants in the early twentieth century.[5]
When the Rouge plant started operations in 1917, for example, Dearborn's
Southend neighborhood became home to a small but growing population of
Arabic-speaking immigrants. Economic diversity further defined the Detroit
metro area. As Oliver Zunz has shown, the townships that became the City
of Dearborn in 1927 (Springwells, Greenfield, and Dearborn) were populated
with both farmers and skilled and unskilled factory workers. Although data

on the race, ethnicity, and class of Greenfield Village visitors is unavailable, Detroit's varied population obviously had easy access to the site, and publicity campaigns encouraged local residents (including Ford Motor employees) to attend.[6]

After the site officially opened in the summer of 1933, a local marketing campaign was initiated. Detroit's clubs were one popular venue for advertising the village and stating its goals. William A. Simonds, the director of public relations, often gave talks to groups such as the Optimist Club, the Business Women's Club, and the Delta Gamma convention, explaining how these potential visitors *should* experience Greenfield Village. In a 1937 speech to the Society of Automotive Engineers, for instance, Simonds said: "Mr. Ford didn't spend twenty-five years making his collections simply to bring a homesick tear to sentimental eyes, nor to serve as a drab contrast against which we may really appreciate the superior way we live today. . . . It is intended to open the eyes of the more thoughtful visitor to some of the values that have been lost in the process of our material advancement." Simonds asked the "thoughtful" visitor to consider Greenfield Village as a celebration of past *values* rather than a depiction of objective facts about American history. Such an approach actually encouraged visitors to interpret the site on their own terms, since each individual might lament the loss of a very different set of values.[7]

By the 1940s, residents were also urged to visit the village through the local media. Detroit's WWJ radio station broadcast the nondenominational service from the Martha-Mary Chapel on Sundays, the *Detroit News* published articles about the village, and Ford promoted the site nationally in his many interviews with popular magazines and newspapers. The availability of local transportation and an affordable entrance fee made a trip to the village attractive. Visitors could either drive to the site or pay twenty-five cents to take the twenty-minute bus ride from Detroit to Dearborn. Annual attendance rose steadily between the opening in 1933 and 1940, when it peaked at 633,296. Staff reported record lows between January 1941 and December 1944, but throughout 1945 attendance slowly increased to over 200,000.[8]

Buying the Village: A Two-Hour Tour

Greenfield Village's official narrative was communicated in a number of ways. Public talks by Simonds, radio announcements, and of course interviews in which Ford discussed his vision and purpose established the values he hoped the village honored. Signs identified the buildings, and the free pamphlet, or the more detailed ones available for purchase, offered visitors a map along with a brief description of each structure.[9] Guides also conveyed the site's official narrative. As I noted earlier, on some occasions visitors met guides when they arrived at buildings that were open for viewing, while on others one guide took a group through the entire village; thus visits were never unmediated.

Between 1933 and 1945, Ford continued to add buildings. During these years, the tour guide script for each building remained virtually the same. Consequently, the 1945 script provides the most complete version that guides used between 1933 and 1947 (the year of Ford's death). Beginning in 1945, one significant change was made: guides were to ask visitors to forget the "atomic age" in which they lived. Still, the general themes of the script remained the same throughout Ford's presidency.[10] Although the tour guide script did not credit an author, it is likely that Simonds, who directed the guides and public relations, wrote it. Themes that the script developed mirrored those Simonds discussed in his public talks. But it was almost certain that Ford reviewed the script, too, given his controlling approach to managing the site.

The 1945 tour script mixed historical information, tidbits from popular culture, and positive cultural tropes. Chronology did not determine the order of buildings visitors viewed, or the information provided to them once inside a home, shop, or laboratory. At the Blacksmith Shop, for example, visitors learned that the art of blacksmithing could be traced to ancient Egypt, heard a line from Longfellow's "The Village Blacksmith," and were introduced to the tools blacksmiths used.[11]

The scripted tour began at the Floral Clock, originally designed in 1893 for one of Detroit's parks and long a city landmark; its face was "composed of between six and eight thousand plants." From there visitors moved through the village in sections, beginning with buildings depicting industry, next those representing commerce and government, then the residential section, and finally the reproduction of Edison's Menlo Park. (Table 1 lists all of the buildings included.) Although visitors were not shown the interiors of all of the buildings, guides provided information about each structure. Within each section, the script developed specific themes that promoted some of Ford's views. Certainly every building did not fit neatly into a thematic structure. For example, at the Susquehanna House (a home from Maryland then believed to be built in the seventeenth century, donated to Ford in 1942), visitors learned that "Marylanders as a whole were not the stern, forbidding puritans our history books describe," but that these settlers were "well-to-do Calvinists, who imported furniture and luxuries from England and kept up with the latest British styles."[12] On the whole, however, the script celebrated self-made manhood, established that small towns were ideal, and touted the importance of industry and technology.

TABLE 1. Buildings on the 1945 Tour, in Order of Appearance

"Ext." indicates that visitors only saw the outside of the building; "opt." indicates that guides could exclude a building from their tour.

1. Floral Clock
2. High School Building (ext.)
3. Luther Burbank Office (ext.)
4. Chemical Laboratory (ext.)
5. Henry Ford Birthplace (ext.)
6. Village Print Shop (ext.)
7. Loranger Gristmill (ext.)
8. Edsel Ford Building and 58 Bagley Avenue (ext.)
9. Armington & Sims Machine Shop
10. Sandwich Glass Plant
11. Hanks Silk Mill
12. Deluge Fire House (ext.)
13. Lunch Wagon (ext.)
14. Plymouth Carding Mill
15. Edison Illuminating Company (ext.; opt.)
16. Blacksmith Shop
17. Kingston Cooper Shop
18. Currier Shoe Shop (ext.)
19. Toll House
20. Smith's Creek Depot
21. Tintype Studio
22. Plymouth House
23. Post Office
24. Village Green
25. Town Hall (ext.)
26. Waterford General Store
27. Gardner House (ext.; opt.)
28. Pioneer Log Cabin (ext.; opt.)
29. Riding Stable (ext.; opt.)
30. Clinton Inn
31. Herb Garden
32. Martha-Mary Chapel
33. Scotch Settlement School
34. Logan County Courthouse
35. Slave Huts (ext.; opt.)
36. George Washington Carver Memorial
37. Mattox House (ext.)
38. McGuffey Group
39. Chapman House (ext.)
40. George Matthew Adams Birthplace (ext.)
41. Steinmetz Camp (ext.)
42. Stephen Foster Birthplace
43. Steamer Suwanee
44. Swiss Watchmaker's Chalet
45. Luther Burbank Birthplace (ext.)
46. Edison Homestead
47. Ann Arbor House (ext.)
48. Noah Webster House (ext.)
49. Secretary House (ext.)
50. Cotswold Group
51. Cape Cod Windmill
52. Plympton House
53. Susquehanna House (ext.)
54. Ackley Covered Bridge
55. Christie Street
56. Fort Myers Laboratory (ext.)
57. Sarah Jordan Boarding House
58. Menlo Park Group (Laboratory, Glass House, Machine Shop, Office and Library, Woodworking Shop)
59. Building Number 11 (ext.)
60. Sir John Bennett Jewelry Store
61. Grimm Jewelry Shop (ext.)
62. Wright Homestead
63. Wright Cycle Shop
64. Magill Jewelry Store (ext.)
65. Miller School

Source: "Greenfield Village Tour: 1945," box 8, accession no. 141, Edison Institute Records, Benson Ford Research Center, The Henry Ford.

Interpreting Self-Made Manhood

The tour script used biographical information and anecdotes to argue that the ideal self-made man came from humble roots, had strong values rooted in Protestant Christianity, and was curious, inventive, courageous, hard-working, and often lucky. The biographies highlighted on the tour often reflected a version of self-made manhood that followed the popular nineteenth-century novelist Horatio Alger's simple formulas of "rags to respectability" and "pluck and luck."[13] For example, inside the small Plympton House, visitors were to learn that the home was built in 1650 by an indentured servant who went on to secure his own home.

The first self-made man visitors learned about, however, was Henry Ford. Several buildings were used to flesh out his biography. Early in the tour, visitors walked by the Luther Burbank Office (1906). Although Burbank's accomplishments in horticulture were mentioned, guides were to highlight Ford's and Edison's relationship with Burbank, whom they "often visited . . . when the office stood at his [Burbank's] nursery in Santa Rosa, California." Similarly, inside the Village Print Shop, constructed in 1933, guides were not only to mention the significance of the press in the American Revolution, but also that the shop was currently used to print Ford's Greenfield Village school newspaper and informational materials for the Edison Institute Museum. As visitors viewed the exteriors of Ford's Chemical Laboratory and the Henry Ford Birthplace, the script painted Ford as a curious boy, a good friend, and a devoted son. Visitors learned that Ford was a pioneer of plastics technology when they viewed the Chemical Laboratory. And the birthplace was used to discuss Ford's devotion to his mother, the script noted, because he included the site to honor her memory. Later in the tour, visitors would learn more about Ford's boyhood. His affection for his teacher John Brainard Chapman was mentioned when visitors viewed the exterior of Chapman's home. And when visitors walked by the Grimm Jewelry Store they learned that the shop "was often visited by young Henry Ford, who stopped in to chat with Mr. Grimm or to buy watch parts."[14]

The Edsel Ford Building and 58 Bagley Avenue further defined self-made manhood through Ford's biography. The replica of a garage workshop that Ford built for his son documented his excellent parenting skills, while the adjacent replica of the Bagley Avenue workshop highlighted Ford's first great invention, the Quadricycle. As they stood outside these two buildings, the script encouraged guides to relate the by-then popular story that when Ford finished building the Quadricycle it was too big to get out of the shop, and that he solved the problem by making the door larger. The message was that Ford was so passionate about work that he forgot practical things, but that his inventiveness often led to quick and amusing solutions.

Visitors were reminded of Ford's precociousness at the exterior of what was then portrayed as the Magill Jewelry Store and inside of the replica of the Miller School, the last two buildings on the tour.[15] When Ford arrived in Detroit in 1879, he soon found a job at Magill's store repairing watches. The script explained that Magill required Ford to work in the back of the store because he feared that customers would not trust such a young workman. When visitors reached the Miller School, they learned that "it was here that young Henry's inventiveness was shown when he and his classmates built a steam turbine in a shed behind the school. The engine exploded and tore off part of the school house." "Here also," the script noted, "the boys constructed a dam and waterwheel; when the boys forgot to undam the mill one night the neighboring farms were flooded the next morning." Thus Ford demonstrated that the self-made man was intrepid, fearless, and full of mischief.

While Ford's life story was often center-stage on the tour, so was Thomas Edison's. The tour script cast Edison, too, as a paragon of self-made manhood. For example, at Smith's Creek Station, built in 1858 near Port Huron, Michigan, where Edison grew up, the development of rail travel took a back seat to tales showing that Edison was brave, adventurous, and lucky. The station "played a prominent part in the early life of Edison," guides recounted; in 1862 the young inventor snatched the stationmaster's son from the path of a moving train. The stationmaster then taught Edison what he knew of telegraphy, and Edison was on his way to becoming a famous scientist and inventor. The script also recounted that it was at Smith's Creek Station that Edison was "thrown from the train by an angry conductor when he set fire to the baggage coach during one of his experiments."

The Menlo Park section of the script furthered the theme of self-made manhood, using popular narratives from Edison's biography. Before making their way to the Menlo Park buildings, visitors walked through the Ackley Covered Bridge and found their way to the village's Christie Street. Guides explained that the original Christie Street was "the first street in the world to be lighted by Edison's incandescent lamp." They then proceeded with the tour of Menlo Park; visitors viewed the exterior of the last laboratory Edison used (the Fort Myers Laboratory), went inside the first home to be lighted by a "practical incandescent light" (the Sarah Jordan Boarding House), and saw the building where the first incandescent bulbs were blown (the Glass House), the world's first power station (the Machine Shop; fig. 7), and the shed used in many of Edison's experiments (the Woodworking Shop). They went inside the site where Edison lit the first incandescent bulb (Menlo Park Laboratory), and saw the exterior of one of Edison's offices in West Orange, New Jersey (Building Number 11).

Inside the laboratory, the script directed guides to identify the objects that captured Edison's career, discuss the building's claims to fame, and recount anecdotes that defined Edison's character. The downstairs contained chemicals, a galvanometer (a device used to measure electric current), and models that Edison submitted for patenting (see fig. 7). Upstairs, visitors saw equipment he used to perfect his systems of electrical heating, lighting, and power. The script suggested that guides remind visitors of Greenfield Village's own history by informing them that "fifty years later Mr. Edison came to the building and in the presence of former President Hoover and Mr. Ford re-enacted the complete scene of the invention." Afterward, the script noted, Ford ordered that the chair in which Edison sat be nailed to the floor. Visitors then were invited to view a phonograph, typewriter, vote-recording machine, and telephone that Edison invented. The stories told at Menlo Park were indicative of the swift movement between chronological periods that defined the script. Menlo Park was a reminder of Edison's accomplishments as a young man, and of Ford's achievement in building a replica of his mentor's laboratory.

Edison was portrayed as congenial and jocular in the script, which mentioned that he and his workmen often gathered around an organ to relax during breaks or after a hard day at work. Concluding the tour, guides were to tell visitors that when Edison arrived in 1929 he remarked to Ford that the re-creation was "99.9%" perfect. When Ford asked Edison what was incorrect, he replied, "Our floor was never as clean as this." The Menlo Park script cast

FIGURE 7. To re-create Menlo Park, Ford was forced to build several replicas, including one of the machine shop. He then located the implements that would have been used by Edison and his employees inside the buildings. Photo by author, 2011.

Edison as immensely productive, hardworking, compassionate, friendly, and funny, and while his achievements were grand, he was presented as a common man, one whose habits could be emulated and whose success could be achieved by any man.

The tour script used Edison to make a case for ideal womanhood cast in the framework of self-made manhood. Women's importance was defined in terms of their relationship to men: "self-made" men had supportive mothers and wives.[16] Inside the Edison Homestead, for example, visitors toured the kitchen and the Sunday parlor, which contained a set of history books belonging to the inventor's mother. "Perhaps," the script said, "Edison would never have become a famous inventor if his mother had not been a schoolteacher, for, as you may remember, young Tom was sent home from school in disgrace because his teacher said it was impossible to teach him. Fortunately, his mother was able to continue his education." Women could be educated and work outside of the home, as long as their endeavors supported their husbands and sons.

Documents from popular culture supported the tour script's narrative. Two films celebrating Edison—*Young Tom Edison,* starring Mickey Rooney, and *Edison the Man,* with Spencer Tracy in the title role—were released in 1940, and much of the footage for each was shot at Greenfield Village. By 1945, the National Opinion Research Center found that Edison placed fourth (after Franklin Roosevelt, Lincoln, and Washington) as the greatest man who ever lived. The same year a Gallup poll ranked Edison sixth, behind Jesus, FDR, Lincoln, Washington, and General Douglas MacArthur, as the "greatest person, living or dead, in world history." In 1947, Edison's wife and daughter opened the Edison Birthplace Museum in Milan, Ohio, and other efforts to commemorate Edison on the American landscape followed in the 1950s. Edison's biographer Wyn Wachhorst has argued that in newspapers, magazines, and film, Edison's humble beginnings were often tied to his success, suggesting that "technological triumph itself was inseparable from the romantic individualism of an earlier and simpler America."[17]

Although all of the homes included on the tour, such as the Luther Burbank Birthplace, suggested that self-made manhood and domesticity were connected, this narrative was most clearly articulated inside the Wright Homestead and the Wright Brothers' Cycle Shop. Placing these two buildings next to each other created a clear link between ideal domesticity and a successful career. The script for the Wright Homestead emphasized the importance of family and education, and it advanced the progressive view that science and religion were not necessarily in conflict. Guides characterized the homestead, which dated to 1870, as a typical middle-class home of the late 1800s. It too had a Sunday parlor decorated with Victorian-era furniture and a living room that served as the "center of the Wright family life." It was here, the guide said, that the Wright boys studied "theories of flight and read the many books owned by their father, Bishop Wright." (The elder Wright was a minister and bishop of the Church of the United Brethren in Christ.) The family was "well educated" and "broad-minded"; for example, the "possession of Darwin's *Origin of Species* . . . was quite daring for a minister."

Visitors then entered the cycle shop and were told that it was the "birthplace of the airplane." The brothers began their bicycle business in 1897 and produced three models that guides discussed, the Van Cleve, the Saint Clair, and the Wright Special. Visitors then heard the story of Kitty Hawk and the first successful motor-driven flight on December 17, 1903. The walls were adorned with photographs showing the first flight, and the office contained the brothers' desk, a safe, and a typewriter used by their father. In the next two rooms, visitors examined storage racks, stands, and equipment for repairing bicycles. Once again, the overall message was that the Wright brothers were exemplary self-made men, curious and pragmatic, who through hard work and experimentation achieved well-deserved economic success.

The script emphasized that men could make great intellectual strides in unexceptional settings, and these included the Steinmetz Camp, the small wooden cabin built in 1896 that belonged to Ford's friend Charles Proteus Steinmetz. Known as the "Wizard of Schenectady," Steinmetz was a mathematician and electrical engineer whose work was integral to the expansion of electric power in the United States.[18] Guides were asked to explain that the cabin "offered a quiet spot for Steinmetz to work on his electrical textbooks."

The script often pointed out that a home was significant because it represented a popular type of architecture, which furthered the theme that exceptional men were often born, lived, and worked in unremarkable places. Outside of the Ann Arbor House, visitors learned that Robert Frost had lived there while on a fellowship at the University of Michigan in the early 1920s.[19] Just as important, however, was that the home was built in 1830 and offered an "excellent example of the Greek Revival influence in architecture." The four columns and pediment on the rather humble home would have made this assertion clear. Visitors were also reminded of the importance of popular building styles when they walked by the Plymouth House, built in 1845 in Plymouth, Michigan. Guides pointed out the return cornices typical of the Greek Revival style and noted that "thousands of homes" like it were built across the Midwest in the 1800s. At the Adams House, home of the newspaper columnist George Matthew Adams, guides were to explain that the two-story home (although built in the 1840s), represented "the architectural style of the later Victorian years."

The tour script tied self-made manhood to English and Swiss heritage at the Cotswold Group, the Swiss Watchmaker's Home, and the Sir John Bennett Jewelry Store. The Cotswold buildings were on the periphery of the village, at the end of South Dearborn Road. Here, the script noted that the Rose Cottage, stable, dovecote, and forge were built in the 1620s and represented a "type of home in which our forefathers might have lived in England." Visitors learned that it was built of limestone, which was both an abundant and an affordable building material. Once inside, guides noted that the occupants of the home were "two families of sheep herders," and that each family would have had its own bedroom upstairs. Guides were to point out the fireplace and fireplace utensils, a long trestle table, and several lamps, and to note that the home had been decorated with furniture from the "Stuart or Jacobean period." Visitors next viewed the stable, dovecote, and forge, as well as descendants of sheep from the Cotswold region.

Inside the Swiss Watchmaker's Chalet, built in 1935, visitors learned that during the nineteenth century the Swiss "led the world in the production of fine watches." The building was "typical of the combined homes-and-work-shops which were found in the Jura Mountains of Switzerland," and contained rooms set up for engraving, silversmith, and stamping work. Later in the tour, when visitors entered the Sir John Bennett Jewelry Shop, they were to be told that the building was a London landmark. (In fact, it was a partial reproduction combining portions of the exterior of the 1846 shop, moved from England, with new construction done at the village between 1930 and 1931.) Visitors viewed a variety of watches and clocks, including an English lantern clock from 1630. The inclusion of buildings either from or linked to England and Switzerland was a striking reminder that Greenfield Village was an invented place, but these structures also connected self-made manhood to western European heritage.[20]

The Stephen Foster Birthplace (later the Stephen C. Foster Memorial) offered visitors a cautionary tale. The script began by observing that the "songs of Stephen Foster are so much a part of our American musical heritage that we seldom stop to think about their author." Sadly, the script said, "Foster lived a short, tragic life and died in poverty and obscurity"; he never knew that "Old Black Joe," "Old Folks at Home," and "Camptown Races" became popular songs. Foster's family, unlike those of many of the other men repre-sented at the village, was unsupportive, and consequently "Stephen grew up to be a charming, kind-hearted, impractical dreamer with little business abil-ity." He was never fully paid for "Uncle Ned" or "Oh! Susanna." And although Foster loved his family, he was "temperamentally unable to settle down" or to provide for his wife and daughter. Foster and his wife "separated several times, and Stephen was alone when he died in a charity hospital in New York. In his pocket were 38 cents and a slip of paper" containing the phrase, " 'Dear

Friends and Gentle Hearts,' perhaps the title of a song he never wrote." Foster's biography was expanded on at the nearby Steamer *Suwanee,* also on the tour, a reconstruction of a stern-wheel steamboat "patterned after one which cruised along the Suwanee River of Foster's song"—though guides were to note that "Foster never saw the river which he immortalized." Foster's failures implied the importance of a supportive family, a pragmatic nature, and a good marriage to achieving economic success.

At the three one-room schoolhouses in the village—the Scotch Settlement School, the McGuffey School, and the Miller School—the script simultaneously lauded institutional education and downplayed its importance in achieving self-made manhood. Visitors learned that the 1861 Scotch Settlement School "was the first school that Henry Ford attended." There, Ford studied the "old McGuffey readers and acquired a great admiration for their author." "It is interesting to note," the script continued, "that Mr. Ford had only four years of formal education, attending this school in 1871–72 and later attending the Miller School," which visitors viewed at the end of the tour. The script explained that the self-made man was often self-educated, worked hard, and practiced self-discipline. The third one-room schoolhouse was part of the McGuffey Group. At the McGuffey birthplace, smokehouse, and one-room school building, the script chronicled McGuffey's humble beginnings and his rise to fame. McGuffey was clearly exemplary of self-made manhood, but his achievements also supported the rise of other self-made men.

The presence of a building honoring George Washington Carver implied that African Americans could achieve self-made manhood, but the script did not clearly place Carver in that narrative. Visitors were to learn that the "cabin was built in the Village in honor of George Washington Carver, the famous Negro scientist." Carver's agricultural inventions were mentioned, and he was "credited with changing the agricultural pattern of the south." That the cabin was based on Carver's memories of his birthplace, however, was not mentioned. Instead, visitors were to be told that "Carver lived in this house for a short while in 1942 as the guest of Mr. Ford," and that it was "unusual in that the front room is paneled with wood from every state of the union." Although this was certainly an interesting feature, the script did not explain its connection to Carver: that the governors of every state had donated wood to help Ford honor his friend. Indeed, the detail actually disrupted the narrative focus on Carver and his accomplishments by highlighting Henry Ford and the home's architectural features. Further, the script did not clarify that Carver was born into slavery and poverty, but had gone on to achieve fame. The notion that Carver was a self-made man was suggested, but not made explicit in the tour script.

The script for the Carver home was far more elaborate than the narrative for the adjacent Mattox House, however. Visitors were to walk by the Mattox home and learn only that it was a "small frame house" that was "used by slave families at the Richmond Hill Plantation, near Ways, Georgia." Further complicating the script for the Mattox house was that the building was, as we saw in chapter 2, inhabited by a black tenant farmer and his family when Ford purchased it. While all of the homes served as symbols of the links between self-made men and domestic life, the script did not always make this narrative explicit, particularly at the homes associated with African American history.

The Small-Town Ideal

Ford intended Greenfield Village to stand in stark contrast to what he saw as the urban blight of Detroit. The tour script celebrated small-town life in several sections of the village, but the Village Green most clearly defined this ideal by suggesting that private institutions and local or state government were preferable to the federal government. Just as one might see in a real New England town, surrounding the green were a town hall, a general store, an inn, a small church, a school, and a courthouse (fig. 8).

The Town Hall (one of the village's original constructions) was the first stop on this part of the tour. Guides mentioned that it was a place where "town business and local politics were discussed." According to the script, the hall was typical of those found in "New England and the southern states" and was now being used as a classroom for third and fourth grade classes at the village's private school system.

While the script acknowledged the importance of the Town Hall, its function was insignificant in comparison to the next site: the Waterford General Store. Visitors learned that it was built in 1854 in Waterford, Michigan, about forty miles north of Detroit, and they were invited to view the products on display. The store, visitors were told, was not only a place where everything "from drugs to dry goods and household furnishings could be purchased," but also an "informal meeting place for the men of the family." While the Town Hall offered formal meeting space, the General Store helped cultivate personal ties among members of the community.

The script then gave guides the option of pointing out a series of small buildings associated with Ford's childhood. In some tours, visitors were told that a distant relative of the Fords originally owned the Gardner House; that the Pioneer Log Cabin was built in the 1820s by John Salter, a "hermit-philosopher" whom Henry Ford often visited as a young boy; and that the Riding Stable once stood on the farm of Addison Ford, Henry's second cousin. In

FIGURE 8. Greenfield Village's Main Street, 1935. Visitors touring the village at this time found a replication of a small town center at the Village Green. On the right is the Waterford General Store; the Town Hall is in the background. From the collections of The Henry Ford (2008.0.1.1)

other tours, the guide might choose to bypass those sites and head straight for the Clinton Inn, constructed in 1832 in Clinton, Michigan, on the Great Sauk Trail, which became U.S. Highway 112.

By the time they arrived at the striking two-story, nine-columned Clinton Inn, visitors likely believed the guides when they said it was a "welcome sight to weary stagecoach travelers in the days when it was the first overnight stop on the Detroit-to-Chicago coach route." The script highlighted the hardships of the past by explaining that "travel was extremely difficult in those days" and that "often the tired travelers had to get out and walk or help push the stagecoach out of the mud." Once inside, visitors learned about the function of the taproom, the everyday parlor, the Sunday parlor, and the objects in each. The script depicted the inn as a model of gentility where "famous people" such as "Daniel Webster, the orator, James Fenimore Cooper, the novelist, and President James Polk" visited. In identifying these men as guests, the script indicated that the inn was also an important locale for public discourse.

Outside the Martha-Mary Chapel, visitors saw a replica of a thirteenth-century Grecian herb garden, called "The Garden of the Leavened Heart," that was based on one Clara Ford had seen in Italy. The garden included eight segments, four of which were heart-shaped. In the center was a brass sundial that bore the inscription "Ye Shadow Teacheth."[21] Once inside the chapel, guides were to inform them that churches once "served as landmarks for travelers and as watchtowers for Indian raids." The script pointed out that religious customs were much stricter in the past, that church services were at one time the only chance for people to see their friends and get the latest news, and that the preacher was often the most important man in a community. "Many times," guides said, "when pastors lost favor with legal authorities and were asked to move, their influence was so great that entire communities packed up and moved with them." The script reinforced the landscape, which also placed the church at the center of small-town life, at the head of the Village Green.

The script for the Logan County Court House, a spare—even severe—two-story vernacular building, chronicled Abraham Lincoln's life and death. Guides were to open by saying that "Abraham Lincoln was just another country lawyer in 1840, when his first cases were heard in the Logan County Court House in Illinois." Lincoln was described as a "tall gawky young man who loved a good story and was a tricky debater—but neither in appearance nor in behavior did he give much hint of his future greatness." Inside the courthouse visitors could see the chair in which Lincoln was assassinated on April 14, 1865 (it was later moved to the indoor museum). "Lincoln's death could not have come at a more tragic time," the script intoned. "The long, weary war with the South was nearly over, and the nation's future looked bright." A detailed account of Lincoln's assassination followed, concluding with an announcement that all of the furniture in the courthouse came from Lincoln's home and law offices. While the Civil War was mentioned, it played an almost insignificant role in the story told at the Court House. Instead, the script emphasized Lincoln's humble beginnings, his intelligence and congeniality, his work in local politics, and his untimely death, and it implied that Lincoln's experience working with the residents of small towns was central to his success.

The next two buildings visitors might see were the exteriors of the Slave Huts, which guides could choose to bypass. If they were included on the tour, their placement next to the Logan County Courthouse suggested their political significance, though the script did not encourage guides to make that connection. Between 1934 and 1940, guides told visitors that the Slave Huts were important because they were featured in D. W. Griffith's 1915 film *The Birth of a Nation,* providing a popular culture framework for understanding the buildings that connected them to the history of the Ku Klux Klan.[22] By 1941, however, research showed that the buildings were not featured in the film, and instead visitors were provided with a set of facts: "These slave huts stood for many years on the Hermitage Plantation just outside Savannah, Georgia, where they were units of a slave quarter containing 52 similar huts." The subsoil around the plantation, guests learned, was "excellent for brick-making" so most of the buildings were brick. A discussion of racial politics was absent from the script, but by placing the Slave Huts adjacent to the Lincoln County Court House, visitors were sent competing and contradictory messages. On the one hand, they could choose to think about Lincoln, his role in the Civil War, and his effort to end slavery, and in that context the Slave Huts were part of a narrative of social justice. Visitors viewing Greenfield Village and the Slave Huts in nostalgic terms, however, might read them as supportive of a social and once legal racial hierarchy.

Celebrating Industry and Technology

Through success stories and cautionary tales, the tour script venerated industrial and technological advancements, just as the village itself did by preserving and replicating buildings associated with long histories. For example, at the Cape Cod Windmill, visitors learned that windmills had "come to America with the Pilgrims." Visitors were encouraged to agree that inventors made products more efficient, safer, and more affordable, and to recognize technology's role in humanity's development.

The script for the Loranger Gristmill placed American mills at the top of an evolutionary chain beginning in ancient times. Once inside, visitors were to learn that the gristmill was a typical example, built in 1832 near Monroe, Michigan. A discussion of the challenges farmers faced getting to a miller was followed by a description of how grain was dropped into bins, carried upstairs through a conveyor system, and sent to the hopper. Milling, the script said, was one of the oldest industries in the world, dating back to the "early days of the Egyptians." By placing the Loranger Gristmill in a history beginning in ancient times (as was also true at the blacksmith's shop), the script promoted Ford's view that industry and technology had long defined daily life.

At the Armington & Sims Machine Shop, guides offered a brief history of the steam engine through this replica of the original 1883 factory in Providence, Rhode Island. "Although the steam engine was invented in 1705," the script said, "the early engines were not too practical and it remained for Armington & Sims to make a truly efficient one." Inside, visitors saw "one of the original Armington & Sims engines," and discovered that "Thomas Edison put the firm on the map when he chose their steam engines for his first commercial lighting station, the Pearl Street Station in New York City." Guides were then to point out that the "lantern-type roof, the overhead crane system, and the belt operated machinery" had been replicated from the original shop. Small companies, the script implied, were imperative to building a world that was more pragmatic and efficient.

The suggested talk at the Sandwich Glass Plant celebrated an older technology while ignoring its demise. For example, on the one hand, the script located American industry at the end of a progressive history beginning in ancient times by explaining that glassmaking dated to 2500 B.C. and was one of the earliest industries brought to America from Great Britain. Visitors learned that the original Sandwich plant, built in 1825 on Cape Cod, was "one of the most outstanding glass companies in America," and that part of the firm's success lay in the fact that "Deming Jarves, the owner of the plant, imported foreign glass blowers who knew more skilled techniques than the American workers did." Inside the plant, visitors viewed a glassmaker at work. Here the long history of industry was reinforced, as was the idea that inventive company owners were central to an industrial business's success. The script did not note, however, that the industry in Sandwich had failed.

In contrast, the script for the Hanks Silk Mill did recognize this industry's demise. Inside the mill, visitors were told that "in the 1600's Britain was importing raw silk for her silk mills at enormous cost from foreign countries, and she could see the great advantage of having a ready supply of raw silk in the colonies." Although they were encouraged to raise silkworms, early settlers found raising tobacco more profitable. The Hanks Silk Mill was built in Mansfield, Connecticut, in 1810 as part of an effort to revive the industry, visitors learned, but was an exception: while "the American climate is suitable for silk raising, we can't compete with foreign labor in producing our own silk." Here guides were to make a subtle argument against importing products that could be made in the United States. Developing industries that made quick money, like tobacco, as opposed to those that required diligence, hard work, and long-term commitment, had significant economic consequences.

Across the street from the silk mill, visitors learned more about technological progress when they viewed what was then called the Deluge Fire House. This building, originally interpreted as a firehouse, had been built in the mid-nineteenth century and moved to Greenfield Village in 1928 from Newton, New Hampshire.[23] The script focused on advances in equipment, noting that "firefighting equipment of the past century was clumsy and inefficient, as you can see from this fire engine, built in 1845." At the next stop on the tour, the Owl Night Lunch Wagon, visitors were given more glimpses into Ford's biography; the script noted that the eatery was "a popular gathering spot for policemen, reporters, and other shift workers," and that "Henry Ford, while working on the night shift at the Edison Illuminating Company, often stopped here for hot dogs and coffee."[24]

At the Plymouth Carding Mill, technological advances took center stage. Within the mill visitors viewed machines documenting the nation's "200 years' progress in the textile industry." Technological advancement was beneficial, inevitable, and by 1945, dominated by American industrialists. At the Kingston Cooper Shop, visitors were told that barrels dated to "1580 B.C." and "played a great part in the romance of the centuries, being used by the Greeks and Romans, by the Crusaders," and "by pirates of the Spanish Main." The Kingston Cooper Shop, which was built in Kingston, New Hampshire, in 1785, was "the oldest craft shop in the Village," and was so valuable that it could be used as part of "the dowry for a marriageable daughter." The tour script made a case that the history of industry should be at the center, not the periphery, of Americans' understanding of the past. Self-made men were presented as heroes refining and improving the industrial technology of ancient civilizations.

Guides had the option of stopping outside the quarter-size replica of the Detroit branch of the Edison Illuminating Company. Visitors learned that the building was a "partial reproduction of the original which was built in 1886 at Washington and State Street." Guides were to relate the structure to Henry Ford's successful rise in the company by noting that "when the Beck steam engine broke down and Mr. Ford repaired it, he received a promotion and a raise in pay." They could also connect the structure to the reproduction of the Armington & Sims building if they told visitors that inside were "two Armington and Sims engines."

As Ford had promised when he announced his plan for the museum, visitors could also learn about industries that created domestic products at the Currier Shoe Shop, the Toll House (another shoe shop), and the Tintype Studio. The script explained that the Currier shop, built around 1870 in Newton, New Hampshire, exemplified "hundreds of such small industries which paved the way for today's modern shoe factories." The Toll House, built in 1828 in Rocks Village, Massachusetts, served multiple purposes. "Since traffic was slow in the long winter months," the script noted, "the toll master spent his spare time making shoes." Finally, inside the Tintype Studio (an original construction), guides were to explain that "nearly every family album contains at least one tintype, with the family in stiff, uncomfortable poses." Visitors learned that the tintype was invented in 1856 and became popular "during the War Between the States, when soldiers sent back pictures to their families." Guides were to point out the posing chair, head rests, tintype camera, and "primping room," before viewing tintypes of famous Greenfield Village visitors.

As visitors viewed the exterior and interior of shops and factories, they were provided with information that pointed to the centrality of industry and technology. The script celebrated the past and the present by noting the unique and important features of, for example, the Armington & Sims machine shop, while simultaneously arguing that great technological strides had been made in the development of firefighting equipment at the Deluge Fire House. Further, the wide range of shops and factories reflected Ford's vision of a museum that recognized the work of ordinary citizens. At Greenfield Village, nineteenth-century shoemakers were celebrated alongside Thomas Edison and Henry Ford.

Visitors' Views

The themes that the tour script promoted, however, were not always the focus of visitors' comments. During the early years of operation, visitors most often linked the buildings and objects on display to their personal memories or interests. They noted most often how their individual memories, knowledge, and politics shaped their trip to Ford's past rather than expressing appreciation for or approval of his various philosophies. That visitors saw the village through their own lens was unsurprising. What was significant, however, was the diversity of these individual experiences and the degree to which such encounters—even those that jarred with or challenged the official narrative— were given credence by guides.

Between 1934 and 1946, guides recorded daily happenings in a series of typed notebooks titled "Greenfield Village Journal." The journals provide a unique glimpse of how visitors used history museums during this period. Despite the growth of museums in the late nineteenth and early twentieth centuries, rigorous studies of visitors were rare. One exception was *Principles of Museum Administration* (1895), by George Brown Goode, assistant secretary of the Smithsonian Institution, which referred to visitors' comfort. Benjamin Ives Gilman, secretary of the Museum of Fine Arts in Boston and president of the American Association of Museums, discussed museum fatigue twenty-three years later in *Museum Ideals of Purpose and Method* (1918), and Edward Robinson, an educational psychologist, expanded on this work in *The Behavior of the Museum Visitor* (1928). Robinson's work sparked a number of other scholarly studies of visitors during the 1930s, such as Arthur W. Melton's examination of visitors at the Pennsylvania Museum of Art (1935), but in general, methodical studies of the experience of museum-goers were few and far between. Despite the dearth of external, systematic analyses of visitors, many institutions kept informal records on their audiences, such as the journals kept by Greenfield Village guides. Of course, these journals are an imperfect source, since the voices of visitors captured there were filtered through the guides. Still, the staff's efforts to document what visitors said and how they behaved at the village provides an invaluable opportunity for understanding how Americans consumed Ford's version of America's history.[25]

Three young male guides identified themselves as authors of the journals between 1934 and 1938. After that, no authors were listed, and after 1941 the entries became sporadic, ceasing altogether by 1946. In general, guides were recruited from the Henry Ford Trade School after 1933, and local high school and college students supplemented the ranks. As the Greenfield Village school extended to higher grades, some of the older girls served as guides as well.[26]

Between 1934 and 1936, Jerome Wilford wrote about daily occurrences at the village in the journal. Wilford was eighteen in 1934 and had just graduated from Dearborn High School; his father was a local real estate agent. In 1932, while still in high school, Wilford was an active member of the debating team; that year, members of the Michigan High School Debating Society were required to develop affirmative and negative arguments based on the question "Resolved that the State of Michigan should enact legislation providing for compulsory unemployment insurance." Wilford had participated in several debates arguing the negative case, and the young man's oratorical skills may have won him the guide position at the village.[27]

In 1937 nineteen-year-old Donald M. Currie took over the journal. Currie was the son of Scottish immigrants; his father, Robert, had arrived in the United States in 1908 and his mother in 1913. One year later the couple had their first child, and five years later Donald arrived, one of a pair of twin boys. In 1930, Robert Currie listed his occupation as "Marine Engineer" on the U.S. Census form. In 1932, when he was fourteen, Donald Currie was enrolled at Dearborn High School, but at some point he and his twin brother were sent to Scotland for two years to attend a boarding school. Currie returned to the United States and began working as a guide as early as 1936, but he did not take over the journal until 1937. By 1940 he was working as a secretary, and had completed one year of college at the University of Michigan. He would go on to become an educator, and in 1962 he became superintendent of the Royal Oak, Michigan, public school system.[28]

Finally, Jack Sullivan, who was the last listed journal author and completed entries in 1938, was most likely Dearborn resident Jack C. Sullivan. Born in 1919, Sullivan was the son of an attorney; by 1939 he was attending the University of Michigan.[29]

In the first year, Jerome Wilford wrote almost daily about the village's activities. He carefully divided each entry into five general sections, beginning with a narrative account of the day, which generally spanned two pages. Entries often started with a description of the chapel service, where guides were notified of their duties for the day as well as any policy changes. Wilford also frequently offered an update on new building construction and completion, recorded notes about the activities of the schoolchildren, and, of course, made comments on visitors. This was followed by a brief discussion of what was happening in the indoor museum, a list of "Special Parties," and a comparison of the yearly attendance rate to date. At the conclusion of the entry, Wilford added a brief sentence describing weather conditions, most likely because it determined attendance and available activities. After 1934, however, while the information included was largely similar, entries were limited to approximately half a page.

Wilford's comments could be mundane statements such as "There have been some complaints by visitors as to the amount of walking distance in the village," or "A guide spoke of the complaints that are raised because of the height of the steps on the large buses from the ground."[30] But they also described the lenses through which visitors viewed buildings and objects. Comments fell largely into two categories: visitors asserting their authority over the past by challenging the site's depiction of it; and visitors noting how the objects and buildings on display evoked personal memories.

Both categories reflected Ford's decision to preserve and replicate buildings that were familiar to him. The material culture of his early life, or the era of his early life, dominated the Greenfield Village landscape. Of course, these buildings and objects were equally familiar to many visitors as well—men and women of Ford's generation who also grew up in Michigan or elsewhere in the upper Midwest. On the whole, comments illustrated visitors' diversity in every sense: they were of different races and classes, and they arrived with various worldviews. The visitor experience was definitively personal, and thus a visit to the village was, at least in some ways, a democratic experience.[31]

Village journal-keepers recorded many encounters with visitors who claimed authority over the site. One way that visitors asserted this power was by suggesting changes. In June 1934, shortly after the village opened to the general public, many made their recommendations to a Mr. Boyle, who sold tickets and merchandise at the center desk in the waiting room. The journal reported that many visitors expressed their desire to be able to do more heritage-inflected shopping when they told Boyle that they "would like to have a catalogue from which they can order the products of the village by mail from points out of town," and that others "suggested placing price tags on articles for sale in the carding mill."[32] Visitors clearly saw the past as a product that could be purchased and sold, but these comments also reflected a sense that the site was for the public, and as such one that could be changed to suit their needs and desires.

In August 1934, the guides met to discuss how to better manage visitors. Eighteen-year-old Wilford told the young guides to avoid making "wise-cracks" in their speeches, and explained how to handle big groups. Guides also debated how best to handle visitors who challenged an object's authenticity. One woman, for example "said she had seen another chair in which Lincoln was sitting when shot." Although Israel Sack had secured and authenticated the chair for Ford in 1928, Wilford wrote that "it was decided that the best thing to do is present the facts, and allow the visitor to draw his own conclusions."[33] Guides were encouraged to allow visitors to express their own opinions, and many who found that the site's version of the past conflicted with their personal experience did not hesitate to question its veracity.

Guides' comments illustrated when and how visitors regularly challenged the village's depiction of the past. Visitors often expressed dismay when they did not encounter objects or products that conformed to their stereotypes or personal experience. During the 1936 summer season, for instance, a guide reported that visitors often asked why objects commonly used to discipline students during the nineteenth century were not in the Scotch Settlement School. The entry stated that "'Where is the hickory stick?' is a question asked by many quizzical visitors at Scotch Settlement School." Another common question at the Scotch Settlement was "Where is the dunce's stool?" At the General Store, many visitors remarked on the "absence of the cracker barrel" and complained that "the place does not look natural without the barrel." In 1943 the journal reported that a visitor claimed the "Logan County Courthouse was incomplete without the Gettysburg Address and Emancipation Proclamation."[34] Visitors were confident that their personal experiences and understandings of the past trumped those on display. Their assuredness disrupted the idea that the official narrative superseded the individual one, and facilitated a more democratic conception of history in which the past was constructed by the visitor, the guide, and the objects on display.

A second category of comments focused on the personal memories of visitors. Wilford was struck by "the way visitors will get more out of seeing something they know all about than seeing something of which they have never heard of before."[35] These personal memories often focused on connections that visitors made between their own lives and the lives of famous men, or were inspired by the more typical buildings at the site, such as the Clinton Inn, the Waterford General Store, and the one-room schoolhouses.

The buildings surrounding the Village Green sparked the most personal memories. At the Clinton Inn, for example, one visitor in 1934 remarked that "she had taken her first piano lesson from Mrs. (Ella) Smith, the previous owner, on the piano in the Sunday parlor." Another visitor in 1936 said that "he used to take his sister to the Inn years ago for her piano lesson, which meant that it was on the piano which is now in the parlor."[36]

Others found the Waterford General Store familiar. Mr. William C. Allen, who was over eighty years old, told guides that his "father leased the Waterford Store from 1861–1867." He also remembered "the men who congregated in the store for news of the war." Allen then recounted that his brother would often ride his horse to the train station to get the paper and then bring it to the "people waiting anxiously to hear from the front." Another visitor announced that he was the son of John G. Owen, who once owned the store, and approved of its restoration by observing that it seemed very "realistic."[37]

Other buildings that invoked personal memories were the Cooper Shop, the Blacksmith Shop, the Magill Jewelry Store, and the Scotch Settlement School. In 1934 a visitor told guides that his father was a cooper in Saline, Michigan, and that he still had some of the old equipment. Another visitor said that her mother had owned some sugar buckets that were similar to those on display. At the Blacksmith Shop, a visitor told guides, "I can remember when I used to play hookey from school and spend the day pumping the hand bellows in the Village blacksmith shop." Mr. J. F. Brewer of Lyons, Ohio, recognized one of the watches in the case at the Magill Jewelry Store and told the guide that "about fifty years ago he traded a four year old horse for a key wound watch exactly like one of those on display. Mr. Brewer said the colt was ugly and hard to break so he was glad to get rid of it." In 1936 the journal reported that the "Scotch Settlement School seems to set as a fuse which fires the memories of our more aged visitors, lighting up the dimming part of them, and leading them to relate their old experiences."[38]

The Lincoln Court House also inspired visitors who had their own material culture related to the president and his assassination. Guides began noting when visitors commented that they possessed a copy of a newspaper from the day that Lincoln was assassinated in the summer of 1936, but by September a journal entry announced, "To-day another visitor claimed possession of an original Lincoln Assassination *New York Herald*. This is positively the last time we shall consider such a common item as news."[39]

Both white and African American visitors had much to say about the Slave Huts. For example, in 1936 the journal reported: "In conducting a large colored party through the Village yesterday, the guide was asked by one lady to show her the Slave Huts. She informed him that her uncle had spent his life in one of the fifty-two huts located on Hermitage Plantation, near Savannah, the very place where those in the Village once stood." Five years later, the journal recorded, "An old darky told one of the guides that he was originally a slave in Shepardsville, KY during the Civil War." The aged visitor said that his name was "Hogoland, taken from the man who owned him, Judge Hogoland," and that he remembered when "Lincoln was shot, because he was in the service of General Lee's daughter Betty at the time, and remained with her for several years after emancipation." The civil rights leader Alain Locke came to the site in 1941 and asked to see the Slave Huts; the journal noted that "a slight gray haired negro, one of the race's most distinguished educators, spent Monday afternoon here, preceding his lecture tonight in Dearborn." Locke's subject that evening was "The Negro's Gifts to America." The journal writer observed, "Of special interest to him were the Slave Huts from Georgia, and the Lincoln Court House. He also spent some time at the Menlo Park Laboratory and the Stephen Foster Cottage."[40]

White visitors' encounters with the Slave Huts varied. One remarked in 1937 that the Slave Huts "look like forerunners of the modern tourist cabins." But the guide recording this entry suggested that this was unusual, writing that he remembered "all the visitors who have pitied the enslaved negroes, and it might not be foolish to wager that many of those visitors are packing their families in trailers and tourist cabins at the present time." In 1940 another guide reported that a visitor was surprised that the Slave Huts appeared to be the same size as temporary homes provided by the Federal Housing Administration during the Great Depression: "When the Slave Huts were pointed out to a visitor this afternoon he wittingly exclaimed, 'Slave Huts! Why, they are the same size as the 'F.H.A.' huts!'"[41] Overall, white visitors' interpretations of the Slave Huts were dependent on their worldviews. The guide offered basic facts about the buildings to visitors—how they were constructed and their original location—but little else in the way of context. An encounter shaped by visitors' personal politics was inevitable.

For many African American visitors, the George Washington Carver Memorial was the village's main attraction. For example, in December 1942 eighteen black men arrived in Detroit from Gary, Indiana, to enlist in the military. Before going to war, however, they wanted to see the Carver building. According to the guide's entry for that day, it was late Sunday evening and just turning dark when they received a call from the young men, who said they had trouble finding transportation on a Sunday but had finally found a way to get there and asked if the village could stay open a bit later for them. The staff agreed, and at 6:12 p.m. the men arrived on a bus. Another bus took them to each building, and they asked to get out and see some of the buildings, among them the Carver Memorial. The men kneeled before the cabin in silent prayer. In August of the same year, three graduates of the Tuskegee Institute arrived at the village, and a Miss Ophelia Hill mailed a picture postcard to Dr. Carver from the Village Post Office. On August 13, the journal reported: "The Carver Memorial Cabin has become very popular with the visitors. Many come to see it especially and many request their guides from the beginning of the trip to show it to them."[42] For black visitors, the meaning of the Slave Huts and the George Washington Carver Memorial was negotiable. African Americans traveled—some, given Jim Crow laws and racism, at personal risk—to Greenfield Village from across the country. They spent their time and money to journey to see Ford's village. When they arrived, black visitors viewing the Slave Huts remembered personal or family memories of enslavement. Some, like Alain Locke, used the inclusion of the Carver building to argue for social and cultural equality. And for the young men from Gary, Indiana, viewing the Carver Memorial was a spiritual experience, one shaped and understood by them alone.

White visitors constructed divergent messages from their encounters with the Slave Huts and the Carver Memorial. Some who saw the slave cabins made personal connections that allowed them to ignore the legal realities of enslavement, while others accepted or even celebrated the end of slavery. Thus the politics of race at Greenfield Village were determined by the visitor rather than by the site's official narratives, and this kind of experience was, for the most part, supported by the staff.

In his analysis of Ford, mass production, and modernity, Ray Batchelor briefly considers Ford's construction of Greenfield Village, arguing that the typicality of the buildings allowed for highly individualistic encounters.[43] Visitor comments recorded by guides support this assertion. In part, the familiarity of the past on display encouraged diverse responses. As they viewed buildings and objects, visitors were captured by their own memories, and it was those memories that shaped their experiences. Guides also supported visitors who offered personal anecdotes relating to the past on display. A wide range of experiences may have also been the result, ironically, of the tour script's emphasis on self-made manhood. The display of exemplary men whose beginnings were humble invited visitors to imagine how their own lives could move from relative obscurity to fame and fortune with a little pluck and hard work. Visitors were consistently placed at the center of their encounter not only by themselves but also by guides, and by the tour script.

The authors of the Greenfield Village journals rarely recorded explicit connections between the past and contemporary national crises. If visitors discussed Ford's negotiations with the United Auto Workers union, guides were clearly unlikely to record them. Still, it seems surprising that the Great Depression and World War II make so few appearances in the pages of the journals. National events clearly shaped at least some visitor encounters, such as the African American servicemen's request to see the Carver Memorial. But according to the guides, visitors focused primarily on the connections between the pasts on display and their own pasts.

In 1931, two years before the village opened to the public, professional historians like Carl Becker called on academics to write histories that spoke to "Mr. Everyman" and allowed for competing perspectives on the past. At Greenfield Village, guides were meeting Becker's challenge by encouraging visitors to act as their own historians. The visitor experience was highly democratic in the sense that visitors could define, understand, and consume the past on their own terms.[44]

Ford hoped to control the past and to shape the present when he built the village. He countered the history presented in textbooks by preserving and replicating the past he valued in Dearborn. During the 1930s, Ford was increasingly nostalgic for his childhood and for the Ford Motor Company before it became a mammoth corporation symbolized by the Rouge Factory. At Greenfield Village, Ford could immerse himself in a landscape that depicted the benefits of industry and technology while celebrating the relationships and cultural traditions he feared were slipping away. When he opened it to the public, Ford likely hoped that visitors would depart with the same sense of the past that he had. But the landscape of the village, with its mix of preserved and replicated buildings from different time periods and different places, opened the door for numerous interpretations. Ford's emphasis on the individual also supported a visitor's inclination to see the past through his or her personal prism. Even guides, who served as the voice of the official narrative, were encouraged to engage in a dialogue with visitors who challenged the site's depiction of the past. The qualitative evidence suggests that visitors were also demographically diverse, and the variety of visitors and the pasts they brought with them ensured that Ford's intended messages were constantly negotiated and renegotiated. At Greenfield Village, every man was—like Ford himself—his own historian.

II

DEARBORN, NOT DETROIT

Greenfield Village after Ford

Our attendance decline for the period May through August accounts to 18.9 percent. In terms of people and dollars this is a significant and disturbing loss. Many reasons have been set forth, but primary blame must be put on the Detroit riots.

— Public Relations correspondence, September 13, 1967

Restore old mills and factories in northwest section, remove unrestored artifacts, encourage more black Americans to attend. More historical detail.

— Visitor comment, summer 1973

4

Searching for an Identity

What is it then? What should the Village be presented as? After wrestling with the problem for many hours, I think the answer is this. . . . Greenfield Village is the tangible evidence of Mr. Ford's interests. It breathes with his spirit. Its heart is his heart. Presented as something else it is unreal and always will be.

— ALLSTON BOYER, 1951

Between 1926 and 1945, Henry Ford was clearly the most important person in the life of Greenfield Village. He chose the buildings and their locations, monitored the schools, and decided when the site was ready for public viewing—indeed, Ford controlled the village. When his health began to decline in 1945, Clara tried to maintain her husband's version of the village, an effort she would continue in the years after his death. Consulting primarily with Ray Dahlinger, Clara preserved Greenfield Village the way she believed Henry Ford intended it to be.[1]

Administrative changes, then, were few in the immediate aftermath of Ford's death. In 1947, Benson Ford, Henry's grandson and the second oldest of Edsel's four children, was appointed president of the board of trustees of the Edison Institute (the corporate name for both the indoor museum and Greenfield Village). Two years later, the board appointed Hayward S. Ablewhite director of the Edison Institute Museum. Ablewhite had served as a deacon, priest, rector, dean, and finally bishop in the Episcopal Church from 1915 to 1940. That year, after a dispute with members of his diocese, Ablewhite found employment in Ford's Sociological Department as an investigator, eventually serving as head of the department from 1946 until it was discontinued in 1948. He then briefly worked as a representative in the Personnel Section until Clara Ford asked him to serve as museum director in 1949. As Geoffrey Upward has shown, however, the addition of new board members and the appointment of

99

a new director of the indoor museum did not significantly alter the day-to-day operations of Greenfield Village.[2]

In January 1950, Clara Ford suffered a mild heart attack, and her involvement in the museum and village declined. She died nine months later, at eighty-four, and she left the Edison Institute a healthy endowment of $9 million. Like her husband, Clara had been a dominant presence at the village. But, as Upward notes, during her illness and after her death administrators began to reorganize the museum and village and to reconsider their goals and purpose.[3]

Contributing to administrative uncertainty was the fact that by 1950 none of the staff members who had played powerful roles during Henry Ford's time as president remained at Greenfield Village. Edward Cutler was gone, as was Frank Campsall (Ford's personal secretary), who had died in 1946, and William J. Cameron (public relations spokesperson), who retired the same year. Francis Jehl had died in 1941, and in 1942 William Simonds (director of public relations and guide manager) had moved to work in Ford's Willow Run factory, southwest of Detroit, to assist with the company's war effort. Fred Smith, who had been superintendent of the museum since at least 1934, took full charge of the museum in 1945, but illness forced him to retire by early 1949. Finally, Ray Dahlinger, who had controlled much of the village since 1945, left in 1950.[4]

Managerial lines of authority remained unclear after Clara Ford's death. In 1950, Ablewhite received the new title of chief curator, and Emil A. Ulbrich was appointed general manager, supervising activities in several areas, including the public relations, curatorial, maintenance, and security departments and the schools. Geoffrey Upward has argued that Ablewhite demanded autonomy, however, which ensured that Ulbrich served primarily as a business manager rather than an interpretive expert. The division in responsibilities further muddied exactly who was in charge at the museum and the village.[5]

The following year, the board appointed Augustus King Mills executive director of both the museum and the village, and William Clay Ford, Edsel's youngest son, became president of the Edison Institute. Mills—known as A.K.—had a diverse professional background. After graduating from the University of Missouri's school of journalism, he worked in a variety of public relations positions. He represented Amelia Earhart in 1928, directed publicity for the first Byrd Antarctic expedition from 1928 to 1930, and worked as European picture editor of *Life* magazine from 1936 to 1938. Between 1938 and 1949 he worked for Earl Newsom & Company, a public relations firm in New York City. Mills's first position with the Ford Motor Company in 1949 was as director of public and employee relations for Ford International. In 1950 he was appointed director of Ford Motor Company's Fiftieth Anniversary Plans

Office, and he helped launch a company-wide archival program in 1951. Like many of those he managed, Mills had no formal training in museum work. Still, his appointment provided stability, and for the first time in years staff began to consider the village's future.[6]

Mills and subsequent administrators were in many ways haunted by Henry Ford's vision of American history. While Ford's intentions and goals for the village were clear to him, subsequent administrators were much less definite about the purpose of the village. Mills began the process of considering the village's future by inviting staff members from its primary competitor, Colonial Williamsburg, to tour and evaluate the site. They offered advice specific to Greenfield Village's unique landscape, but their recommendations were also grounded in broader shifts that were occurring in the field of public history.

Public History in the Post–World War II Era

In the decades after the Second World War, Greenfield Village administrators worked in what was a quickly expanding and dramatically changing public history profession. American history museums were increasingly administered and funded by federal dollars and run by men with degrees in art, architecture, history, anthropology, or other fields that marked them as "experts." The amateurs who initially drove the movement to preserve the past in the United States now competed with or worked alongside professionals.[7]

Preservation also moved into the hands of the federal government. The National Trust for Historic Preservation was established in 1949, but it became a much more powerful institution in 1966 with the passage of the National Historic Preservation Act. The new law created the National Register of Historic Places and established the Advisory Council on Historic Preservation, and it required each state to develop a preservation plan and appoint a State Historic Preservation Officer. Before demolishing a site listed on the National Register, federal offices were required to consult with the Advisory Council.[8]

The years immediately following World War II also saw a shift in rationales for preserving and presenting the past. Many administrators at outdoor history museums expanded their efforts to depict industrial history that put common men and women at center stage. Often they did so with support from officials in federal agencies who identified history as a useful weapon in the Cold War. For example, at Colonial Williamsburg, John D. Rockefeller III initiated several programs throughout the late 1940s and early 1950s intended to link Williamsburg with Americanism. In 1950 he proposed a new orientation program for soldiers in the U.S. Army: enlistees would visit Colonial Williamsburg and be educated in the values and ideals that America stood for so that they could explain them to the enemy if captured. Seven years later, the production of the film *Williamsburg—The Story of a Patriot* and the opening of a new information center made the site's Americanist ideology explicit.[9]

At what would become Historic Deerfield, Henry Flynt's Heritage Foundation adopted a similar interpretive theme. In 1957 Flynt and Samuel Chamberlain published *Frontier of Freedom*, a largely pictorial history of Deerfield Village that claimed to offer a visual counternarrative to communism. "There is a legion of . . . replies to the vilification of the Communists," the authors wrote, "and they do not need to be couched in calumny or hollow phrases." In fact, they argued, "visual truth speaks louder than words in contradicting propaganda," and a New England village "can be the most eloquent response to the strident falsehoods poisoning the air today."[10]

Politicians, too, believed that histories linking democracy to industrial and scientific progress were particularly powerful counterarguments to communism. In 1955, President Eisenhower signed a bill approving the addition of the Museum of History and Technology to the Smithsonian Institution. When it opened in 1964, the museum displayed objects representing the armed forces, science and technology, culture, the arts and industries, and civil history; in many ways, it indicated the triumph of Henry Ford's vision.[11]

By the mid-1960s, however, the notion that museums should offer a wholly patriotic vision of the American past was challenged. The successes of civil rights activists and second-wave feminists soon led to calls for changes in the academy and in history museums. Not only was it essential to chronicle the lives of ordinary people, they claimed, but it was also imperative to question American exceptionalism, to represent diverse racial and ethnic histories, and to understand how oppressed people found ways to control their own lives.[12]

Museums responded to these calls in a number of ways. African American history museums were established throughout the 1960s and into the 1970s, interpretive programs were altered, and the National Register expanded to include more vernacular architecture associated with the histories of women, people of color, and the poor. One of the most dramatic efforts to acknowledge traumatic and painful American pasts occurred at Colonial Williamsburg. In 1977, Williamsburg president Carlisle Humelsine hired Cary Carson, a specialist in American history with a doctorate from Harvard, to revise the site's interpretive program with the express purpose of acknowledging the community's history of enslaving African Americans in the eighteenth century.[13]

America's other outdoor history museums and privately run historic house museums were swept up in these changes as well. Many worked to adapt by hiring professional architects and academic historians, and by rewriting interpretive scripts. Unlike federally funded sites, however, private museums relied heavily on visitor dollars, and their administrators did not always view the goals of meeting new professional standards and attracting more visitors as complementary.[14]

At Greenfield Village, administrators sought to find their institution's place in a rapidly changing field. The stability brought by the Mills administration allowed for a complete reassessment of collections, management, and interpretation. It was at this point that village administrators asked for assistance from their sister institution—and now the interpretive and economic leader among outdoor history museums—Colonial Williamsburg.

Reflection and Expansion

As Mills considered the village's future, he commissioned two external reviews from staff at Colonial Williamsburg. In 1951 he invited Allston Boyer, who served as assistant to Kenneth Chorley, then Williamsburg's president, to review Greenfield Village, the Village School, and the adjacent indoor museum. Boyer was an expert in resort development rather than curatorship or education, and his review's focus on visitor perceptions, profits, and management spoke to that background. Perhaps the choice of Boyer was also indicative of village administrators' primary focus on increasing attendance at the site.[15]

Boyer began his thirteen-page report by describing his and others' reaction to Ford's idiosyncratic landscape. Boyer was convinced that the site created "confusion in the minds of almost every" visitor with whom he spoke—an interesting finding given that Greenfield Village was experiencing a growth in attendance. Because the village did not depict one real place or time, Boyer declared that it could not be understood as a museum about the past. To him, the site made little sense in a linear historical framework because it was based on one man's "historical" interests and inspirations. Boyer thought the problem of meeting standards set by others in the field could be avoided by explicitly telling visitors that the village was Ford's unique understanding of the American past on display for the public.[16]

Boyer offered several recommendations to clarify the mission and operation of the village, as well as many suggestions for maximizing its profits. He encouraged administrators to hire younger staff members: "You can never balance your budget if you have throughout your organization a state of mind which accepts the cleaning of an eight-and-one-half acre room with 36-inch brooms pushed slowly by old gentlemen." Expanding the village's limited season was also proposed as a tool for increasing revenue; at that time the site was closed between November 1 and April 14, which meant over five months of lost ticket sales. Boyer also recommended adopting more modern approaches to maintenance and instituting a more rigorous accounting method. He suggested closing several buildings, posting more signs outside, and making the interiors visible from the windows, and he encouraged administrators to adopt the Colonial Williamsburg model by boarding staff in some of the houses in the residential section to produce additional income.[17]

In August 1952 a second reviewer, Holmes Brown, offered a critique of Greenfield Village. Perhaps administrators had always planned for two reviews, or perhaps after reading Boyer's report they wanted a second opinion. Like Boyer, Brown was not trained as a museum professional; he had a long career as a public relations expert and social activist. While working at Colonial Williamsburg from 1950 to 1952, Brown became famous for opening the Williamsburg Inn to African American visitors. After leaving Williamsburg, he went on to work for a host of corporations, including Ford Motor Company, and to participate in the foundation of the educational organization Head Start.[18]

Brown's analysis was more favorable. There were several points during his tour of the village, he reported, when his "spine tingled." He found the Stephen Foster Birthplace particularly moving; "Tears came to my eyes," he wrote. But he also admitted that at other buildings he was "bored stiff," and that by the end of his tour he was "exhausted physically and mentally." He commented on the mix of constructed and preserved buildings, noting that "it's hard to tell what is an authentic building and what is not." In fact, Brown's own experience was shaped by one of several historical inaccuracies that further muddied the village's terrain. It was just a year after Brown's visit that staff discovered that the Foster Birthplace, which Brown found so moving, was not the house where Foster was born. To alleviate the problem of discerning between replicas and preserved buildings, Brown cleverly suggested that the "background color of the descriptive sign be the same color for all authentic structures."[19]

Like Boyer, Brown urged staff to focus on the life of Henry Ford rather than that of Thomas Edison. By the time he left the village, Brown said, he had a "pretty good picture of what Tom Edison was like," but he knew "literally nothing of the personality, ambitions, successes and failures of Henry Ford." He urged administrators to open the interior of the Ford Homestead; although it was included on tours, visitors saw only the exterior. Finally, he recommended that "the garage housing the First Ford . . . be made the climax of the trip."[20]

The decision to invite Boyer and Brown to review the site reflected the long-standing relationship between the village and Colonial Williamsburg. Administrators continued to see the Williamsburg site as a sister institution. As a reconstruction of an actual place and time, however, Colonial Williamsburg followed very different narrative and interpretive trajectories, and

Greenfield Village administrators could not follow Williamsburg's path to success because they were confined by Henry Ford's broadly defined approach to preservation and collection. Perhaps unsurprisingly, the two reviewers suggested approaches that would make Greenfield Village more closely resemble their own museum, but they also encouraged administrators to develop a unique identity by embracing and celebrating site's connection to Ford.

Mills took many of Boyer's and Brown's suggestions seriously. In 1952 the Edison Institute was renamed The Henry Ford Museum and Greenfield Village to more accurately reflect the collection's relationship to Ford. In 1953, as the fiftieth anniversary of the founding Ford Motor Company was being celebrated, the Ford Homestead in the village was opened to the public. Curators and the Ford family designed and installed "Henry Ford—A Personal History" on the second floor of the museum. While Thomas Edison remained an important figure on the Greenfield Village landscape, the site's biographical focus was now more obviously tied to Ford.[21]

That same year the Heinz family, made famous by their mass production and sale of condiments, donated the Sharpsburg, Pennsylvania, birthplace of H. J. Heinz, the company's founder. Heinz's parents were middle-class German immigrants, and their son's rise to fame and fortune paralleled that of many of the other men celebrated on the Greenfield Village landscape.[22] Like the other birthplaces at the village, the Heinz house linked middle-class domesticity to capitalist success. The addition of the house suggested that administrators were willing to alter the village landscape, as long as it followed the interpretive model established by Ford.

In 1954, A. K. Mills died suddenly, and in November Donald A. Shelley, who had been serving as fine arts curator, took over as executive director. Shelley, born in 1911 in York County, Pennsylvania, was the first academic at the helm of the museum and village. He held a master's degree in art history from Harvard and a doctorate in American art from New York University, and he was the first curator of paintings and sculpture at the New-York Historical Society. While acting as executive director of the Edison Institute, Shelley also served as vice president of the American Association of Museums, the field's leading professional organization, from 1962 to 1968.[23]

Shelley's academic training clearly influenced his management approach, and he led his staff in a number of changes that reshaped both the Henry Ford Museum and Greenfield Village. With his guidance, curators conducted research on the museum's holdings and acquired new objects in order to fill gaps in the historical record. In 1955, Shelley spearheaded an oral history program to document the history of the museum and the village. By then, the museum's permanent exhibits included "Agriculture," "Crafts," "Machinery," "Power," "Communications and Lighting," and "Transportation," as well as several displays featuring various styles of furniture design, and the "Street of Early American Shops," which recreated the interiors of typical trade, crafts, and businesses of the eighteenth and nineteenth centuries. One of Shelley's most significant projects, however, was organizing the Ford Archives, which were given to the Henry Ford Museum by Ford Motor Company in 1964. Administrators began to organize millions of documents, including transcripts of over three hundred oral reminiscences by those who knew Ford best.[24]

At the village, starting in the mid-1950s, several historic homes, such as the Noah Webster House, were updated with more historically accurate furnishings under Shelley's guidance. Shelley also oversaw the addition of yet another building. In 1959 the Howards, a Michigan family, donated their father's doctor's office, which dated to 1839. This building supported Ford's original intent to celebrate entrepreneurs and the small town as an ideal. Administrators called in Edward Cutler to help with the restoration process, and in 1963 the Howard Office opened to the public. Like the Heinz house, it reinforced the messages Ford had hoped the village would send.[25]

Shelley served as executive director until 1968, when his title was changed to president. He continued as president until 1976, when he was replaced by Frank Caddy, who had worked at the village since he was a student at the Henry Ford Trade School in 1932. Caddy had received a degree from Detroit Business College while he continued to work at the village, and after graduating he held a number of positions in various departments. In 1940, Caddy worked in the Payroll and Accounts Payable department, and five years later he was named controller of the department. He continued to move into more prestigious positions; in 1951 he was appointed to the board of trustees as treasurer, and the following year he became director of administration under Mills. When Shelley retired in 1976, Caddy was appointed president, an office he held for five years.[26]

During Shelley's and Caddy's tenures, the site's administration continued to expand. In 1950, Emil Ulbrich oversaw forty-one positions. By the end of the 1970s, Caddy managed seventy positions, including vice presidents of education, collections and presentation, corporate services, and public affairs. A total of 350 full-time employees worked at the site. The addition of new positions and employees marked a dramatic shift from the time of Ford's presidency.[27]

Henry Ford had used Greenfield Village to celebrate his version of the past, and he cared little whether it met the needs and desires of public history professionals or visitors. Those who administered the site after his death faced a difficult challenge. As Boyer had noted, Ford's vision for the village lacked coherence. It was clear that his management style could not continue, and additional staff and procedures were accordingly added and refined. The village landscape itself posed a problem that indoor museums did not face: although it could be changed, adding or removing buildings was a daunting and expensive proposition. Common sense suggested, then, that the best approach was, as Boyer recommended, to present the site as a reflection of Henry Ford's interests. The administrators of the post-Ford era, however, also made decisions to appeal to new audiences. Mills, Shelley, and Caddy demonstrated a desire to be taken seriously by other museum professionals and to attract new customers. To meet both goals, administrators shifted the village's narrative focus to Ford himself while expanding the site's educational offerings and leisure activities.

Education or Entertainment?

Another aspect of the administrative expansion that marked Greenfield Village in the post-Ford years was the establishment of the Department of Education, which followed trends in the museum profession at large. George E. Hein observes that although many museums in the United States had expressed their missions in educational terms since the late nineteenth century, it was after World War II that museums began developing specific programs and departments aimed at educating the public. Erik Christiansen notes, for example, that during the 1950s the Smithsonian Institution's "mission radically changed from its prewar role as national repository" to a "public-learning complex." At their 1958 annual meeting, the Southeastern Museum Conference followed suit when they adopted the principle that museums are obligated to "interpret their collections," for the public.[28]

Greenfield Village was part of this national trend. In 1950 the Education Department issued a report titled "Plans and Progress." The report began on a high note: "Many well-informed individuals claim that the Henry Ford Museum and Greenfield Village are unmatched anywhere in the world in variety, number, and quality of facilities and resources." But it went on to contend that "the component problems which combine to relegate the Village and Museum to an insignificant role in the field of education can be resolved, essentially, into the paradoxical situation of an *educational institution without an educational program.*" The report advocated expanding the literature available for teachers, distributing that literature to a national audience, and designing a program for "creative kinds of activities such as educational conferences and research."[29]

During the next two decades, educational efforts followed the department's suggested paths. In a concerted effort to raise national awareness of Greenfield Village among educators, administrators distributed films about the site, developed relationships with other educational and professional organizations, and expanded outreach programs to public schools.

By the mid-1950s, for example, administrators used television to market the museum and village. They were particularly thrilled on April 18, 1955, when NBC's *Today Show* featured a segment on the museum's collection of carriages and antique cars. In the fall, the village began broadcasting its own show, *Window to the Past,* on Detroit's educational station, WTVS. The show was brief—only fifteen minutes long—and depicted life in the nineteenth century. On October 25, NBC crews returned, and the *Today Show,* Arlene Francis's *Home* show, and *Howdy Doody* (a popular children's television show featuring a puppet) aired segments from the village.[30]

The Department of Education also hired staff with professional training in the field, and by the late 1950s many held advanced degrees in history or education. The department's list of responsibilities also reflected the impact of the "Plans and Progress" report. Education staff were primarily responsible for analyzing and evaluating the educational content of exhibits and preparing pedagogical materials for national distribution.[31]

The Department of Education also built strong relationships with other educational and professional organizations. For example, in 1959 students in Wayne State University's education department were invited to learn how to use the museum and village in their classrooms. Enrollment in the special course reached fifty-four that year, and it was repeated annually from 1960 to 1963. In 1962 the museum and village hosted the annual conference of the American Association of Museums. The following year the Education Department announced a partnership with the Rackham Graduate School at the University of Michigan in Ann Arbor, located a short thirty miles away. The program would include an internship at the museum and village as part of a master's degree in museum practice. But although staff reviewed several applications, no candidates were selected, and the initiative was abandoned. Still, this effort reflected administrators' desire to build relationships with external institutions more explicitly aimed at education.[32]

As Greenfield Village expanded its educational outreach programs to both children and adults, the village school system was struggling. As we've seen, Ford initially envisioned the village as his personal educational laboratory, which included replicating his childhood education in one-room schoolhouses. But tuition did not generate a significant amount of revenue for the village; in 1952 the high school closed and in 1969 the elementary school followed suit. At the same time, however, educational goals aimed at serving children continued to drive administrators. Children from public and private schools across the metropolitan area still made up a large and important part of the site's visitors in the post–World War II era. Throughout the 1950s and 1960s, the site welcomed over two thousand school groups annually.[33]

The Education Department's relationship with guides also changed during this period. Between 1950 and 1951 the site's guides (whose number continued to reach 150 or more in the summer) reported to Hayward Ablewhite, who was by then chief curator. In 1952 the guides began to report to the Guest Relations Department within the Department of Education. Beginning in 1969, however, the Guest Relations unit was eliminated and visitors reported instead to the Visitor Relations manager, who worked in the Special Events Department, and this arrangement continued throughout the 1970s. Although it is unclear why the management of guides moved to Visitor Relations, it suggests a changing view of the role that education played in the interactions between village audiences and guides.[34]

The director of education continued to play an expanding role in the management of the village throughout the 1970s, however. The director's responsibilities included supervising the adult education manager, the audio-visual manager, the school services manager, and the theater arts manager. As with other institutions in the post–World War II era, under Ulbrich, Mills, Shelley, and Caddy the site's educational mission, goals, and programming were refined using a variety of techniques. Necessarily, however, educational goals were balanced with the need to generate revenue.

While the Education Department focused on developing and expanding its goals, other departments focused specifically on entertaining visitors, particularly through the addition of special events and leisure activities. Like many other institutions, Greenfield Village did its part to support the Cold War by adding programming that blended history and nostalgia in order to promote America's industrial achievements, the entrepreneurial spirit, and patriotism. These themes, were, of course, strikingly similar to Ford's own notions of self-made manhood, the small town as an ideal, and the benefits of technology and industry.

During the 1950s, staff identified automobile collectors as an important and potentially lucrative audience. The Old Car Festival, first held in 1951, was a particularly useful way of tapping into an identifiable and expanding market of visitors interested in collecting and purchasing antique automobiles. At the festival, visitors were invited to display their antique cars and enter them in a variety of competitions, including ones that awarded prizes for the cars that were the most authentic. In some years a pageant depicting the first thirty years of the development of the automobile was held.[35]

The institution of the Old Car Festival captures how administrators in the post-Ford era managed the village. As we've seen, Henry Ford wanted to depict America before the arrival of the automobile, when horse-drawn carriages were the primary mode of transportation; he insisted on keeping the car out of the village. But Mills's administration, and those that followed, recognized that the village's audience was changing. By the 1950s the village landscape was far less familiar to audiences; unlike those who visited during Ford's lifetime, many had never traveled by horse. To continue celebrating the nation's industrial achievements, it was necessary to move the village forward in time by making connections with a new generation whose childhoods were spent riding in the back of Ford's Model Ts. The car festival identified an unforeseen benefit of Ford's refusal to focus his site on a specific time period or place: because he chose to restore or replicate buildings spanning five centuries, the addition of events tied to more recent histories did not disrupt the site's narrative. The village could continue to serve as a conduit between the past and the personal memories of visitors because administrators were willing to veer slightly from Ford's original vision.

The car festival also facilitated administrators' efforts to shift the village's meaning to fit present needs. During the 1950s, the heroic age of the auto industry, visitors could interpret the Old Car Festival through the lenses of both nostalgia and progress. As the 1950s wore on, however, Detroit lost auto industry jobs to suburban areas and outsourcing. By the mid-1970s, America was in the midst of a recession initiated by skyrocketing oil prices, and the auto industry (and the Ford Motor Company in particular) suffered further. As the economic state of the auto industry changed, however, visitors at the Old Car Festival could still enjoy themselves by reminiscing about the good old days or imagining economic recovery. Or they could forget about the present altogether. The Old Car Festival removed the automobile from the factory (the location of continuing labor disputes and anxiety) and placed it in a setting where it was venerated as a relic and a work of art.[36]

Another annual event, and one of the most successful, was the Country Fair. First held in 1961, the fair invoked nostalgia for small-town life and was designed to both educate and entertain. The annual report for 1961 described the fair as "old-fashioned" and "fun-packed," boasting "all the trappings and color of the late nineteenth century." It was designed as an "educational-recreational project for school children of the metropolitan area," and school groups were invited to attend. Staff engaged in craft demonstrations, and there were also animal exhibits, band concerts, and demonstrations of early American and Maypole dancing (fig. 9). Each day of the weekend-long event began with a "parade of transportation milestones." Some aspects of the fair were historical in one sense, but for the most part the activities were a celebration of the rituals that may or may not have defined small-town life.[37]

"Let Freedom Ring" was a Fourth of July celebration, begun in 1963, that tied

FIGURE 9. Country Fair of Yesteryear in 1969 on the Village Green. Performances invoking cultural tropes of small-town life, such as dancing around a Maypole, defined the event. From the collections of The Henry Ford (P.B.52611).

the site explicitly to national patriotism. The ceremonies took place in front of the entrance to the Henry Ford Museum, and local and state public officials often attended; in 1964 Michigan's governor, George Romney, was the featured speaker. The celebration included a parade of men and women dressed in Revolutionary garb. Visitors were encouraged to contemplate the events of 1776, while simultaneously enjoying a communal experience with their family, friends, and fellow Americans.[38] "Let Freedom Ring" was a unique event for the village because it moved the site's historical narrative more directly toward national political history and historical themes that spoke to the concerns of the Cold War era. The exterior of the Henry Ford Museum, a replica of Independence Hall in Philadelphia, certainly evoked patriotic sentiments. With the exception of the Lincoln Court House, however, Greenfield Village did not directly remind visitors of the nation's political past. "Let Freedom Ring" connected the village's celebration of self-made manhood, technology, industry, and the small town to the American Revolution.

The Old Car Festival, the Country Fair, and "Let Freedom Ring" were just a few of the special events held at the village. Others included the Village Turkey Shoot (1955) and the Famous Early Movie Festival (1961).[39] In part, these events were aimed at a local audience, as they made a visit new and different for repeat customers. The brand of entertainment administrators provided also pointed to their understanding of the village visitor as interested in the auto industry, fascinated by positive cultural tropes that defined small-town life, and patriotic.

The Country Fair might have been particularly attractive to local visitors who wanted to forget the problems that increasingly defined Detroit's landscape. By the late 1960s the city's public image had been stained by racial conflict, poverty, and the failures of the industrial economy. But inside Greenfield Village a different America was on display, one that allowed visitors to escape into a past where machine and garden were in harmony.

While special events supported the administration's interest in constructing a leisure experience, the Capital Improvement Campaign made this goal explicit. On October 21, 1969, William Clay Ford, the chairman of the Edison Institute's board, announced plans to spend $20 million expanding and developing Greenfield Village. Shelley and Caddy would oversee some of the most dramatic changes to the site since Ford's death. Grounds improvements were one focus of the campaign; new brick sidewalks and benches were added in 1972, and the following year the gatehouse was remodeled and enlarged and the Pond 'n' Coop restaurant opened near the Ackley Covered Bridge. The two largest projects were the construction of a perimeter railroad, which opened in 1973, and the addition of a turn-of-the-century amusement park, Suwanee Park, which opened in 1974. It included a bandstand, a lagoon, a railroad station, an ice cream parlor, a gift shop, and a new restaurant. A Herschell-Spillman carousel, built around 1913, and a raft ride to Suwanee Island completed the park. In 1975 the village's craft center received attention with the addition of a bakery and a demonstration center. Finally, the campaign provided funds to move and reconstruct an early eighteenth-century saltbox-style house from Andover, Connecticut, to fill what administrators felt was a gap in the history of house architecture; it opened in 1978.[40]

While the capital campaign did not focus entirely on entertainment, a majority of efforts could not be interpreted in any other terms. The rides, the addition of new restaurants, and the loose associations with the past indicated that administrators, or at least the board, believed that the key to garnering new visitors was the addition of entertainment facilities. And new visitors were essential. The 1977 annual report noted that museum and village revenue came from two primary sources: the endowment (27.8 percent) and public support (72.2 percent). Public support revenue included contributions to the collection and donations from friends, but 63.6 percent came from on-site sales.[41]

Village staff were increasingly concerned that Detroit's image as a site of racial conflict discouraged new visitors from attending. At the time, however, Dearborn itself had developed a reputation as one of the metro area's most racist suburbs, suggesting that the public image of the smaller city where the village was located complicated the visitor experience even further. The racial politics of both Detroit and Dearborn constructed new lines between the urban core and Greenfield Village, and between audiences who, depending on their personal politics, might have identified either Detroit or Dearborn (or even both) as a reason to avoid a trip to the village.

"Keep Dearborn Clean"

The residential segregation that began to define the Detroit metropolitan area in the 1920s was entrenched by the end of the 1970s. Thomas Sugrue has shown that a number of factors facilitated the urban crisis in Detroit. Between 1949 and 1960 the city experienced four recessions related to the loss of manufacturing jobs. Further, when African American Detroiters attempted to move into all-white neighborhoods, whites created alliances with elected officials, businessmen, and realtors to maintain the color line. Sugrue notes that the "results of housing segregation, in combination with persistent workplace discrimination and deindustrialization, were explosive." The National Advisory Commission on Civil Disorders (better known as the Kerner Commission) warned in its 1968 report on the causes and consequences of urban racial unrest that "our nation is moving toward two societies; one, largely Negro and poor, located in central cities; the other, predominantly white and affluent, located in the suburbs and outlying areas," a prediction that was already all but fulfilled in the Detroit area.[42]

Dearborn, perhaps more than any other suburb in the six-county metropolitan area, became a bastion of white flight and racism. Orville Hubbard capitalized on that racism when he ran for mayor in 1942 with the slogan "Keep Dearborn Clean"—a phrase that many interpreted to mean he would keep Dearborn white. There were rumors throughout his first campaign that he was a member of the Ku Klux Klan and the Black Legion, a notorious vigilante group. Hubbard's reputation and the reputation of Dearborn more generally appears to have affected the racial makeup of its population. When Hubbard was elected, only 35 of Dearborn's 63,584 residents were black. In 1980, two years after he left office, the situation had not changed much; the number of African American residents was 83 out of 90,660, or less than 0.1 percent of the population.[43]

Initially, Hubbard's racist policies revolved around housing. In September 1948 the John Hancock Life Insurance Company proposed the construction of a $25 million, twelve-hundred-unit multi-family housing development in the Springwells Park neighborhood of Dearborn, which had itself been built on Ford-owned land beginning in 1939. The new development was to be located on 930 acres of land owned by the Ford Motor Company and the Ford Foundation, and, as Hubbard's biographer David L. Good notes, it was advertised as "a model town within a town." A poll conducted by the *Dearborn Press* found that a majority of the city's residents were in favor of the development, which promised to bring construction work and tax revenue to the area, and it appeared that the city's planning commission would readily approve the necessary zoning change from business to residential use.[44]

Hubbard, however, quickly announced his opposition to the project, insisting that the "model town" would be anything but. Apartments and duplexes, he argued, attracted undesirable residents. Hubbard claimed that 95 percent of Dearbornites supported his position because they realized that the new residents would include renters who would not have a stake in the community. At a city council meeting in October, he made explicit his concern that the development would bring African American residents to the city. He read a telegram sent to him by William R. Hood, a recording secretary of the UAW-CIO's Local 600 and an African American, who requested information about the project and asked whether the homes would be available for purchase by blacks. Hubbard argued that the telegram was evidence that the development would lead to a "race problem," and again claimed that the majority of Dearborn's residents were opposed to it. When the *Dearborn Press* found that 75 percent of the city's residents in fact supported the idea, Hubbard mounted a campaign to change their minds.[45]

Both Hubbard and his opponents agreed that a vote on the issue, although it would have no legal standing, would decide whether or not John Hancock could proceed with its plans. As Good notes, before the vote took place, Hubbard sent city department heads and their aides, along with some Civil Service employees, to distribute flyers across the city. One demanded "KEEP NEGROES OUT OF DEARBORN . . . PROTECT YOUR HOME and MINE!" Another leaflet explained that none of the approximately 1,500 black employees of the Rouge lived in Dearborn (most, in fact, still lived in nearby Inkster, the town Henry Ford tried to "rehabilitate" in the 1930s), and that Hancock would have to rent apartments to them.[46]

In the end, Hubbard's tactics worked: 15,948 voted against the project and only 10,562 for it. Hubbard had changed the minds of a considerable number of Dearborn's residents by appealing to racism. The city council agreed that they would not grant the rezoning request, and Henry Ford II canceled the land contract with Hancock. The win drew permanent lines between Hubbard and the Ford Motor Company and illustrated Hubbard's talent for cultivating racist sentiment among many Dearborn voters.[47]

Although Hubbard built a strong base among Dearborn's voting population, in 1950 he faced a recall campaign that accused him of "using strong-arm men to break up public meetings, putting cronies in city jobs, refusing to submit city books to public audit, practicing favoritism in tax assessments and in the selection of city contractors, and breaking the city with his fiscal policies." Those supporting Hubbard's removal included the Detroit and Dearborn newspapers, five of Dearborn's seven councilmen, and the Ford Motor Company. To demonstrate their support, several Ford Motor Company officials contributed $150,000 to the effort to oust Hubbard as mayor. Anti-Hubbard billboards were permitted on company property, and Ford employees living in Dearborn helped gather signatures on the recall petition. Despite the 7,775 signatures obtained and the backing of the Ford Motor Company, Hubbard remained mayor in a 16,872–12,732 vote. In fact, the events solidified Hubbard's base and encouraged him to maintain his dictatorial approach to the office of mayor.[48]

Changes at the River Rouge plant had a further impact on Dearborn's population. The Rouge had long brought a racially, ethnically, and economically diverse population to Dearborn during the workweek. As Sugrue has noted, for example, the Rouge was the city's largest employer of African Americans until the late 1940s. Ford Motor Company's experiments with automation and decentralization, however, forever changed a factory that had defined the industrial age. "Ford officials," Sugrue explains, "hoping to weaken union strength on the shop floor, targeted the Rouge for automation," and "stamping, machine casting, forging, steel production, glassmaking, and dozens of other operations were shifted from the Rouge to new Ford plants throughout the 1950s." In 1945 the Rouge employed 85,000 workers, but by 1954 that number had fallen to 54,000, and six years later to 30,000. The factory that had brought diversity to Dearborn five days a week was on the decline.[49]

Hubbard continued to be known as a racist throughout the 1950s and early 1960s. In 1956 he told an Alabama reporter that he was "for complete segregation, one million percent." It was during the 1960s that Hubbard engaged in some of his most openly racist activities and received the greatest support from Dearborn's residents. A leaflet from Hubbard's 1961 mayoral campaign stated that if reelected the mayor would keep "persons and problems who would lower property values" out of Dearborn. Another piece of literature promoted Dearborn's public park as "37 hours away from Africa and 37 minutes from Belle Isle," Detroit's main public park. In 1967, Hubbard was accused of violating Michigan civil rights laws by posting clippings derogatory to black

Americans on city bulletin boards. The state's civil rights commission filed a
case in Wayne County Circuit Court when Hubbard refused to comply with
the commission's request to remove the clippings. Hubbard finally agreed and
the commission dropped its suit.[50]

That same year, racial conflict in Detroit reached a boiling point. On July
23, police raided an illegal after-hours bar on Twelfth Street, where they found
eighty-five people celebrating the return of two African American soldiers
from Vietnam. They placed the patrons under arrest and called for reinforce-
ments. Soon a crowd of almost two hundred people gathered to protest what
was seen as the latest injustice in a long history of persecuting black residents.
Conflict between the police and the crowd continued throughout the evening
and by 8 a.m. over three thousand people had found their way to Twelfth
Street. Soon the city was enveloped in a full-fledged riot. In Dearborn, Mayor
Hubbard set a curfew and announced that looters and arsonists would be shot.
The insurrection finally ended five days later through the combined efforts of
law enforcement personnel, federal troops, and National Guardsmen. Forty-
three people were killed, 7,231 men and women were arrested, 2,509 buildings
were burned, and $36 million in insured property was lost.[51]

Hubbard's response to the riot typified his approach to race relations in
Dearborn. The following week he addressed the city council and told them:
"This is war. The only way to stop it is with guns. . . . [W]hen you have mad
dogs running around, brute force is needed to cope with the situation." "My
advice to Dearborn residents," he continued, "is to learn to shoot, shoot
straight and learn to be a dead shot." The city began to sponsor inexpensive
gun courses that included instruction in handguns, rifles, and shotguns, and
a class on the history of arms from ancient China to the twentieth century.[52]

Hubbard's racist practices continued in 1969. He authorized the sale of a
small park for residential development rather than rehabilitating the space,
claiming that improving the park would be "an open invitation for nonresidents to invade our city." Although he supported (unsuccessful) black Detroit
mayoral candidate Richard Austin, just a few months later he refused to travel
to predominantly black Inkster for the Mayors' Day Exchange program. That
year the city also hosted a meeting of the United Klans of America, one of the
largest Ku Klux Klan organizations.[53]

While Hubbard's administration succeeded in preventing African Americans from living in Dearborn, Arabs had been immigrating to Dearborn
since Ford opened the Rouge Factory in 1917. By the 1960s a thriving Arab
American community had been flourishing in the Southend section of the
city for generations. In 1964 the city began a "community development" program intended to move industry into the Southend by eliminating existing
housing. Six years later, Dearborn's Arab American community was ready to

challenge the city's plan to turn a residential area into an industrial landscape and formed the Arab Community Center for Economic and Social Services (ACCESS) to lead their opposition. When city officials argued that the effects on South Dearborn's residents had been minimal, they filed a federal suit. In December 1973 the federal courts prohibited the City of Dearborn from acquiring further property except by condemnation. ACCESS was one of the few groups to successfully oppose the Hubbard administration. Unlike African Americans, who were effectively prevented from living in Dearborn, as longtime and newly politicized residents Arab Americans would become an increasingly powerful presence in the city.[54]

Hubbard's continued campaign to maintain segregation in Dearborn was more successful. In 1971 he joined the anti-busing campaign in Michigan, arguing that those who supported busing were communists. Two days after Hubbard's speech, federal district judge Stephen Roth directed the Michigan Board of Education to prepare a package of school integration proposals, including one that recommended busing students to and from suburban districts in the metropolitan area.[55]

By January 1972, Dearborn and several other suburban districts joined together to challenge Roth's busing plans. In March the city council placed three advisory propositions on the May presidential primary ballot. Constituents were asked to vote on the following question: "Are you in favor of amending the United States Constitution to prohibit forced busing and guarantee the right of each student to attend his neighborhood school?" The noted Alabama segregationist George Wallace used Dearborn's anti-busing sentiment to garner support for his presidential campaign. In a rally at the Dearborn Youth Center, Wallace called on the approximately three thousand people inside the building and another three thousand outside to oppose "busing, big government, and liberals." In attendance that day was a Milwaukee busboy and janitor named Arthur Bremer. Six days later, while Wallace was campaigning in Laurel, Maryland, Bremer shot him in the back, paralyzing him for life. The following day, Good notes, Wallace "swept every precinct in Dearborn's Democratic primary," and Dearborn voters "also approved Hubbard's anti-busing question, 29,037 to 5,409."[56]

In 1974, Hubbard suffered a stroke that left him largely incapacitated. That same year, Coleman Young became Detroit's first black mayor, and in *Milliken v. Bradley* the Supreme Court ruled that busing suburban residents could not be used to integrate public schools in Detroit. While many hoped that Young and his colleagues would integrate the city and suburbs, his administration was marked by racial turmoil. Hubbard's term ended in 1978, and he died four years later.[57]

During Hubbard's tenure, many local residents came to associate Dearborn not only with the Rouge Factory, Henry Ford, and the Ford museums, but also with one of the most racist mayors in the metro area. While the Ford Motor Company was keenly aware of, and dismayed by, Hubbard's power over Dearborn, Greenfield Village officials did not express concerns about Hubbard's or Dearborn's reputation in their written records. But by late June 1967 the staff was increasingly worried about the public's perception of Detroit as a potential tourist destination.

The Cities and the Village

After the 1967 riot, Greenfield Village administrators identified Detroit's public image as something they would have to overcome to attract new visitors. That fall, the Public Relations Department reported that "primary blame" for an almost 19 percent decline in attendance "must be put on the Detroit riots." In contrast, the site's leadership did not see Dearborn's growing reputation as a bastion of white flight as a potential liability.[58] The lack of concern about Dearborn's public image might have been related to the staff's conception of the site's audience. It is plausible that, with the exception of schoolchildren, African Americans did not make up a significant percentage of village visitors.

Despite the initiation of visitor surveys in the late 1960s, administrators did not gather statistics on race, making it difficult to determine how many African American adults or families visited, but photos taken at special events suggest that the number was fairly low (fig. 10). In seventy-six crowd shots containing hundreds of visitors taken at special events between 1948 and 1967, only twenty-five visitors appeared to be African American. Although it is difficult to determine an exact number, these photos certainly suggest that few African Americans visited Greenfield Village during this period.[59]

These low numbers might have been connected to Dearborn's reputation, to declining employment at the Rouge Factory, or to the expansion of historic sites more directly related to African American history. As the historian Andrea Burns notes, the black power movement of the 1960s led to the construction of new black history museums in many urban areas, including Detroit. In 1965, Dr. Charles H. Wright and a host of community organizers opened the International Afro-American Museum in a basement apartment on West Grand Boulevard. Throughout the late 1960s and into the 1970s, the museum's staff developed numerous exhibits, expanded its collections, and increased outreach efforts.[60]

Detroit's public schools and universities were also expanding their efforts to depict black history. When the black community identified opportunities for accessing this history, however, Greenfield Village was not among them.

FIGURE 10. Country Fair of Yesteryear in 1970. Note the two African American men in the background. This is one of the few photos from the period in which black visitors are visible. From the collections of The Henry Ford (P.B.55677).

During 1968, the city's African American newspaper, the *Michigan Chronicle*, noted that "Afro History" topics were included in the curriculum at Hillger Elementary School. An "Afro-American History class" was introduced at the University of Detroit after students submitted a petition. And the *Chronicle* confidently announced "Negro History Week Now an Obsolete Device," because "more and more black children are finding the pathway to knowledge about their past illuminated by newly published books; and by enlightened teachers often using homemade materials resulting from their own search for information about Afro-American culture." The same year the *Chronicle* also noted Thomas Edison's achievement with a four-page spread titled "Thomas A. Edison Cleared Way for 'A Century of Progress.'" Throughout this detailed accounting of Edison's achievements, the author never mentioned that readers could travel to Dearborn to see a replica of Menlo Park, let alone the slave quarters and other buildings that could serve as documents of African American history. Despite the proximity of a re-creation of the site where the

"Century of Progress" began, the *Chronicle* did not list it as a potential place to visit and learn more about Edison, perhaps because they knew that African Americans traveling to Dearborn might have to face discrimination before they reached the Greenfield Village gates.[61]

Despite the salience of race in and around Dearborn at the time, the available records tell us nothing of village administrators' views on the number of black visitors. Their actions, however, suggest that they believed their primary audiences were not interested in at least two of the buildings that depicted black history at the site. In 1968 there were calls from the public to open what were then called the Slave Huts, which had been part of official tour guide scripts since the earliest days but were rarely made available for public viewing. The year after the Detroit riot, a reader from the suburb of Oak Park wrote to the *Detroit Free Press*'s "Action Line" section to ask: "Why are the slave huts at Greenfield Village closed to the public? Are they trying to hide one of the uglier aspects of American history?" A *Free Press* staffer responded: "They'll be opened if enough people write indicating interest in them. . . . If they get enough requests, they'll open 'em and include them on the guided tours."[62] It is unclear how many requests Robert Dawson, the village's public relations director, received, but he responded to each request with a form letter claiming that interest in the Slave Huts was minimal:

> Thank you for your recent letter to the Director of Collections at Greenfield Village concerning the Slave Huts. Your letter was one of a very few received as a result of an article which appeared in "Action Line." I'm enclosing some information which may be of interest to you concerning the Slave Huts and the Village and Museum in general. You will note in the descriptive material that the Slave Huts are in an area of related exhibits. These include the Logan County Courthouse, the George Washington Carver Memorial, and the Mattox House. The latter was a plantation overseer's cottage. Although there is still very little public interest in the Slave Huts, we are opening them to visiting school classes on special request.[63]

By the mid-1970s administrators saw themselves in conflict rather than in partnership with other Detroit-area tourist destinations and organizations. Despite the national recession, marketers suspected that many Americans would choose to make Greenfield Village part of their Bicentennial celebration. The marketing and public relations departments accurately predicted that the site would receive at least 1,725,000 visitors that year. The report's authors identified, however, what they believed to be a "growing resentment (or, more accurately, jealousy) on the part of such Detroit groups as Central Business District Association, the Chamber of Commerce, . . . and, occasionally, but to a lessening degree, the Convention Bureau."[64] While the village continued to attract visitors, tourist organizations in downtown Detroit suffered. Administrators recognized that their location outside of the city was a benefit when advertising to national audiences, and they chose to embrace an approach that focused on the site's location in Dearborn rather than in the broader Detroit metropolitan area in order to draw audiences who might have avoided a visit to the village because of anxieties about the safety of Detroit.

Despite the successful efforts to attract visitors during the nation's Bicentennial, administrators continued to be concerned that Detroit's reputation was a prime impediment to the site's growth. In 1977, Brewer Associates, the village's longtime marketing firm, produced a report for Dearborn's Chamber of Commerce titled "Tapping the Tourist and Convention Market," recounting their concerns that Detroit's reputation was keeping visitors away: "In view of the negative press coverage of Detroit's myriad problems, and the anticipated 1978 opening of Michigan's Cedar Point, a competing amusement park, a strong 1977 effort on Dearborn's part would appear just the opening gambit in the long-term struggle for the tourist and convention dollar."[65] Marketers argued for an approach that tied the Henry Ford Museum and Greenfield Village to Dearborn by establishing the city as a "desirable and interesting travel destination," and as a "convenient . . . site for meetings and conventions." The Brewer Associates team was not, however, concerned with Dearborn's local reputation as a racist community. Administrators believed that the village appealed to their visitors because of its location in Dearborn, not in spite of it.

After Henry Ford's death, subsequent administrators struggled to define the purpose of Greenfield Village. Changes to the site's program offerings and landscape were driven both by shifts in the field of public history at large and by their audiences. Staff developed stronger relationships with other museum professionals, expanded their educational programs, and developed new special events. Administrative decisions were also shaped, however, by events in the metro area. After 1967, the village's public relations and marketing teams placed significant blame for any declines in attendance on Detroit's public image. Despite mounting evidence that Mayor Orville Hubbard's local reputation as an ardent segregationist identified Dearborn as a bastion of racism, village officials did not include Hubbard's activities, nor the reputation of Dearborn, in their list of concerns.

During the late 1960s, public historians faced a new challenge. Many leaders in the field called for more representations of women, people of color, and the poor. The Greenfield Village landscape offered opportunities for such interpretations, but administrators asserted that their audiences were uninterested in viewing, for example, the interiors of homes inhabited by enslaved people. The 1969 capital campaign might have focused on adding more historical depth to the village, but instead additions expanded the site's opportunities for leisure and entertainment. By the late 1970s, the actions of both Shelley's and Caddy's administrations suggested that the leadership's answer to the question Allston Boyer asked in 1951—"What is it then?"—was that Greenfield Village was a museum whose primary purpose was to please its audiences.

5

Visitors Respond

I love no place more and would walk a mile over hot coals to get there. . . . It's got Disneyland beaten in every way. It's real.

— Visitor from Alberta, Canada, 1976

In 1954, two months after Donald A. Shelley took over as president, the Henry Ford Museum conducted a visitor survey. Between August 18 and August 26, staff distributed survey forms in the museum's lobby; respondents were asked to complete the forms and return them by mail. By late October, 594, or roughly 20 percent, of the approximately 3,000 surveys distributed were returned. The survey asked visitors what they liked best and least, and they were also asked to rate the sections in the museum, indicate whether they planned to return, and identify their income range and the population of the city or town where they lived. It is unclear exactly how Shelley and his staff used the results, but the questions asked point to an increasing interest in identifying who was coming to the museum and what they enjoyed about their visit.[1]

Throughout the early 1960s, surveys with similar questions were distributed, albeit sporadically, to visitors at both the museum and Greenfield Village. By 1969, Brewer Associates was asked to gather data on visitors. During the winter and fall surveys were sporadic, but the Brewer team collected information from visitors each summer between 1969 and 1979, and these eleven years of surveys tell us much about how visitors encountered Greenfield Village during this period. They established that a majority of visitors were fairly homogeneous in terms of age, income, and employment status. Their experiences were also strikingly similar. In their comments about the village's homes, shops, and attractions, for example, visitors used consistent language to both praise and critique the site's landscape and interpretation.

The Context

Greenfield Village administrators' interest in assessing the visitor experience followed national trends. As we've seen, after World War II many museum professionals and academics turned their attention to visitors. This new interest came from many directions; as George E. Hein observes, some professionals "were drawn to the field by intellectual curiosity," while "more were thrust into the 'business' of evaluating programs and exhibits" with the goal of acquiring external funding from government sources. Others became interested in visitor studies, Kenneth Yellis has noted, as a result of the Cold War–era "concern with ideology," which led scholars to investigate the "ways in which museums could induce attitude change." For example, in *The People's Capitalism Exhibit* (1956), Robert Bower examined how international visitors interacted with this U.S. Information Agency exhibit. The following year, Alvin Goins and George Griffenhagen published "Psychological Studies of Museum Visitors and the U.S. National Museum," which studied visitors' emotional responses to museum exhibits. In 1968 two educational scholars, William Cooley and Terrence Piper, published their pioneering work, "Study of the West African Art Exhibit of the Milwaukee Public Museum and Its Visitors," which examined the exhibit's effect on visitors' racial prejudices. In the same year, Harris H. Shettel and his colleagues released their study of the United States Office of Education exhibit *The Vision of Man.* According to Hein, the Shettel study offered a template for other scholars interested in assessing whether an exhibit had achieved its educational goals.[2]

Similarly, Greenfield Village and other private museums began to replace the informal documentation of visitors with more prescribed processes. The staff at Colonial Williamsburg, for example, conducted visitor surveys as early as 1940. The organization's Hostesses program questioned visitors to determine their ticket-buying patterns and their reaction to the newly released Hollywood motion picture *The Howards of Virginia* (1940), much of which had been filmed at the site. By the mid-1950s Williamsburg was conducting more regular studies of their visitors; the Public Information Department took quarterly "readings" of visitors by asking them to complete and mail back questionnaires handed out at their various facilities and at local motels. They were asked to react to the site's advertising, signage, available hotels, prices, food, tours, and exhibition sites. Williamsburg also hired public relations and marketing firms to administer visitor surveys beginning in the 1960s.[3]

At Old Sturbridge Village in Massachusetts, administrators used surveys to determine how visitors were using the site and to assess how Old Sturbridge fared when compared to other outdoor history museums. In 1958 staff asked visitors to assess the site's ability to educate, to compare it to other outdoor history museums, and to offer suggestions for improvements. In general, visitors were satisfied with their trip to Old Sturbridge. Of 305 respondents, only three said that the re-creation of America's past did not provide them with a "new understanding and appreciation of American culture and history."[4]

Visitors were also asked to compare Old Sturbridge Village to Colonial Williamsburg, Greenfield Village, and Plimoth Plantation in eastern Massachusetts. Like the leadership at Greenfield Village, administrators at Old Sturbridge found that their primary competitor was Colonial Williamsburg. Of those who responded, 107 said that Colonial Williamsburg was "better than Old Sturbridge Village," 36 viewed the Greenfield Village experience as better than or equivalent to Old Sturbridge, and 14 said that it was "not as good." Only three preferred Plimoth Plantation to Old Sturbridge. Administrators at Old Sturbridge would continue to conduct internal surveys to gather visitors' input throughout the 1960s and 1970s.[5]

Rather than using internal surveys to document and understand the visitor experience, the staff at Greenfield Village turned to marketing firms, which suggests that they planned to use the surveys to expand their customer base. Thus Brewer Associates collected data that identified the segment of the population most likely to visit the village, an approach that had consequences for how audiences interpreted the site's representation of the past.

Lizabeth Cohen has shown why so many companies adopted the market segmentation approach after World War II. During the early twentieth century, marketers used the mass-market paradigm; Henry Ford and other successful industrialists made their millions by selling affordable products to a customer base whose needs and desires were assumed to be similar. But by the early 1950s marketers were concerned that this model would constrict business growth as companies competed for the same customers. Many marketers turned to social science research to better understand their customers' desires. What they found was that within the masses there were actually many significant differences (later translated into market segments) related to a customer's demographics, such as age, gender, race, and income. The market was not a mass, but was actually rife with subgroups to which retailers and manufacturers could appeal by creating products geared to meet a variety of specific needs and desires. Cohen argues that "segmenting the mass market thus helped democratize it, allowing sub-cultures to shape markets around their own priorities."[6]

By the late 1960s, then, Americans were used to being sold a wide variety of goods tailored to their interests, including public history venues. Further, they were well prepared to evaluate not only material goods but also experiences as products. In the age of what Cohen calls the "Consumers' Republic," Americans saw purchasing and evaluating purchases as part of their civic duty. "In

the postwar Consumers' Republic," she maintains, "a new ideal emerged—
the *purchaser as citizen*." Consumer purchases, even though motivated by
personal wants, "actually served the national interest." Cohen argues that
marketers and advertisers played a particularly central role in propelling the
Consumers' Republic. And according to Marguerite Shaffer, even tourism was
affected by the focus on consumption; after World War II, tourism in general
changed from a "cultural experience to a more recreational and therapeutic
experience."[7] The leadership at public history sites, then, expected visitors to
bring this consumerist point of view with them and responded accordingly.

Although administrators at Greenfield Village were interested in how and
what their visitors learned, they also hoped to glean information that would
help them increase attendance. The questions posed in surveys by Brewer
Associates indicated which segment of Americans was visiting the village, and
administrators used this information to attract new visitors and to encourage
those who had visited to return.[8]

Maintaining a high attendance rate was essential to meet the site's financial
goals. In order to maintain their classification as a publicly supported foundation, administrators needed to be able to report that two-thirds of the site's
operating funds came from visitors and donors. Increasing revenue from ticket
sales became particularly important during the 1970s. Almost one-third of the
museum's and village's income was generated by interest on the endowment,
which was heavily invested in Ford Motor Company stock. The company's
stock had long been a relatively safe investment, but as Douglas Brinkley has
noted, during the 1970s Ford faced a number of challenges. In 1973 the nation's
energy crisis forever changed American attitudes about energy as well as the
future of the automobile industry. Early in the year, a gas shortage raised prices
across the country; then, in the fall, an embargo by OPEC (the Organization of Petroleum Exporting Countries, most of whose members were Arab
nations) led to a dramatic shift in the automobile market. For the first time,
many American drivers chose to purchase smaller automobiles because they
had good gas mileage, and those models were largely of foreign make. Despite
efforts to introduce its own smaller, more fuel-efficient models, after 1973 the
Ford Motor Company struggled and the village's interest from the endowment
declined. As the 1970s wore on, then, administrators focused their efforts on
identifying who was most likely to buy a ticket to the museum and village.[9]

The Typical Visitor

As we've seen, in 1969 the public relations department and Brewer Associates began to conduct a series of surveys aimed at defining the segment of the
population that was visiting Greenfield Village and the Henry Ford Museum.

Visitors were asked questions about their hometowns, their careers, their annual income, and what they enjoyed most and least about their experience; they were also asked to comment on their visit.

In January 1981, Brewer Associates submitted a cumulative report titled "A Decade of Marketing Activities at the Edison Institute: 1970–1980," which summarized visitor attendance and marketing efforts at both the village and the museum. According to the report, the typical visitor tended toward the "high side of the normal demographic profile in education, age, income, and profession," and lived in a small town or suburban community outside of the metro area; thus visits to the site usually involved an overnight stay.[10]

The surveys indicated that the visitors were more likely to buy a ticket to the village rather than the museum. From 1969 to 1975, only 20 percent of visitors bought tickets only for the museum; 34 percent purchased a ticket only for the village, and the remaining 46 percent bought tickets for both. Thus Greenfield Village was more often the primary destination for visitors. Perhaps it was because the village offered something very different from a traditional museum experience, one more directly aimed at satisfying the typical visitor's desire to be entertained during an educational trip. Or perhaps parents felt more comfortable bringing their children to an outdoor space where they could explore. Administrators certainly believed that their visitors valued the entertainment that the village offered, since they continued to add opportunities for play throughout the 1970s, most obviously when they opened Suwanee Park in 1974.[11]

During the 1970s, about half of visitors to the village and museum were coming for the first time. The other half, the repeat visitors, evidently saw their experience as worthwhile and returned again. Administrators clearly sought to identify the aspects of the village that visitors enjoyed and to enhance those aspects in order to retain and increase the number of repeat customers. They added special events and objects, especially ones that they believed would attract new visitors, while appealing to those who had already made one or more trips. For example, while the Old Car Festival, the Country Fair, and "Let Freedom Ring" were different in many ways, each followed the thematic trajectory of nostalgia for an imaginary and ideal small town.[12]

The cumulative report indicated that most visitors came from cities and small towns within a five-hour drive. Although one of the "major markets" was the Detroit metropolitan area, many visitors were not local residents. In their decade of marketing activities, the museum and village were "more productive in drawing visitors from a 1–3 hour drive time distance than from a 0–1 hour drive time." As figure 11 indicates, an analysis of visitor surveys administered between 1975 and 1977 confirms the cumulative report's findings. During this two year period, over 80 percent of all visitors traveled more than one hour to get to the museum, the village, or both. Approximately 46 percent traveled five hours or more, and another 34 percent traveled between one and four hours.[13]

Administrators used the data collected on visitor's travel time to make advertising decisions. The market-segmentation approach ensured that advertising campaigns targeted audiences primarily in the "0–5 hour" range. As the Brewer Associates report concluded, "Within a matter of a few years after the marketing effort was organized . . . the role of paid advertising into the target market evolved" into several segments, "with only minor variations." Greenfield Village was advertised in travel pages and women's pages in newspapers within the "0–5 hour drive time market" in March and April to generate "family visitations during spring break and summer vacations." Ads were also placed in regional editions of family and travel magazines, such as *Women's Day, Family Circle, National Geographic,* and *Better Homes and Gardens.* Smaller ads appeared in *Smithsonian* magazine, *Americana,* and *Early American Life* to appeal to an even more focused market of visitors interested in early American antiques and material culture. Finally, administrators also targeted visitors in the "0–3 hour drive-time markets" for special events.[14]

The report's identification of Detroit as an impediment rather than an attraction further explains the degree to which staff identified their primary audience as nonlocal. For example, the 1980 cumulative report explicitly blamed declining sales on the public image of Detroit. During the Bicentennial, the village and museum reported a record-breaking total of 1,751,126 visitors. By 1979, the total dropped to 1,570,853 (see fig. 1 in the introduction). The decline in overall attendance, the report argued, was related to several factors, including the Detroit riot and several well-publicized muggings at Detroit's convention center. Marketers argued that Detroit's reputation deterred their primary market: visitors from suburbs and smaller cities.[15]

The lack of local patrons shaped visitor encounters inside the site, too. Most visitors came from small towns and suburbs across Michigan, Indiana, Ohio, and Pennsylvania, and their presence supported a Greenfield Village narrative that remained largely separate from Detroit and its residents. While a few brought local historical knowledge with them, most were tied to other places and other local pasts.

The typical visitor also reported a relatively high annual household income. In 1976 the national median income for American families was $12,686, but as figure 12 shows, more than 70 percent of Greenfield Village visitors in that year claimed household incomes of at least $15,000, and almost a full third, just under 33 percent, claimed $20,000 or more. Only about 8 percent reported annual incomes of $10,000 or less.[16]

The surveyors found that visitors' self-reported careers were in fields that

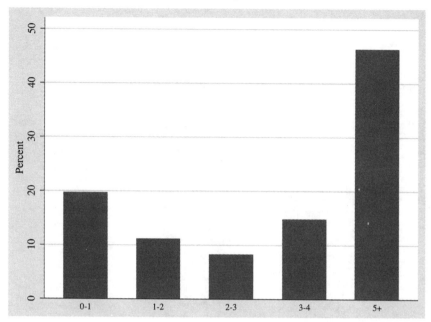

FIGURE 11. Average hours visitors traveled, 1975–1977. Source: Data collected from Greenfield Village visitor surveys.

FIGURE 12. Visitor self-report of household income, 1976. For comparison, the median U.S. household income in 1976 was $12,686. Source: Data collected from Greenfield Village visitor surveys.

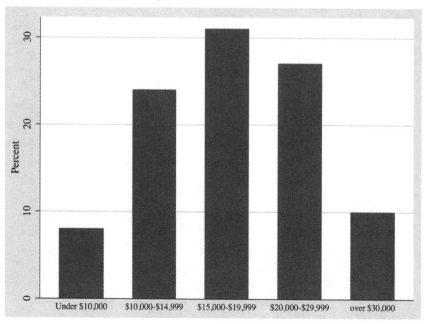

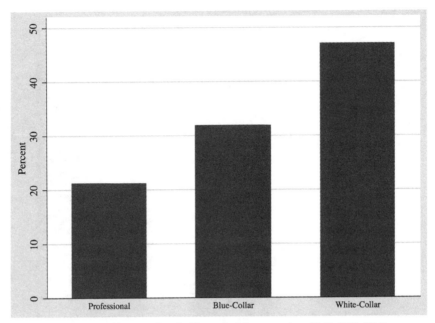

FIGURE 13. Visitor self-report head of household occupation, 1969–1971. Visitors selected the head of household's occupation from these three choices. Source: Data collected from Greenfield Village visitor surveys.

FIGURE 14. What visitors were most interested in, 1969–1977. Visitors selected from a series of attractions. No data were collected in 1971 or 1975. Source: Data collected from Greenfield Village visitor surveys.

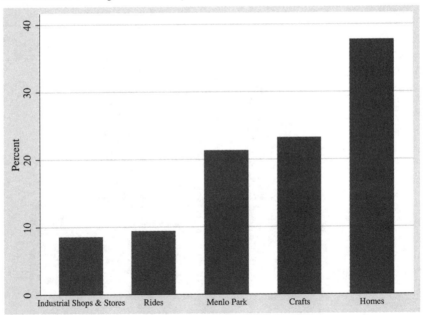

corresponded to higher wages, as figure 13 shows. A total of 68 percent were identified as working in one of the two better-paying categories of white-collar (47 percent) and professional (21 percent) jobs. Thus even though many visitors complained about the cost of tickets and food, administrators saw them as making a sufficient income to afford to vacation and to spend money on gas for the trip, buy tickets for the entire family, purchase food and beverages, and pay for a souvenir.[17]

In many ways, the typical visitor to Greenfield Village was much like the typical visitor to museums in general. During the late 1960s the Smithsonian Institution Museum of History and Technology conducted surveys of its visitors, who averaged over 750,000 in each of the summer months. According to Erik Christiansen, "despite the modest efforts to engage visitors of all backgrounds," these surveys showed that the average visitor was "white, male, middle-aged, and upper middle class" with "an above-average education." Similarly, in a study of approximately 2,400 overnight guests at Colonial Williamsburg in 1975, the Kansas City–based Midwest Research Institute found that Williamsburg was typically visited by families consisting of "a husband and wife, 25 to 34 years of age; two children, 10 to 12; with a family income over $15,000." "Of the husbands," the report continued, "more than 82 percent attended college or hold graduate or postgraduate degrees," and "almost two-thirds listed occupations as professional/technical or management positions." Midwest Research concluded that "in comparison with current socioeconomic statistics, the Colonial Williamsburg visitor is well above the national average both in education and income."[18]

Finally, as figure 14 demonstrates, the typical Greenfield Village visitor was consistently more interested in the homes than in any other aspect of the site. Offered a list of attractions at the village, a remarkable 38 percent of visitors chose the homes as the one they liked best, followed by the crafts section and the Menlo Park group, with the industrial shops and stores trailing far behind. The recently added rides did not fare well, either; they drew a mere 9 percent of visitor votes. Of course, the surveys were completed by adults rather than children, which may account for the poor showing. Even so, the low percentage may have contributed to later decisions by the board and the staff to move away from the focus on entertainment.[19]

Why were the industrial shops and Edison's Menlo Park not as interesting to visitors as the homes? Certainly most of the structures at the village were homes, which may account for their consistent popularity: there were simply more homes to see. But perhaps for most visitors, material culture from the industrial era was part of a too-distant past. During the 1970s, a majority of visitors were identified as white-collar or desk workers. Even blue-collar visitors who labored in large industrial factories would find Menlo Park unfamiliar. Homes, however, were recognizable both as buildings and as symbols. Even if a home contained unfamiliar objects, during the post–World War II era home ownership was celebrated as a powerful weapon in the Cold War and had also become an important front in the battle for civil rights. The home, then, was a potent icon to which many visitors could relate.[20]

Visitors' Comments

The surveys also invited visitors to add any "General Comments" they might have about their time at the village. To learn more about the visitor experience I examined 3,837 comments made on summer surveys between 1968 and 1979, and I found that they generally fell into seven categories I characterize as "nostalgia," "patriotism," "Ford," "appearance," "overall value," "education," and "leisure" (fig. 15).[21]

Overall, these comments illuminate what visitors expected to see and experience, what they enjoyed, and how they thought their trip could be improved. They also expose the criteria visitors used to evaluate their experience at the site. As we saw in chapter 3, the comments recorded by guides in the 1930s had focused primarily on how the objects and buildings on display sparked memories that democratized the past by infusing it with personal, political, or even spiritual meaning. But it was primarily issues of consumption that drove the comments made in the 1970s. For example, many visitors compared the village to other outdoor history museums like Colonial Williamsburg or Old Sturbridge Village. Visitors remained empowered in the sense that they felt confident challenging the portrayal of the past, but their experience was shaped most by an assessment of Greenfield Village as a product.

Nostalgia, Patriotism, and Ford

Few visitor comments were related to Henry Ford (less than 2 percent), patriotism (just under 1 percent), or nostalgia (2 percent). Despite the efforts of administrators to make the connection between Ford and the displays explicit and to develop themes of patriotism using special events, very few visitors mentioned the link in their comments. More surprising was that visitors made few comments related to their personal nostalgia for the past, perhaps reflecting the degree to which a new generation of visitors, one less familiar with the objects and buildings on display, dominated the village's audience.

A few visitors mentioned Henry Ford or the Ford Motor Company. For example, some criticized the admission price, given the profits of the Ford company. Many visitors believed that Ford Motor or the Ford Foundation funded Greenfield Village, a misperception pervasive enough that adminis-

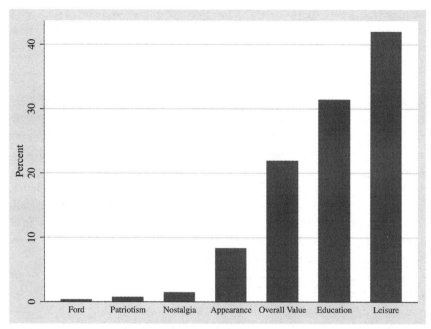

FIGURE 15. Topics mentioned in visitor comments, 1969–1978. Source: 3,837 comments collected from Greenfield Village visitor surveys.

trators included a question on the surveys between 1976 and 1979 that asked, "Did you know that Greenfield Village and Henry Ford Museum are not connected to the Ford Motor Company or the Ford Foundation?" Approximately 50 percent of respondents reported that they did not.[22] Disabusing visitors of this notion was important to administrators, given comments like this one from a visitor in 1971:

> An excellent exhibit but too much money. I don't believe that Mr. Ford or Mr. Edison ever intended that the public be gouged by high prices, especially when the site rests on charity land and when help could be received through the Ford Foundation. $1.00 per adult and 50¢ per child should be sufficient to make ends meet, cut the surplus of help which was observed all over the place, and too [much] commercialism such as cones, pop corn, etc. I will recommend this to my friends but I will advise about the prices. We have found Williamsburg, Washington and the Detroit Zoo more in keeping with the thought expressed. Our family will never return to Dearborn and next year our camper will be pulled by a Chevrolet instead of a Ford.[23]

This visitor asserted that both privately and publicly funded institutions should be affordable for the average consumer. At Colonial Williamsburg, visitors could at least walk through the site free of charge, and clearly the

Washington Mall was free; the Detroit Zoo did charge an entrance fee of 50 cents, but at Greenfield Village tickets now cost $2 for adults and $1 for children. This visitor also assumed power and agency by claiming that he or she would oppose the site's high fees by not buying another Ford.[24]

Visitors were also less likely to comment on patriotism. Even during the bicentennial year, when a national publicity campaign encouraged Americans to show their patriotism by touring museums and historic sites, and Greenfield Village reported over 1 million visitors for the first time, audiences were unlikely to ground their critique or praise of the village's exhibits in a discussion of patriotism. Perhaps by 1976 Americans were inspired to visit public history sites because of patriotic marketing campaigns, but were ultimately engaged in, as Marguerite Shaffer has argued, a "quest for self-indulgent individual pleasure and hedonistic personal freedom in a culture of mass consumption that revolved around spectacle, fantasy, and desire," rather than one to connect with the "collective national identity."[25]

Finally, while visitors' experiences in the 1930s and 1940s were defined largely by personal nostalgia, by the late 1960s and 1970s only a few visitors were reminded of their childhood when they toured the village. One factory worker who visited in 1969 said that the village "brought back memories of my youth with some of the farm machinery and many things my grandparents used, such as butter churns, coffee grinders, etc." When personal connections were made, they were more likely to be linked to family heirlooms rather than direct personal experience. For example, one bicentennial-year visitor wrote, "Historically, we enjoyed all of it as to our age, [and] memories of things exhibited proved this, as we have things passed on by our parents and grandparents that were also in the museum and village for comparison."[26]

Appearance

About 8 percent of visitors indicated whether the site met their expectations in terms of appearance. For many, the staff's ability to maintain a manicured space determined whether they had a pleasant experience. These comments often included remarks about whether the village met a visitor's standard of historic authenticity.

Cleanliness was the focus of many comments about the site's appearance. For example, in 1969 a policeman noted that the "surroundings were well kept—people friendly." Others were less satisfied. The same year a salaried Ford Motor Company employee wrote: "This was our second visit, the first being three years ago. We were surprised and disappointed by the lack of service and maintenance since our prior visit." The writer continued with a series of examples: "muddy parking facilities (inspite [sic] of the fact that the ground in the other lot had dried from the rain); appalling restrooms (no toilet tissue, overflowing receptacles, dirty floors); snack lunch counters under-staffed (by more than 50% of facility capacity)." Horse manure was a frequent topic in comments on appearance. Visitors often suggested, as did this one in 1972, "Have somebody go around picking up the horse manure."[27]

It seems that visitors expected to see an authentic version of America, but not an unpleasant one. Definitions of historical authenticity excluded unsanitary conditions and inconvenience. The sanitized version of the American past was maintained, then, not only by administrators but also by the demands of visitors.

Overall Value

Many visitors (approximately 22 percent) wrote comments assessing the site's overall value, focusing on whether the trip met their expectations in terms of experience and cost. As we saw earlier, they often compared Greenfield Village to venues that they felt were similar to it. While some of these sites were obvious (Colonial Williamsburg and Old Sturbridge Village), comparisons to Disneyland were suggestive of the degree to which many visitors blurred the line between the village and an amusement park.

Visitors purchased a product when they bought a ticket to tour the village. Brief assessments of whether they enjoyed their experience or not, decisions about whether to make another visit, and comparisons between the village and other history museums or theme parks that required a fee indicated visitors' understanding of the museum as a commodity. One wrote: "Liked it much better than Sturbridge Village. As good as Williamsburg, Va." A bicentennial-year visitor was less pleased, however, complaining that while "the Village and Museum was a nice weekend trip . . . as far as history and points of interest was concerned, we were slightly disappointed," and adding, "We feel that Williamsburg has Greenfield Village beat. There were too many things in the Village and Museum that were not interesting to us." The site fared better when a 1973 visitor compared it to Disneyland: "I'm tired but happy. I think you've excelled Disneyland and Disney World. That should make you happy." These visitors expected that their individual needs would be met and that if they were not, their voices could and would facilitate the changes they identified as necessary.[28]

Education

Approximately 31 percent of visitors offered comments about the site's educational qualities. Observations included the words "educational," "interesting," "realistic," and "historical." Other comments noted the degree to which guides were informative and the extent to which buildings and historical details about those buildings were accessible, or made recommendations for improving the site's historical narrative.

Visitors had somewhat different and sometimes irreconcilable visions of exactly how a historic site should educate its audience. Most often, remarks on educational value assessed the village's authenticity or realism. For example, in 1973 a visitor praised the site's "overall excellent display," and added, "Keep the Village as realistic as possible." Another 1973 visitor expressed a common view that historic sites were clean, but should not be not commercial, advising, "Don't emphasize the rides. You're destroying the historical atmosphere. You're making it into an amusement park." Another 1973 visitor drew the line between commercialism and historical authenticity differently when he or she wrote: "Sell more varieties of film, sell fish sandwiches and beer. Make an old-time tavern. Don't modernize too much. Get more old buildings. Garden room needs redecorating. Smell of horses." Visitors' critiques also addressed whether the site met their personal standards of authenticity. For the 1977 visitor, a constructed old-time tavern would add to the site, but "too much" modernization would not, although what counted as "too much" was unclear.[29]

Others commented on the site's historical value indirectly when they challenged or supported the approach to historic preservation. In 1969 a "Doctor (M.D.)" wrote, "The fact that the Lincoln Assassination chair is in this museum and not at the Ford's Theater in Wash. D.C. is inexcusable. It should be where it belongs." Another visitor, not realizing that the Menlo Park buildings were replicas, expressed shock and concern after viewing them: "How did you get the State of New Jersey to go along with your taking most of Edison's historical buildings and articles from New Jersey?" Yet another assessed the village in terms that Henry Ford would have enjoyed, praising its preservation not only of buildings, but also of a worldview: "The project is I believe a valuable contribution to education and to the preservation of certain values in our culture."[30] These visitors evaluated how well the village's representation of the past met their personal definitions of history, which were often contoured by their politics.

Visitors also characterized their educational experience based on the appearance of guides and staff. They often encouraged staff to adopt more of a living-history approach. One wrote: "I think if the guides wore period costumes they would give you more of a feeling that you were back then. Even though your exhibits are from different eras, I would love to see clothing of the different periods." Another recommended an addition to the paddleboat ride and more costumes to transport them into the past: "Would like to hear

Stephen Foster songs on paddleboat," and see "Western show girls in cos-tume."[31] In general, visitors defined the ideal educational experience as one that re-created an atmosphere of the past. For some, such as the visitor who wanted to see Western showgirls, the ideal historic atmosphere was grounded in stereotypes and nostalgia rather than fact.

Visitors frequently expressed satisfaction or dismay depending on whether the site met their informational needs. Closed buildings prompted many adverse comments. One woman complained that her "husband was disap-pointed in the blacksmith's shop" and frustrated that neither the harness shop nor the sawmill were working. She also criticized the interpreters, noting that "the talks and demonstrations in the trades were not informative enough." Visitors wanted more interaction; the same woman wrote that she "would have loved to have seen a demonstration of quilting by a talkative woman instead of her just sitting there hand stitching pieces." Another visitor was dissatisfied with the absence of history relating to the Old West: "I think you should continue to add more of history including the western pioneer days which I did not see." Visitors often blamed guides for less-than-stellar educa-tional experiences; one wrote that "guides seemed unenthusiastic at times, too many people in one house at one time[,] would have liked to see more of each house."[32] The desire for historical authenticity shaped other comments con-cerning commercialism. While many complained that the village contained too much information, for others there was not enough.

On the whole, comments on the site's educational value focused on whether it met visitors' personal definitions of history, guides' performance of the past, and visitors' access to information. Visitors offered suggestions and recommendations guided by their expectations and understandings of what counted as historic. Further, those who made comments saw themselves as authorities on the past and how it should be displayed and represented.

Leisure

A plurality of comments (42 percent of the total) related to Greenfield Vil-lage as a leisure experience. Visitors shared concerns about cost, souvenirs, food, rest areas, and the rides. They were most concerned with the degree to which their trip was a pleasurable one, and they offered a number of solutions if it was not. As with the comments on education, however, these suggestions were often incongruous, even oppositional.

As I mentioned earlier, visitors frequently focused on assessing whether the site cost too little or too much. Many used their comments to recommend alternatives for how the staff could raise more money. The entrance fee for the village (which, for adults, increased from $2 in 1969 to $4.75 by 1980) was the target of many complaints. Specific solutions were offered: a visitor employed by Ford Motor Company, commenting in 1969 that the high admission fee meant he or she spent less on souvenirs, added, "If your prices were lower on things you would sell more and perhaps acquire a larger profit." And in 1971 a visitor wrote, "Entrance fees expensive for us on budget and limited incomes. I'd like to suggest you offer a season pass." A 1977 visitor from Ohio offered a long list of suggestions to make the trip more affordable for "Mr. Average Man and his family." He encouraged administrators to add a "McDonald's 'Golden Arches' enclosed in a suitable frame or brick building for the low budget eater and his five children in the Village," selling "a bumper sticker for the visitor to adorn his car as he leaves," and offering "'T' shirts for the small fry at cost."[33] This visitor's point was that a more commercial approach would increase value and appeal for those he identified as the village's primary customers: the average suburban family.

Souvenirs also played an important role in defining the experience. For many, a trip to Greenfield Village was incomplete without the appropriate memento. In 1969 a plumber wrote that he "wanted to buy glass articles" from the Sandwich Glass Plant, but the site "wouldn't sell" them to him. A few visitors found their experience at the souvenir shop less than satisfactory when they discovered that the shop sold items made overseas. A 1973 visitor wanted to purchase items relating to both the Henry Ford Museum and the village: "Would have liked a booklet of more complete history and coverage of both places, (a souvenir). Also a souvenir (knick-knack) made there and of special interest of both places, rather than foreign made articles." And a 1975 visitor from Michigan remarked, "Souvenir shops shouldn't sell Japanese junk." Perhaps this comment was related to the dawning threat that the Japanese auto industry posed to what had long defined the Rust Belt's economy.[34]

Many commenters voiced concerns about the quality or availability of food, but in different terms from those of the 1977 visitor from Ohio. A 1973 visitor quipped that the village needed "more food facilities, less manure." While the 1977 visitor from Ohio recommended the addition of a McDonalds, a 1975 visitor criticized the food because it "compared to McDonalds."[35] Frequent comments on the site's dining facilities reflected the divergent and sometimes irreconcilable visions of what a historic site should be, but nonetheless they demonstrated that most visitors were focused on the village's ability to satisfy their desires.

The size of the village posed a challenge for many visitors, like the 1971 tourist who wrote that it "was interesting, could not see all completely in one day." One 1975 visitor suggested the addition of "moving sidewalks," and the same year another remarked that "they need more benches in the Village." Another visitor announced: "I love the Village so much that on my next trip to the Detroit area I plan to visit alone, so no one can force me to go home before I see it *all*. This year my daughter became ill at the park and that is why we were only there 3 hours."[36]

Visitors focused a majority of their comments on the site's ability to serve their needs as a leisure space. For most, price, souvenirs commemorating the trip, food quality, and comfort surpassed other concerns. They expected service along with education during their visit to the village. What constituted good service, however, was inconsistent. For some, more rides and opportunities to buy souvenirs improved the experience, while for others it disrupted the site's historic atmosphere. The goals were quite similar in that these visitors were primarily in pursuit of a leisure experience, but they often approached the village with different aesthetic values and assumptions.

Race, Ethnicity, and Gender

Of the 3,837 comments submitted between 1969 and 1979, very few criticized the site's representation of race, ethnicity, or gender, illuminating the degree to which visitors shared the administration's perspective on these themes. But the few comments on these subjects demonstrate that a small number of visitors thought about American history. For them, the site failed to adequately address the nation's diverse past and present.

Racial politics shaped the comments of seven visitors who urged the site to hire more African American guides or to work to attract more black visitors. One recommended adding "dressed up people, (except slaves)." The same person also suggested that the site "hire more black people." Another wrote in 1971, "The absence of black guides is noticeable." And in 1975 a visitor from Ohio called for more stories about black Americans (in the midst of a critique of the site's commercialism): "Hopefully in the future you won't go too commercial—amusement parks are already plentiful. These few captured hours of America in the past should remain just that. Have you considered recognizing more blacks from the 1800s?" In the wake of the urban riots of the late 1960s, a few visitors were looking for representations of the past that offered more diversity, recognizing that the introduction of black guides and African American histories would raise timely issues. In 1973 a visitor encouraged administrators to "restore old mills and factories in northwest section, remove unrestored artifacts, encourage more black Americans to attend. More historical detail."[37] While it is not possible to determine whether these visitors were black or white, the comments demonstrate the degree to which some visitors—their awareness perhaps raised by racial unrest—noticed the absence of African Americans on the front lines and in the audience.

Comments from other visitors suggest an emerging historical consciousness shaped by the social movements of the time. For example, Native Americans were the focus of two visitor comments. One asked: "What happened
to the American Indian? Aren't they part of our history too?" The second
encouraged the addition of historical narratives that covered the history of
Native peoples: "Village could be more diversified, could take in more of the
U.S.A. i.e. Indians, few people get to go out West and other cultures and areas
of U.S. development." Two visitors spoke about the roles of men and women at
the site. One commented on the difference between men and women in terms
of labor: "Girls and boys should hold same positions (information, driving
buggies, other vehicles)." The second called for more stories about women and
minorities, writing that "there should be some aspects of the Village representing the role and contribution of American women," and adding, "I further
stress the need to give credit to minorities. This country is a melting pot. I saw
the replica of G. W. Carver home—what about Mary McCloud Bethum [*sic*],
Betsy Ross and others."[38]

These comments pointed to the possibility of politically progressive
encounters at the village. But such remarks were rare. During the 1970s, the
village's administrators were convinced by the data collected by their marketing firms that their visitors were uninterested in altering the site's largely
consensus narrative. Given their desire to please what they saw as their typical
visitor, it was unlikely that administrators would respond to these few requests
for more representations of the nation's diverse history.

As Lizabeth Cohen has argued, market segmentation democratized everything from product development to political campaigns, but at Greenfield
Village this process had a slightly different effect.[39] During Henry Ford's
lifetime, the visitor experience at the village, as reported by guides, was wide
ranging. The recent history on display ensured that visitors' diverse and
sometimes divergent personal memories shaped their responses to the site's
official narrative. By the late 1960s and 1970s, much of the past on display
was unfamiliar to visitors, and instead of being guided by personal memories they were more likely to draw on other contexts as they encountered the
village's material culture. Once Brewer Associates identified the typical visitor, staff focused on attracting new customers from the same demographic.
Between 1969 and 1979, visitors' encounters continued to be democratic in
the sense that visitors interpreted the material culture on display on their
own terms, but the comments from surveys indicated that for most, those
terms were similar.

Greenfield Village succeeded when it met visitors' expectations as a leisure experience. The ideal leisure space carefully balanced authenticity and commercialism. Where that line fell was inconsistent, but what was important was that each visitor anticipated that administrators would understand how to respond to a comment that, for example, called for more realism but warned against adding too many rides. Further, with the exception of a very few visitors, authenticity did not mean considering the complicated histories of race, class, and gender. Finally, visitors were confident that their sense of how the site should present the past by blending historical authenticity, modern convenience, and entertainment was the right one.

Administrators certainly attempted to meet the needs expressed by their customers. For example, the data collected through marketing surveys explains, in part, why village leadership used $20 million to build Suwanee Park in 1974. Given that most comments assessed the site's quality as a leisure experience, it was unsurprising that Shelley and his staff used additional funding to add the Herschell-Spillman carousel and the raft ride. Suwanee Park was educational in the sense that the activities it offered were related to the American past, but it was also clearly aimed at entertaining the typical Greenfield Village audience.

During the 1970s, most visitors who paid to see the village were from similar backgrounds, expressed similar desires, and used the site for similar purposes. The rare exceptions, however, highlighted the degree to which a more diverse audience could significantly alter encounters with the past. When a few visitors called for more African American interpreters, or noted the lack of women's history at the site, they established the possibilities for broadening the historical narrative at the village. Although we don't know the details of how these visitors interacted with others and with guides when they walked through Menlo Park, for example, it is possible that the questions they asked and their conversations challenged the audiences around them to think differently about the objects on display. Again, however, the comments show that such visitors were the exception, not the rule. With a largely homogeneous customer base, visitor experiences likely confirmed rather than challenged one another.

Interestingly, the typical experiences of 1970s visitors seemed to reinforce many of the messages that Henry Ford had intended to send. Visitors couched their critiques and praise for the site in terms that Ford would have understood and appreciated. They enjoyed seeing a positive portrayal of small-town America, of inventor-entrepreneurs, and of traditional crafts. Ford would likely have sympathized with visitors' requests for a more authentic and convenient experience; he too wanted to preserve the past using his own unique definition of what counted as authentic history. But Ford also lauded the efficiency and convenience of the present. In many ways, visitors evaluated their experience at Greenfield Village along similar lines; they defined their trip as a success or failure based on their individual notions of what constituted the perfect balance between historical authenticity and modern day comfort at an outdoor history museum.

6

The New History at an Old Village

We're not an industrial museum. We're not a museum of technology. The thing that's most unique at our museum and village is that this can be, and must be, the great American museum of change. The period in which America was transformed from a rural, agrarian economy to an industrial, urban, technological world power really signaled one of the basic shifts in how people lived and worked. It was a profound transformation. I feel we have an opportunity— indeed a responsibility—to help people understand the great change.

— HAROLD K. SKRAMSTAD JR., 1981

In 1980, Larry Lankton, who had curated the Henry Ford Museum's power and shop machinery collection from 1972 to 1974, published "Something Old, Something New: The Reexhibition of the Henry Ford Museum's Hall of Technology" in the journal *Technology and Culture*. Lankton was deeply critical of the new exhibit. He described the renovation, which cost $2.4 million and took five years to plan and construct, as "exhausting" and "ultimately monotonous." Although his primary critique was directed at the museum, he also found fault with Greenfield Village's emphasis on entertainment. While Lankton acknowledged that the Edison Institute competed only indirectly with other outdoor history museums, and more directly with "the likes of Lake Michigan beaches, the Detroit Tigers, and the Cedar Point Amusement Park in Ohio," he argued that it was "disconcerting to see" Greenfield Village "struggle with schizophrenia, posing one minute as an educational institution and the next minute as a turn-of-the-century Disneyland."[1]

Lankton's article did not go unnoticed by the board of trustees. As Frank Caddy neared retirement, the board hired a headhunter to find a new president for the Henry Ford Museum and Greenfield Village. Soon, thirty-nine-year-old Harold K. Skramstad emerged as an ideal candidate. Skramstad's credentials included a PhD in American civilization from George Washington University, as well as management positions at the Smithsonian Institution and the Chicago Historical Society. He had built a strong reputation among other museum professionals, and the trustees hoped his expertise and management style would address some of the problems that Lankton, and staff at Greenfield Village, had identified. Initially, Skramstad was reluctant to accept the position. He later recalled that what changed his mind was a visit to his home in Evanston, Illinois, from a board member, Sheila Ford, and her boyfriend (and later husband) Steven Hamp, who was then working in the museum's Education Department. In Skramstad's words, Sheila Ford "convinced me that this was potentially a great museum and that we have to make it that way." After their conversation, Skramstad said, "the challenge" of remaking the museum and the village "was irresistible"; he accepted the job and began his term as president in 1981.[2]

The Skramstad era forever changed Greenfield Village. During his tenure, staff conducted research to verify the history of each building, added new placards explaining in detail each structure's original site and use, opened a working historical farm, and instituted the African American Family Life and Culture program. Visitors initially expressed annoyance about changes to street names and maps (as well as increased attendance fees), but they generally accepted modifications that altered the site's interpretive program.

History Wars

Skramstad's appointment reflected broader shifts in the public history profession as well. By the early 1990s, millions of visitors would encounter what many academics referred to as the "new social history" at museums, in national parks, and at historic sites. For many institutions, the addition of new history programming led to controversy and conflict.

During the early 1980s, many public historians embraced the "new social history." As Eric Foner wrote in 1997, "new histories" emphasized "the experience of ordinary Americans, [and] the impact of quantification and cultural analysis," and signaled "the eclipse of conventional political and intellectual history." In fact, as Ellen Fitzpatrick has argued, the new history that emerged in the late 1960s shared much with the new history approaches that academics like James Harvey Robinson had called for in 1912, Carl Becker echoed in 1931, and numerous others had practiced during the early twentieth century. Both Robinson and Becker urged academics to turn their attention toward research that documented the lives of ordinary Americans. In many ways more progressive academics were engaged in work similar to that of amateur preservationists and curators, including Henry Ford.[3]

For many institutions, new history initiatives resulted in the addition of African American history. At Colonial Williamsburg, social historians hired in the late 1970s began planning a series of ambitious programs that became, by the early 1980s, a significant component of the site's interpretive plan. Rex Ellis, who was the founder and first director of the department of African American interpretation, spearheaded the implementation of the "Other Half Tour," which represented the lives of the enslaved Virginians who had accounted for almost half of Williamsburg's population in the late eighteenth century.[4]

Other outdoor history museums instituted similar programs. In 1985 staff and actors at Old Sturbridge Village re-created a public meeting in which an interpreter portrayed the abolitionist Abigail Kelley, an event that received widespread praise. And at Freetown Village in Indianapolis, a theatrical troupe dressed in late-nineteenth-century costumes to re-create a celebration of emancipation and a black wedding ceremony. Again, the public responded positively.[5]

During the 1990s, however, the academy's influence on public history marked it as a major battlefield in what James Davison Hunter dubbed America's "culture wars." The Smithsonian Institution in particular was targeted when it announced plans for exhibits that openly contested patriotic versions of the American past. In 1991 "The West as America: Reinterpreting Images of the Frontier, 1820–1920" asked viewers to consider visual representations of the frontier in the context of new historical interpretations of western settlement that emphasized the region's history of cutthroat entrepreneurialism and city boosterism, as well as the federal government's policies concerning Native Americans. While comment books showed that visitors' reactions to the wall texts were mixed, opponents published articles in the *Washington Post, Time,* the *Boston Globe,* the *New Republic,* and the *Times Literary Supplement.* At the exhibit opening it was, ironically, a historian who made one of the most serious charges against it. Daniel Boorstin, who initially supported new social history agendas, had become an ardent critic of the political left's influence on the academy. Boorstin wrote in the comment book that the Smithsonian had created a "perverse, historically inaccurate, destructive exhibit." And Senator Ted Stevens from Alaska alleged that the exhibit bred "division within our country."[6]

The reaction to "The West as America" paled in comparison to the grass-roots opposition, beginning in 1993, to the planned "Enola Gay" exhibit at the Smithsonian's National Air and Space Museum. Veterans and politicians organized when they learned that curators suggested exhibit panels on historians' debates about the decision to drop the atomic bomb on Hiroshima, which effectively ended World War II. They also intended to include panels with information about the number of Japanese civilians killed, the number of those who died from radiation poisoning, and a discussion about the legacy of the atomic bomb. In 1995, after two years of negotiating with veterans and politicians, the Smithsonian scrapped the original script, and the director of the Air and Space Museum, Martin Harwit, resigned. Conservative politicians pointed to the proposed "Enola Gay" exhibit and "The West as America" as evidence that public historians were disconnected from their audiences and driven by a liberal political agenda.

The political questions raised by African American interpretive programs at Colonial Williamsburg culminated in 1994 when interpreters and administrators at the site made plans to reenact a slave auction. As word of the plans spread, a number of groups expressed concern and dismay. In contrast to the controversies at the Smithsonian, at Williamsburg the most forceful opposition came not from conservatives, but from members of Virginia's branch of the NAACP, who argued that the re-creation would turn a traumatic chapter of the American past into entertainment. The director of the interpretative program, Christy S. Coleman (who also played an enslaved woman at the auction), defended the event by arguing that it was "just the natural progression of what we've been doing." She noted that despite the emotional nature of the issue, it was also "real history, and it distresses me, personally and professionally, that there are those who would have us hide this or keep it under the rug."[7] For Coleman and others at Colonial Williamsburg, the event offered the opportunity to personalize the trauma of slavery and deepen the impact of their interpretive program.

On the day of the auction, approximately two thousand supporters, three-quarters of them white, arrived at Colonial Williamsburg along with numerous protestors. After the performance, Jack Graveley, the political director Virginia's NAACP chapter, announced that witnessing the auction had changed his opinion; he said that at the reenactment "pain had a face, indignity had a body, suffering had tears." Claude L. Gilmer, a brewery machinist and an African American, said that he appreciated the auction because he attached "a certain reverence" to it, and he added that "it's a period we're paying for dearly, to this day."[8]

While new histories at the Smithsonian Institution and Colonial Williamsburg led to controversy, at Greenfield Village the addition of similar programs did not yield similar results. In some ways, the lack of controversy spoke to the limits of new history. The changes Skramstad initiated, and visitors' responses to them, illuminated the challenges public historians across the country faced as they tried to alter the experience of visitors by presenting them with histories of women, people of color, and the poor, histories that challenged the inevitability of American progress and contested nostalgic versions of the past.[9]

A New Curriculum, a New Village

Skramstad spearheaded changes that affected every part of the Henry Ford Museum and Greenfield Village. For example, in the museum, he would remove the "Street of Early American Shops" and oversee the opening of the 65,000-square-foot, $6 million exhibit "The Automobile in American Life." But the first alterations that Skramstad made were financial. In 1979 the endowment left by Clara Ford to the museum and village, which was still heavily invested in Ford Motor Company stock, yielded $4.4 million in interest. This sum met operating costs not covered by income from admissions, donations, and concession sales. But in 1980, when Ford stock dipped significantly, so did the endowment's interest, and by 1982 it had fallen to only $1.7 million. Skramstad responded with a number of changes. With support from the board, he raised the price of admission. Three investment companies were hired to manage the endowment, and the organization's investments in Ford stock dropped from 75 percent to 7 percent. Other fundraising efforts included a campaign that targeted representatives from foundations and corporations, who were invited to tour the complex. Skramstad also put the village on a hiring freeze between 1981 and 1983. By 1983 he was able to report a balanced budget to the board.[10]

Skramstad later recalled that as he proceeded with some of the most dramatic changes instituted at the village and museum since Henry Ford's era, the board gave him unfailing support. During his tenure as president, he noted, the board operated "much more like a for-profit board in which the CEO is given a lot of latitude." The board's trust in Skramstad and their willingness to let him take innovative approaches to exhibit design was exemplified by their support of revisions to the Henry Ford exhibit in the museum. According to Skramstad, the new exhibit placed "the spinning wheel that Gandhi sent to Ford" alongside copies of the anti-Semitic *Dearborn Independent*. The board agreed that it was important to represent a more complete biography of Henry Ford, even if it was one that included troubling aspects of the industrialist's life.[11]

In 1981, Skramstad began what can only be described as a complete overhaul of the museum's and village's interpretive program. He began by borrowing Colonial Williamsburg's approach and appointed a curriculum committee to review the site's holdings and interpretation. The committee determined that the site was plagued by nostalgia, an attitude that was reinforced by a marketing campaign that defined a visit to Greenfield Village as a visit to "the good old days." The new curriculum, they argued, should not "deny the nostalgic impulse," but "take that emotional reaction and build upon it an understanding of historical truth as much as it can be known." They encouraged others to embrace Skramstad's vision of the village's collections as architectural documents of the "shift from a pre-industrial to an industrial society." While committee members recognized that the village landscape precluded a complete rejection of nostalgia, they hoped to move visitors toward more rigorous historical thinking.[12]

The curriculum committee came up with a series of suggestions. Among them was a list of alternative lenses through which the village might be viewed: "History as Inquiry," "History as Meaning," and "Modernization." These themes, they observed, made historical sense of a confusing landscape that mixed time and place, fact and fiction. They recommended remapping the village to reflect these themes, developing a living-history farm program, and making changes to existing interpretive scripts. Committee members were aware that their findings might disappoint some and "outrage others," but they were optimistic about the potential to improve the site's reputation and offer a more educational experience to visitors.[13]

The committee argued that services should more directly reflect the educational mission of the museum and village. "Many of the programs and services provided to the public by the Edison Institute," they observed, "relate less to our role as a historical agency than to a role as a community center." When the public was allowed to use the facilities for weddings, banquets, and meetings, for example, the site was functioning outside of its role as an educational institution.[14]

Rethinking administrative approaches to the "problem of Detroit" was another theme targeted by the committee:

> Related to the view of The Edison Institute as a tourist attraction is the ever present "problem" of being located in the Detroit area. In the past this has often been sidestepped by emphasizing our location in Dearborn, but there is no use kidding ourselves that we are not part of the Detroit scene for better or worse. Despite the continuing problems of Detroit, we must be an active part of the effort to vitalize the metropolitan area. This may mean developing better relations with the various relevant agencies in the city and the general area.[15]

In the past, administrators and marketing teams had hoped to sever associations with Detroit by focusing on the site's location in Dearborn. But a new history approach, which argued for foregrounding race, class, gender, and power relationships, logically led curriculum developers toward strengthening their relationship with Detroit, a city that in the early 1980s remained at the center of a national urban crisis.[16]

Interpretive issues were another focus of the report. One member of the committee suggested integrating the stories of Henry Ford and transportation. Others proposed focusing on food, clothing, and shelter in the homes to establish common ground with visitors before teaching them about the ways modernization affected the domestic experience. Another recommended using the carousel and Village Green to explore the history of leisure, popular arts, and entertainment that exploded at the turn of the twentieth century. At Menlo Park, the committee suggested focusing on Edison's invention of the modern laboratory. "Instead of one man doing all the work," they pointed out, Edison "pioneered the creation of a lab at which each member of the staff worked on only part of a problem."[17]

To achieve their goals, the committee recommended remapping the village into thematic areas: Agriculture, Domestic Life, and Pleasure and Entertainment. They also suggested developing the Henry Ford Birthplace into the Ford Farmstead and presenting it as a living-history farm. The Ford Farmstead would introduce visitors to the site and set the stage for Greenfield Village as an "immersion into the midwestern rural world of the late 19th century."[18] With the exception of the Ford birthplace, however, interpretive rather than structural changes would make up the bulk of revisions to the site.

Special events were also reviewed by the committee, which recommended that the Country Fair be dropped since it had "no legitimate historical basis in this setting or at this time of year." Instead, they proposed that staff host a series of three-day weekends drawn from the themes of transportation and manufacturing. They also recommended moving the Old Car Festival to May and reframing the popular Colonial Military Muster, Fife and Drum Muster, and Muzzle Loaders Festival in the context of Independence Day.[19]

The committee saw much of its vision become a reality beginning in 1982. After learning that 85 percent of the collections at the museum and village dated to between 1800 and 1950, Skramstad and his team determined that the village's interpretation should focus on the Industrial Revolution. Skramstad recalled that the committee found that "the story of Greenfield Village" was a "story of agricultural towns and communities" that became industrial giants, and that narrative "gave us our gyroscope for the next decade." The museum and village narrative would offer a complex view of how changes in technology altered daily life. At the time, Skramstad told a reporter that "displaying furniture and decoration, the things of daily life, is important, but our challenge is to have people in those houses carrying on the chores of daily life, so the visitor understands the complex social and economic system."[20]

Skramstad's goals for the village were tempered by pragmatism, however.

He knew that visitors arrived looking more for leisure than education, and he told a reporter that he recognized that Greenfield Village was a "tranquil, safe, park-like setting where they can have a nice walk." To slightly challenge the village's idealized qualities, his staff took steps to remind people of the "grim realities" of the past through details. Village staff were told to "leave the horse manure on the road a while, . . . [and] dump ashes out beside the house," and to "point out how people constantly got mangled in the machinery." "People were sick and in pain much of their lives," Skramstad said, "so it was a different existence in many ways, but the life of the mind, the soul, was much the same." He hoped that demonstrating the similarities between the interior lives of people in the past and the present would lead to a more political leap and that visitors would depart with empathy for people who lived in the past.[21]

The village was also remapped, as the curriculum committee had recommended. The Village Green and the Commercial Area were renamed the Community Area, and the Early Industrial Area was renamed Trades and Manufactures. The titles reflected the staff's efforts to create a new historical experience for visitors; for example, visitors were encouraged to view the Village Green and its surrounding buildings as a collective space. The new title both suggested and amplified Henry Ford's view that institutions like the general store, inn, church, and town hall worked in concert to create a sense of community for small town residents. In the Trades and Manufactures area, visitors' attention was focused on how industrialism changed the economy and daily life. In contrast to Ford, who used Greenfield Village to celebrate self-made manhood and the inventor-entrepreneur, the new curriculum emphasized the degree to which small-town residents depended on one another.[22]

In 1983 the Martin Agency, a marketing firm based in Richmond, Virginia, was commissioned to assess the recent changes at the village. According to the firm's report, the average visitor to Greenfield Village was similar to the typical visitor of the 1970s; he or she was between the ages of twenty-five and sixty-four, was accompanied by a spouse or family, belonged to a household with an annual income of $20,000 or more, had a high-school education or higher, and possessed some knowledge about the village prior to arrival.[23]

The typical visitor of 1983, however, was unhappy with the new changes to the site. Although the Martin Agency attributed the recent decline in attendance to higher national unemployment rates and strained travel budgets, the report also noted that Skramstad's decision to increase prices in 1981 from $4.75 to $8 was not well received. It mentioned another factor as well: "Attendance has also been discouraged by the Museum's decision to cut back on some of the programs that the public has traditionally favored (e.g. the handcrafts program)." Visitors were also disgruntled by the elimination of the Country Fair as a special event. The agency observed that "until recently, the Museum and Village have had difficulty getting a handle on what kind of attraction it ought to be to the public." It was advertised as a "comfortable serene retreat, or as the home of American enterprise." But now the real problem was that "changes brought about through the leadership of Harold Skramstad, affecting pricing, programs, exhibits and the public's access to certain areas have confronted the visitor without first providing him with some understanding of how these changes will improve the establishment. Many people are confused, if not irritated." Other weaknesses noted by the consultants included insufficient revenue, a lack of private and corporate donations, and—again—the reputation of Detroit.[24]

Visitors did offer some positive feedback, however, and these comments foreshadowed what would become a general acceptance of changes and additions to the site. Visitors identified the decision to start operating the Armington & Sims machine shop, the Circular Sawmill, and the Loranger Gristmill, and the new interpretive programs at the Connecticut Saltbox and the Edison Home as improvements. A rise in attendance by the end of the 1983 season also suggested support for Skramstad's initiatives.[25]

In 1984 the village received its biggest financial boost to date when the National Endowment for the Humanities (NEH) announced a $1 million challenge grant to the village and the Henry Ford Museum. If the site could raise $3 million in new or increased funding over the course of three years, the NEH would match it with another $1 million. Skramstad said that the grant acknowledged the staff's "efforts to get through financial difficulties of the early 80s," and was a "real recognition that we have a nationally important institution here." Skramstad and his staff used the grant to restore several buildings, such as the Noah Webster house and the Menlo Park laboratory. The funding was also used for repairs to the Henry Ford Museum and to replace part of the $4 million administrators had borrowed from the endowment between 1980 and 1983.[26]

The NEH grant was just the first in a series of grants staff succeeded in winning from state and federal institutions. For example, in 1984 the Michigan Council for the Humanities provided funds for the reenactment of a 1912 Chautauqua tent session. The event was cast as a replacement for the now defunct Country Fair, whose loss the year before visitors lamented. It featured actors playing William Jennings Bryan, Clarence Darrow, and Theodore Roosevelt, as well as musical performances, dramatic readings, and humorists in a two-thousand-seat tent on the Village Green. By applying for and winning grants from institutions that supported historical research to enrich the village's depiction of the past, Skramstad and his administration worked not only to add more educational programming but also to alter the site's image.[27]

FIGURE 16. The Firestone Farm opened to visitors in 1985. Photo by author, 2011.

In 1985 the village opened the Firestone Farmstead, which had been under development since 1982 (fig. 16). Raymond Firestone decided to donate his family's 1828 summer homestead to Greenfield Village largely because the Firestones and Fords had a long-standing personal and business relationship. Harvey Firestone, Henry Ford, and Thomas Edison, along with the author and naturalist John Burroughs, made several camping trips together during the 1920s, and they had visited the Firestone farm in Columbiana, Ohio. The Firestone Company provided the first two thousand sets of tires for Ford's Model T, and in the 1980s continued to supply a majority of Ford tires. Moving the family farm from Ohio to Greenfield Village seemed natural. The Firestone Foundation provided $2 million to disassemble, move, rebuild, and maintain the home.[28]

During its dedication in 1985, fifty relatives representing four generations of the Firestone family stood alongside former president Gerald Ford and the chairman of the Edison Institute's board, William Clay Ford. For Raymond Firestone, the farm represented a nostalgic image of his father, one that emphasized hard work and self-made manhood. He told a reporter that as a young boy, while on vacation at the farm, he had to "work eight hours every day." For Skramstad, however, the farm's significance extended beyond the Firestone name; it was an opportunity to re-create a living historical farm, one of the most popular representation techniques already used in well-recognized outdoor history museums such as Colonial Williamsburg. Under the guidance of project director Nancy Bryk, staff developed programming and interpretive scripts to stress the links between domestic life and techno-logical progress. The Firestone farm, however, in some ways exacerbated the interpretive challenge that many of the village buildings associated with the biographies of famous men already posed. The notion of celebrating a great man did not fit well with the new curriculum's emphasis on the experiences of ordinary people. To emphasize histories beyond the Firestone family, staff dressed in period clothing, cared for the animals on the farm, and prepared daily meals from the adjacent garden, marking the site's first permanent foray into third-person living history. While interpreters recognized the contribu-tions of Firestone at the home and farm, they underscored that the structures were representative of those used by middle-class families during the nine-teenth century.[29]

The Firestone farm marked the most significant architectural addition, but staff also focused on reinterpreting existing structures by altering the training of guides and writing new scripts to help redefine familiar buildings for visi-tors. In 1985, Candace Matelic, who had recently left her position as manager of the interpretive program to direct the Cooperstown Graduate Program in New York State, published an article assessing the new training of the museum and village guides in the *Journal of Museum Education*. She outlined the rig-orous, three-month-long program offered to interpreters, and she argued that, "interpretive training must include method as well as message," and that "interpretive information and training should be conceptual in approach and focus." In the Menlo Park buildings, for example, project director John Bowditch faced the formidable challenge of deemphasizing the celebratory narrative of Thomas Edison that had defined the interpretation of the replica since 1929. Bowditch's new script highlighted the important role that collabo-ration played in Edison's success. The Sarah Jordan Boarding House, where Edison's employees slept and took their meals, was also reinterpreted, with the new script focusing on the important role women played in helping Edison's male employees to succeed.[30]

The reinterpretation of the Susquehanna House, a former plantation home, most dramatically altered the site's representation of African American his-tory. Since Henry Ford had moved the building to the village in 1942, the Susquehanna home had been used to depict the colonial past by represent-ing the lifestyle of a planter living in Maryland during the mid-seventeenth century. But a renewed effort to ground each building's interpretive program in more thorough historical research led to an investigation of tax records, maps, and an archeological dig at the Maryland site. After researchers discovered that the building dated to the mid-nineteenth century and that Henry Carroll, a wheat and tobacco planter who relied on slave labor, once owned the Susquehanna, staff closed the building while research was completed and developed a new interpretive manual. Curator Peter Cousins and others also asked for assistance from Rex Ellis, a historian and the head of African-American programs at the Colonial Williamsburg Foundation.[31]

When the newly named Susquehanna Plantation reopened in 1988, public relations manager Nancy Diem admitted that the new exhibit focused primarily on the life of its former owner, Henry Carroll, rather than on slavery. Instead of placing enslavement at the center, "reminders" of human bondage, such as a bedroll in the kitchen, appeared throughout the house. Guide talks noted that the modest home reflected Carroll's obsession with building his human capital. Peter Cousins told a reporter that the staff "tried to make the point that this system of slavery kind of perverted the way people lived because they became so obsessed with value in human beings and in land." Interpreters wore 1860s-style dress and used third-person interpretation as they pointed out, for example, that the enslaved African Americans built the home and that the owner's "comfort" depended on "human labor."[32]

The critique of slavery in the new interpretive program was certainly limited. Enslavement moved around the edges of guide talks, home furnishings, and likely, visitors' consciousness. Still, expanding the interpretation of enslavement at Greenfield Village was groundbreaking in the site's own history. While visitor encounters with the slave cabins were often mentioned in the journals kept by guides during the 1930s and 1940s, tour scripts listed the interpretation of these buildings as optional. As I noted earlier, the cabins remained closed, except on special request, through the 1970s. To frame slavery as unjust in a new location was a bold move at Ford's village.[33]

That same year, John M. Staudenmaier's article "The Giant Wakens: Revising Henry Ford's History Book" was published in *Technology and Culture*. The essay was a response to Lankton, who had referred to the museum as a "sleeping giant." Staudenmaier was an associate professor of the history of technology at the University of Detroit and often brought his students to the village and the Henry Ford Museum so they could work with the curatorial staff. Now, eight years after Lankton's article appeared, Staudenmaier wrote that "signs abound that Lankton's 'sleeping giant' is waking." He identified Skramstad's managerial style as the force behind the shifts, but he also pointed to the retirement of many senior vice presidents and the rise of several junior staff members, including Steven Hamp, who had become chairman of collections, as well as the directors of the public program, exhibit, and public affairs divisions. Although there were "some not-surprising signs of frustration on the part of personnel who find their normal work time squeezed by project pressure," on the whole the staff supported changing the museum and village. Staudenmaier identified the addition of the Firestone Farm, the reinterpretation of Menlo Park, and the reinterpretation of the Susquehanna Plantation as major accomplishments. "When I first began to take students through the museum and village in 1983," he wrote, "the ideology of linear progress often dominated verbal presentations so that I occasionally used the language of interpreters as examples of 'progress talk' and contrasted them with contextual history." But five years later, he reported, interpretive scripts worked toward providing visitors with "a glimpse of life in a different culture, one with different burdens and different amenities."[34]

In 1991 a more extensive program aimed at representing black history began with the institution of the African American Family Life and Culture program, coordinated by Nikki Graves Shakoor. The Susquehanna Plantation became part of that program, and staff developed new interpretive scripts for the Hermitage slave cabins and the Mattox House. According to Skramstad, the impetus for the program developed from a growing awareness of their collection of buildings associated with African American history: "Here was a cluster of buildings that carried some very powerful themes. There was really no story there so we tied them together with a theme and a story and it sort of emerged out of that. It was not that we decided to focus on African American history, but that we recognized that here is a set of buildings that will add to our curricular offerings." As staff began to develop these programs, they relied not only on historical research but also on focus groups, interviews with visitors, and questionnaires distributed to visitors, educators, children, parents, and other audience segments.[35]

Shortly after the African American Family Life and Culture program opened, the site's public relations director, G. Donald Adams, published an article in the professional journal *Visitor Studies: Theory, Research, and Practice* reporting that a primary challenge staff faced as they developed programming on black history was the reputation of Dearborn: "Many black residents of the City of Detroit and the Detroit area feel they are not welcome in Dearborn."[36] Given that one of the goals of the program was to draw more local African American visitors to the site, staff began their project by hiring marketing firms to conduct audience research. As Skramstad put it, "Our challenge was: how do you make African Americans in Detroit feel more welcome. It's not just permission to come, it's an invitation to come."[37]

Understanding how visitors might respond to an interpretive program centered on black history began with the creation of a consulting panel that included experts on African American history, museum professionals experienced in interpreting African American history, and educators from the Detroit public school system. According to Adams, panel members generated ideas for potential special events and daily audiovisual presentations. They also "clearly established that the history of Dearborn required proactive 'bridge building' with several important constituencies in the metropolitan Detroit area." Consequently, Shakoor was appointed manager of the site's new Community Relations department.[38]

An African American–owned research firm, Moore & Associates, also conducted four focus groups for the staff: one with suburban African Americans, one with suburban Euro-Americans, one with Detroit African Americans, and one with Detroit Euro-Americans. All participants had children between the ages of eight and fifteen, and all had "participated in a cultural place or activity in the last three years." When asked about the "general image of Henry Ford Museum and Greenfield Village," Euro-Americans used words like "great," "educational," and "fun," while African Americans were more likely to use such words as "cars," "inventions," and "white folk." When asked about Dearborn, some African Americans said they were not comfortable going to Dearborn, but others said that they did not generally see the museum and village as part of Dearborn.[39]

The focus groups urged the site to depict the histories of "resilience and resistance, and other positive characteristics rather than the horrors of slavery." African Americans were particularly concerned that the village was going to show "only a low point in the culture without referencing earlier periods of high culture." Participants argued that the "exhibit should demonstrate the proud history of these people." Further, African Americans expressed concern that this was a "one-shot program for marketing purposes, rather than an ongoing and broad institutional focus." They did not, however, view the goal of increasing attendance by black visitors as "necessarily negative." African Americans also indicated that "museum and staff members were sending out damaging non-verbal messages," which indicated to the administration that sensitivity training was necessary. When they viewed the plans for the exhibit, participants felt that "knowledgeable African Americans in period costume" should conduct the interpretation at the Mattox House.

To test the potential success and impact of the African American Family Life and Culture program, the assessment team conducted random interviews with visitors and distributed questionnaires. Many visitors felt that the exhibit would be more credible if there were more than two African Americans among the site's interpreters, who numbered over a hundred. Consequently, administrators hired sixteen additional African American interpreters. True/false questionnaires given to visitors, educators, children, and parents found that many believed that the words "slave" and "black" were synonymous. Curators responded by changing all references in the developing interpretive scripts to "enslaved people." Further, many respondents believed that enslaved families were "not allowed to live together," and that "enslaved people would not have written stories and books." None were aware of the history of industrial plantations and few had any sense that enslaved people could be skilled laborers.

As administrators and staff proceeded with the development of the African American Family Life and Culture program, they kept the concerns of visitors, and potential visitors, in mind. Administrators spent $450,000 to restore the buildings, conduct oral history research, and write new interpretive scripts. Skramstad and his staff used funds from the NEH grant and the Skillman, Hudson-Webber, and Knight Foundations to complete the buildings. In 1991 the site inaugurated the program as part of a three-day weekend celebration of the signing of the Emancipation Proclamation that became a mainstay at the site.[40]

The two slave cabins were renamed the Hermitage Slave Quarters to connect them more explicitly to the Hermitage plantation in Georgia, where Henry Ford first found them. Interpreters and staff used the cabins to place enslavement in a local and national context, while at the same time providing specific details about life under the original plantation's owner, Henry McAlpin. In one cabin, a running tape presented readings from the slave narratives of Elizabeth Keckley, Jacob Stroyer, Frederick Douglass, Olaudah Equiano, and Henry "Box" Brown; wall panels summarized the life of each speaker. In the second cabin docents used third-person interpretation or played a tape to tell the story of everyday life on the original rice plantation, where approximately two hundred enslaved peoples lived. The interior was furnished with a cot, several gourds, some tools, and a gun. Interpreters noted that they used the houses to locate the experiences of "a generic family of enslaved African-Americans . . . within the general setting of African-American rural life in the 1850s." They also sought to "dispel the collective myths, stereotypes and misconceptions of 'slavery'" that visitors brought with them by giving them a "sense of connection with real individuals and families," and to show "how African-American individuals and families resisted the inhumanity of bondage, developed and exercised coping mechanisms, maintained family relationships, preserved and expressed their culture, and, in some cases, escaped to freedom."[41]

The new interpretation at the Mattox House drew on historical research as well. As we saw earlier, when Henry Ford purchased the house in Georgia in 1943, it was inhabited by an African American tenant farming family, the Mattoxes. Now, as staff worked to craft a new interpretation for the home, researchers located Carrie Mattox (granddaughter of Andrew and Charlotte Mattox, the original owners) and a family friend, Charles Boles, in the hope of finding out what the interior of the home had looked like (fig. 17). Boles said that the house resembled the "old building," but that it was in "much better shape." He also explained that the family wasn't "able to keep it up," because they were "poor and illiterate," and that they suffered from "illnesses and diseases."[42]

Boles also led researchers to an uncomfortable past that was included in the new manual for interpreters. The manual explained that while Ford bought the Mattox family a new house and new furniture, he never supplied them with a new deed. The proprietors of a paper mill purchased the land after Ford's death, and without paperwork to prove their ownership of the home, the Mattox family was evicted.[43]

Interpreters using the new script were provided with another talk that emphasized the Mattox family's accomplishments and successes. When interpreters later evaluated the African American Family Life and Culture project, they said that their goal was to use the house to tell the Mattox family's story' "within the general setting of African-American rural life between the two world wars."[44] Ideally, the manual asserted, interpreters would "populate visitors' imaginations with stories of specific people" who had owned their land and home, earned their living through resourcefulness, sustained important family relationships, maintained a sense of dignity and propriety, valued religion and education, and preserved and expressed their culture, while simultaneously struggling to triumph over racism and poverty." To help tell these stories, interpreters drew on the furnishings of the home and its surroundings, which included a field in front of the house, crops, a grape arbor, fences, and a birdhouse.[45]

The recommended talk for guides, however, never mentioned the harsh social, economic, and legal realities of the Jim Crow south, perhaps because focus groups, and African Americans in particular, had urged staff to focus on positive historical narratives. Instead, the story of the Mattox family fit neatly with the other long-standing narratives at the village. Guides were to recount that Andrew and Charlotte Mattox built the home and passed it along to their son Amos, and that Amos and his wife, Grace, were upstanding members of their community and hard workers. "In order to provide for his children, Amos Mattox usually worked two or three jobs. He worked for Bryan County and the Atlantic Coastline and Seaboard Railroads as a mail carrier (until he was injured by lightening)." Mattox was also a "farmer, barber, cobbler, and preacher at the same church his grandfather founded." Grace Mattox was presented as the ideal mother and wife: she was "a meticulous homemaker who crocheted and did 'fancy hand work' embroidery. She canned vegetables

FIGURE 17. Inside the Mattox House at its opening in 1991. Charles Boles, who knew the Mattox family, was interviewed during the reinterpretation of the building with the goal of providing audiences with a more historically accurate interpretation and a sense of its original interior. From the collections of The Henry Ford (B.107738.5).

for needy neighbors and helped tend the sick or ailing. A devoted mother, part of her daily routine was to prepare a 'proper hot lunch' for her two children, Carrie and Amos, pack it in a picnic basket, walk to school (a distance of one mile) and wait for them to finish eating. Upon returning home, she would prepare the family supper." The families of Carrie and Amos Mattox continued to play an important local role and were "contributing members of the Savannah community."[46] In short, the script described the Mattoxes as industrious workers and strong community members who were devoted to their families.

Finally, in 1994, Skramstad and the staff reopened the general store, now rechristened the J. R. Jones General Store to reflect the name of its original

owner. Curator Donna Braden pointed out that the "building was from Michigan, the Elias Brown sign was from upstate New York and the stock was from
old stores all over the country."[47] Curators set to work correcting these "historical inconsistencies," and when the store reopened an interpreter played the
role of J. R. Jones. First-person interpretation had been used at special events,
but this was the first time staff planned to use this approach regularly. Some of
the goods displayed included 1880s-style bolts of cloth, straw hats, and cans of
vegetables. Another curator, Mary Seelhorst, had worked with staff to provide
more than 2,500 reproductions for the store. Braden told a reporter that the
"new old store makes the point that the 1880s were a pivotal time in the development of consumer goods." The store fit with the new curriculum's focus on
explaining how the Industrial Revolution altered daily life.[48]

Visitors Respond to the New Curriculum

Almost immediately following their opening, Skramstad oversaw the establishment of three teams to evaluate the visitor experience at the slave houses
and the Mattox house. One included the original exhibit design team, representatives from the School and Community Programs department, and staff
members from Program Development. Another team consisted of interpreters who had worked at each building. A third team included Detroit-area
teachers participating in the 1991 National Endowment of Humanities Summer Institute on "African and African-American Heritage."[49]

Interpreters who worked at each building noted some of the most common
comments made by visitors. In the furnished slave house (fig. 18), interpreters said that when the recorded tape was used, several visitors commented
that "slaves didn't have it so bad," or that "many poor whites didn't live this
good." Another interpreter reported that "most visitors accept all furnishings"
as historically accurate, with the exception of "the bed and gun." Interpreters identified some of the most popular questions asked by visitors: "Was
this owner more kind, gentler than others?" "Did they really have a gun?"
and "How many people lived in the house?" The number-one question that
children asked was where the enslaved children slept. Almost all of the interpreters interviewed mentioned that visitors were "surprised" that the cabins
were believed to be the only double-walled slave cabins in the United States.
In a series of questions about responses to the unfurnished cabin, interpreters noted that many visitors just walked through to get to the furnished
building, and others said that visitors did not ask many questions about that
building. The metro area teachers attending the NEH Summer Institute made
comments similar to those of the interpreters. Some feared that the material
culture on display in the furnished slave house was such that, as one teacher

FIGURE 18. Inside one of the the Hermitage Slave Houses in 1992. The home was furnished with the material objects by then identified as common to enslaved African American households. From the collections of The Henry Ford (P.B.108755.3).

worried, students might leave the exhibit thinking that "slavery was not so terribly bad after all."[50]

Visitors fit their encounters with the cabins into their own preconceived notions about enslavement, whether that meant that the furnished Hermitage slave house was too nice or not nice enough. While staff hoped that white visitors would find common ground with the enslaved and then move toward a recognition of the horrors of human bondage, visitors seem instead to have identified with the material conditions of enslavement, compared them to their personal understandings and definitions of extreme poverty, and stopped there.

In the Mattox House, visitors noted the similarities between their own or their family's material history and the past depicted. For example, one interpreter said that older visitors often made comments like "I know about the newspaper on walls. I lived in a house like this." Other comments centered on a visitor's personal memories associated with the material objects in the home. Interpreters noted that many visitors said things like "My mother had a trunk like that"; "We played checkers with bottle caps"; "This furniture reminds me of the furniture that my family had." It was clear that some visitors made strong connections between their personal or family histories and the Mattoxes, but did not necessarily recognize the vast differences between their legal rights and those of the Mattox family.[51]

Visitors who did not connect with the Mattox family because they did not come from a similarly impoverished background reacted by challenging its veracity or attempting to fit it into the site's long-standing narrative of self-made manhood. The most frequently asked question listed by interpreters was "Did they really have newspaper on the wall?" And the second was "What was Mr. Mattox famous for?" Again, visitors imposed their understandings of the past, or museums about the past, onto unfamiliar terrain.[52]

Why did the new history programs at Greenfield Village have limited success? Staff followed the tenets of new history by asking the local community for feedback, conducting historical research, and addressing the stories of people long ignored by consensus versions of the past. Still, visitors' responses indicated that these encounters were not as complex or historically nuanced as those who wrote the "New Curriculum" might have hoped.

One of the impediments to achieving the goals of new history at the village was the narrative's focus on material conditions. At the slave houses, white visitors saw the physical conditions of enslavement but not the legal ones. And at the Mattox home, visitors related to the newspaper on the walls and the family games played at the kitchen table without recognizing that outside of the home Amos Mattox could not sit at the same lunch counters, drink from the same water fountains, or send his children to the same public schools as whites.

The rest of the village landscape also worked against the tenets of new history. The majority of the other buildings depicted the humble beginnings of men who went on to amass large fortunes. Even the one other building depicting African American life at the site, the George Washington Carver Memorial, was presented as part of Carver's success story. It was difficult, then, for visitors to shift narrative gears. Life was "grim" for most Americans, but most Americans were not depicted on the Greenfield Village landscape.

"Hostile Suburbs"

Another impediment to new history at the village—which Skramstad and others in his administration recognized—was the world outside the village gates. Even after Orville Hubbard stepped down as mayor of Dearborn in

1977, the city's politics continued to be defined by racism. In fact, many Detroit residents claimed that most of the surrounding suburban communities were unwelcoming, even openly racist, in their treatment of African Americans. In 1986, when proposals were made to impose stiffer gun control measures in Detroit, Coleman Young, the city's first black mayor, announced that he would "be damned" if he was "going to let them collect [i.e., confiscate] guns . . . while we're surrounded by hostile suburbs." Young said that his assertion was based on recent actions by suburban governments in the area. According to Young's press secretary, Bob Berg, Dearborn was one of the offenders and had a "reputation for being a whites-only enclave."[53]

At the time, Dearborn officials were fighting to keep nonresidents out of the city's public parks. In November 1985 the city's voters passed an ordinance banning nonresidents from almost all of its parks and playgrounds; violators faced fines of up to $500 and ninety days in jail. The Detroit branch of the NAACP quickly announced its opposition to the ordinance, arguing that it was designed to prevent African Americans from using Dearborn's parks. Talks between Dearborn city officials and NAACP members resulted in an agreement to postpone enforcing the ordinance, but the city's mayor, John O'Reilly, refused to sign it. The NAACP responded by calling for a boycott of all Dearborn merchants, including the Henry Ford Museum and Greenfield Village, and by filing a joint lawsuit with the American Civil Liberties Union in Wayne County Circuit Court.[54]

Skramstad was immediately concerned about the potential effects of the boycott and called on the Ford Motor Company to intervene. Initially, Ford Motor executives were unfazed by the boycott, assuming that the troubles of Dearborn were largely unrelated to Ford Motor's success. Skramstad recalled that he "called someone higher-up in the company" and urged Ford officials to engage in the conversation by predicting that "one day, the national media was not going to refer to Dearborn as a gritty industrial suburb of Detroit, but as the world headquarters of the Ford Motor Company." "At that time," Skramstad said, "they realized that they needed to talk to people in Detroit."[55]

There were hints that Dearborn's newly elected mayor, Michael Guido, would agree to negotiate with the NAACP in 1986. Although Skramstad described Guido as a real "helpmate" as Dearborn's businesses worked to end the boycott, and Guido personally opposed the ordinance, he did not fully agree with the NAACP's demands and vowed that he would not cooperate by signing a temporary injunction against the ordinance as long as the lawsuit continued to include allegations concerning the city's past policies of racial discrimination. Guido told a reporter, "What I read in there are about two sentences on the parks ordinance and four pages on Dearborn's reputation and history."[56]

The parks ordinance clearly raised issues about the definition of public space. But intertwined with that was the matter of when and what histories should count. No one, not even proponents of the ordinance, could deny Dearborn's history of segregation and racism, but there was a concerted effort to forget that past. For the black community and their supporters, Dearborn's history added new and troubling layers of meaning to the ordinance.

In February, Mayor Guido announced an end to his negotiations with the NAACP and hired Detroit lawyer William Saxton to defend the city ordinance in court.[57] When the case went to trial with Wayne County Circuit Judge Marvin Stempien presiding, Saxton argued that calling up the Hubbard legend served "no purpose and does not prove that enforcement of the ordinance is unconstitutional." Wayne State University law professor Robert Sedler, who represented the coalition opposing the ordinance, argued that Dearborn's past was evident in the population of the present. He pointed to 1980 census figures that showed that only 83 of Dearborn's ninety thousand-plus citizens were black. When asked about how the city would enforce the ordinance, Guido said that there were no firm plans. Some options included fencing the parks and requiring all entrants to present Dearborn identification, having rangers make sweeps of the parks and ask users to show identification, and having rangers check permits of large groups holding functions in the parks.[58]

In September 1986, Judge Stempien ruled that it was unconstitutional to arbitrarily ask park users to produce identification and that the ordinance could be used to discriminate against black Americans. The NAACP accepted the ruling and ended the merchant boycott. Coalition members said that they would not pursue legal action against other Michigan municipalities that had similar ordinances, such as the Grosse Pointes, Flat Rock, Gibraltar, and Clawson. When asked why, the Reverend Adams said that Dearborn was "unique in its capacity as a 'public city'" because of the high volume of commuters." "Fairlane Mall, the Henry Ford Museum, Greenfield Village, Ford Motor Company and the University of Michigan–Dearborn are just some of the entities in the city that attract more than 300,000 commuters daily," he added.[59]

With the boycott over, Skramstad, Adams, and other community and religious leaders from Dearborn and Detroit organized an informal musical performance called the Friendship Concert, featuring a large choir of singers from Dearborn and Detroit churches. In a memo proposing the concert to board president William Clay Ford, Skramstad noted that the parks issue had negatively affected school visitation, "since many of our groups come from Detroit." He went on to explain that the coalition between Detroit and Dearborn had been "quietly facilitated" by the Ford Motor Company. "While this event has a small element of risk," he wrote, "the potential benefit to us is tremendous." The event would not only help reconcile the communities of Detroit and Dearborn but also "position the museum as 'high ground': a historic site where historic things happen."[60]

On June 25, the *Detroit Free Press* covered the Friendship Concert on the front page, noting that "some good is going to come of this Dearborn parks controversy, even some genuine feelings of love between black and white bound together in faith." Over 2,500 guests gathered together on the Village Green to listen to the choir, which included members of twenty-eight churches in Dearborn as well as two of Detroit's Baptist churches. Skramstad recalled that "it was the perfect evening," because "people came together not for politics but as a kind of community gathering." For him, the event marked a turning point at Greenfield Village. "The black community started coming to the Village" he said, "and felt welcomed and at home." The event also "helped pave the way" for the Village's future "programs with the black community."[61]

During 1986, Dearborn scrambled to reshape its public image. City and business leaders released a twelve-minute video titled *Destination Dearborn*, aimed at reversing the city's image as racist and isolationist. The president of the Dearborn Chamber of Commerce, Peggy Campbell, said that "the outside image of Dearborn was like Oregon, where they have signs that say 'We want you to visit us, but don't stay.'" The campaign also coincided with the Ford Motor Land Development Corporation's plans to develop more than 2,300 acres, over half of them in Dearborn. Richard Routh, Ford Land's representative, admitted that "we have some selfish interests in (promoting Dearborn) because we still have 1,400 acres to develop." According to Routh, the issue of the city's racism often came up in talks with business owners who were considering relocating to Dearborn: "We tell them that we do everything we can to promote what our company stands for, and that's equal employment opportunities and aid to minority businesses." City officials also developed a homestead plan, offering six vacant lots for $99 each to people willing to build on them during the 1987 construction season.[62]

But public relations campaigns and victories in the courts did not reshape the persistent image of Dearborn as a racist community in the minds of many African Americans. And many Dearbornites either continued to applaud or chose to ignore the long history of segregation that Orville Hubbard had worked so aggressively to maintain. In 1989 a $60,000 bronze statue of Hubbard was erected in front of City Hall. The statue was indicative of the complicated process of historical forgetting that often occurs on the landscape. In celebrating a politician who was an ardent segregationist, those in power implicitly supported his views.[63]

In 1992 and 1993, Reynolds Farley, a sociologist specializing in population studies, conducted an extensive statistical analysis of racial relations in Motor City and its suburbs. Combining his research with statistical analyses conducted by the University of Michigan's Detroit Area Study, Farley identified a long and persistent history of racial division. Dearborn was described as one of the suburban enclaves least welcoming to blacks. In the 1992 Detroit Area Study, white and black residents of the metro area were asked to identify whether current residents would welcome blacks moving into Dearborn. Of those surveyed, 58 percent of white respondents and 86 percent of black respondents said that blacks would not be welcome. In a more complex survey, white and black residents of the metro area were asked to categorize why they found specific suburbs undesirable. Only 29 percent of white residents said they found Dearborn undesirable because of the residential environment, and a similar proportion, 27 percent, said they found it undesirable for racial reasons. Of those who identified racial reasons, 11 percent pointed to the racial prejudice of residents and 19 percent pointed to the racial composition of the suburb's residents. Black respondents more decidedly identified racial reasons in their answers to this question; 83 percent said that they found Dearborn undesirable for racial reasons.[64]

At the Henry Ford Museum and Greenfield Village, however, Skramstad and his staff continued to work toward bridging the gap between suburban and urban residents and institutions. In 1995, Skramstad initiated a partnership that spoke to the museum's growing commitment to local visitors and cultural institutions. The Motown Historical Museum in Detroit and the Henry Ford Museum formed the Motown Museum Partnership to create a duo-site exhibition titled "The Motown Sound: The Music and the Story." As the Motown Historical Museum was renovated over the course of two years, the Henry Ford would host a more elaborate exhibit documenting the accomplishments of Motown Records and its performers. Visitors arriving at the museum encountered an 11,000-square-foot installation divided into three sections: a twenty-minute-long multimedia introduction, a series of interactive displays, and a hall that placed Motown's history in the context of global events. The Motown Historical Museum, which was once the home and studio of famed record producer Berry Gordy, expanded on the narrative at the Henry Ford Museum using the historic house format. Inside, visitors toured a photo gallery, Gordy's second-floor apartment, and, in the basement, the technology that Gordy used to make so many groups famous—a record-cutting machine, boom mikes, a sound booth, and other equipment.[65]

The Motown Museum Partnership not only exemplified the unique projects that could be completed when the Henry Ford Museum worked in tandem with Detroit's cultural institutions, but also foreshadowed the degree to which the museum would be used to depict more recent American histories. The staff was prompted to work on the Motown exhibit, Skramstad explained, because it was a story of "innovation, ingenuity, and resourcefulness." It was a story "that originated in Detroit, but had international significance."[66] At Greenfield Village, most of the structures reflected a time when African Americans were slaves, and for Skramstad and others, this posed a problem. As surveys of African Americans showed, black visitors wanted to see celebratory depictions of more recent political and cultural accomplishments alongside the painful history of enslavement. The new curriculum demanded, however, that the village's interpretation be confined to the Industrial Revolution. The adjacent museum offered a solution. Curators could acquire new objects and create new exhibits drawn from a more broadly defined past. Subsequent administrators would follow Skramstad's lead and use the Henry Ford Museum to exhibit more contemporary African American history.

Under Skramstad's leadership, dramatic shifts were made to the Greenfield Village landscape and interpretive program that reflected many of the tenets of new social history. Staff engaged in historical research with an eye toward exposing histories that were uncomfortable and even painful. Special events that appealed to nostalgia, like the Country Fair, were dropped. The village map was reorganized in a way that challenged the site's long-standing celebration of the small-town landscape and self-made men. The new map illustrated the relationships that allowed early industrial America to flourish and the hardships that previous generations faced. Skramstad also oversaw the addition and interpretation of the Firestone Farm, where staff used living history to interpret the past, and visitors learned about the hard work required to maintain a nineteenth-century farm. Finally, the African American Family Life and Culture program added well-researched and thoughtful interpretations of African American history to the site. Skramstad's team used the buildings associated with black history to broaden the village's representation of the past and to build a stronger relationship with the metropolitan area's African American residents. These innovations urged visitors to encounter the past as much more than a leisure experience. Yet despite these and other changes, surveys conducted shortly after the program opened showed limited success.

The surveys revealed little about African Americans' responses to the interpretation at the Hermitage Slave Quarters and the Mattox House, in large part because they did not identify a respondent's race. Still, given the reputation of Dearborn, in 1993 it was likely that the number of black visitors to Greenfield Village continued to be low. As G. Donald Adams noted, the local black community called for bridge-building efforts from the museum and village.

Village administrators agreed, and they subsequently hired more African American interpreters and forged relationships with important members in the local black community. But both the African American community and the village administration recognized that, at the very least, the reputation of Dearborn discouraged black visitors from coming to the site. Although Orville Hubbard had stepped down as mayor in 1977, many argued that the policies of the new mayor, Michael Guido, were also driven by racism. Guido was criticized not only for his response to the parks ordinance, but for his attitude toward the city's large Arab American population. During his 1985 campaign, he had published a brochure called "Let's Talk about City Parks and the 'Arab Problem,'" in which he claimed that some Arabs had a "gimme, gimme, gimme attitude."[67] Guido's controversial politics, along with the placement of a bronze statue honoring Hubbard in front of City Hall, ensured that the city's history of prejudice continued to shape its public image and to affect Greenfield Village during the early 1990s.

The village's landscape itself also posed a challenge to reshaping the interpretive program. While Detroit and Dearborn were strong points of departure for conversations about racial, economic, and social power structures, Greenfield Village transported visitors away from the local present and past into an imaginary small town. Only a few buildings tied the landscape specifically to the Detroit metropolitan area. The physical structures that told the troubled stories of Detroit and Dearborn—industrial factories, interstate highways, deteriorating downtown buildings, and segregated suburban housing—were absent. Since Skramstad and his staff were driven by a desire to ground their interpretation in historical facts, new scripts only emphasized the geographical diversity of the buildings on display. Neither the interpretation nor the physical space encouraged visitors to make connections between the past and the local present. Perhaps for this reason, few did.

7

From History Museum to History Attraction

Borrowing ideas from theme-park attractions like Disney World and Sea World, the redesigned Greenfield Village has the look and feel of the real deal—a destination that inspires, educates, and entertains while leaving an indelible impression.

— FRANK PROVENZANO in the *Detroit Free Press*, 2003

In 1996, Harold K. Skramstad ended his fifteen years at the helm of Greenfield Village. "I have always felt that CEOs tend to stay too long," he remarked at the time. "It's time to turn over leadership to the next generation." He noted that during his tenure he had improved the museum's financial condition and taken it from a traditional museum to one "that can truly inspire people." Skramstad would go on to become an influential national voice in the museum movement. In 1999 his essay "An Agenda for American Museums in the Twenty-first Century" was published in *Daedalus*, the journal of the American Academy of Arts and Sciences. The article—now a classic text that is widely read among museum professionals and scholars—reflected Skramstad's progressive approach and his belief in the inherent links between the past and present. "The great age of collection building in museums is over," he wrote. "Up to now much of [museums'] time has been devoted to building their collections and sharing them through 'outreach' to the larger world. Now they must help us create the new world of 'inreach,' in which people, young and old alike, can 'reach in' to museums through experiences that will help give value and meaning to their own lives and at the same time stretch and enlarge their perceptions of the world."[1]

After Skramstad's departure, Steven K. Hamp (whom we met briefly in chapter 6) was appointed president; he had begun working at the village in

1978 as an intern. Under his leadership, staff continued to expand many of the programming initiatives that drew heavily on the new history paradigm. But they also sought inspiration from places like Disneyland and expanded the site's opportunities for entertainment. The recent history of Greenfield Village elucidates the site's contemporary approach to interpretation and what its visitors seek from their encounters with the past.

The Hamp Administration

During his twenty-seven-year career at the Henry Ford Museum and Greenfield Village, Steven Hamp saw himself as part of an effort to translate new histories to the public. He later recalled that "there was a lot of self-consciousness about walking the fine line between making our museums more academic and at the same time more accessible to the public."[2] When he first began working at the site in 1978 as a paid intern in the curatorial program, Hamp was studying for a master's degree in museum practice at the University of Michigan; he also held a master's in folklore from Indiana University and a BA in American history from Butler University. After completing the Michigan program he was offered a post in the Education Department and served in a number of different positions over the years, including chairman of collections and director of education. During Skramstad's tenure, Hamp recalled, he became "the kind of number two guy." Hamp also had direct ties to the Ford family: he had married Sheila Firestone Ford in 1981.[3]

Under Hamp's leadership, Greenfield Village moved in directions that would have resonated with Henry Ford. While working under Skramstad, Hamp spearheaded an initiative to return the village and museum to their former use as schools. A year after he began as president, a charter school, the Henry Ford Academy, opened inside the Henry Ford Museum as a public high school with a college-prep curriculum. The first charter school developed through a partnership between a global corporation, a public educational system, and a nonprofit cultural institution, the academy was funded by the Ford Motor Company and the Wayne County Educational Service Agency. Hamp echoed Henry Ford's views on education when he told a reporter that "the academy's goal is to provide students interested in manufacturing arts and technology with an education emphasizing mathematics, science, communication skills and problem solving in a real-world context." Like the village's schools, the academy used the resources of the Menlo Park laboratory and other buildings at the site to provide students with hands-on learning experiences. In this and other innovations, Hamp drew on Ford's wider sense of the activities for which the complex could be used. But he also saw the high school as part of the effort to build relationships with the Detroit metro area community. As he later noted, administrators had participated in several initiatives to "really focus on making connections to larger civic activities going on in Dearborn and Detroit," which was "part of the impetus to create a high school."[4]

In 1998, Hamp announced that the Henry Ford Museum and Greenfield Village would undergo a $40 million improvement campaign. The campaign had begun twenty months earlier as staff and administrators collected pledges from board members (a total of $5 million), members of the Ford family ($10 million), the Ford Motor Company ($5.8 million), the Knight Foundation ($1 million) and the National Endowment for the Humanities ($2 million). The Kresge Foundation in neighboring Troy also offered a $2 million challenge grant. These diverse institutions reflected administrators' dual goals of educating and entertaining their visitors. Hamp planned to channel the money into several projects, including climate control for the Henry Ford Museum, improved lighting throughout Greenfield Village, and a revitalized Village Green and train system. The funds would also be used to enlarge the Benson Ford Research Center, expand the Henry Ford Academy, and develop an Internet-based education program.[5]

Of all the changes to the museum and village, the opening of an IMAX theater in the museum in 1999 best symbolized the use of technology to expand the site's mix of entertainment and education. Hamp told a *Detroit Free Press* reporter covering the IMAX opening, "We're making a concerted institution-wide attack on the basic nature of the experience in the village and the museum. Think of a Disney World with real, authentic, path-breaking exhibitions."[6] The same article noted that during Skramstad's presidency, "longtime patrons believed his attempts to make the museum more accessible were changing 'their' museum." Administrators recognized that Hamp's changes might elicit a similar response, but believed that ultimately they would increase attendance. As Mary Lynn Heninger, the director of program research and development, put it, "The mission of the museum is not just to serve the specialists. You want them, but the additional purpose is to evoke interest and curiosity and maybe even passion in the people who don't know about it yet." The changes were based in part on research indicating that only a quarter of the institution's visitors were under the age of twenty-five, compared to 43 percent of national museum-goers. Hamp and his colleagues were willing to risk losing some longtime customers to expand their audience.

The *Free Press* also observed that the administration's decision to undertake such an expensive enterprise was surprising. Earlier alterations and improvement programs had been financially conservative. Maureen Martin, the site's director of development, compared Hamp's managerial style to that of his brother-in-law William Clay Ford Jr., who at the time was chairman of the board of Ford Motor Company as well as of the Edison Institute. The two men had a twenty-year friendship and frequently traded compliments. Hamp described Ford as an "active impatient guy," who "wants it all now" and inspired the same response in those around him. Ford called Hamp a "visionary."

Hamp and his staff continued to support the African American Family Life and Culture program. At the Susquehanna Plantation, the Hermitage Slave Cabins, and the Mattox House, interpreters who focused on the experiences of African Americans during enslavement and the Jim Crow era were a daily mainstay. The Emancipation Day celebration in August continued as an annual special event. Participants now included members of the 102nd U.S. Colored Troops reenactment group, who stationed themselves near the Scotch Settlement School and chatted with visitors about the black soldiers who fought in the Civil War. In February 2000, as part of Black History Month, the site invited Howard Paige, author of *Aspects of African American Foodways*, to prepare African American dishes throughout the month and to talk about how African Americans shaped American cuisine. That summer, the village collaborated with the Arts League of Michigan to create a program called "The Idlewild Clubhouse Show." From June 18 to August 19, visitors could learn about Idlewild, a northern Michigan resort community, founded in 1912, that became "a meeting place where national and community leaders gathered to discuss issues relevant to African Americans" and "an important local and regional link to the Harlem Renaissance." Along with re-creating the resort's clubhouse, the village hosted poetry readings, music shows, and social discussions related to the Harlem Renaissance. In their application for external funding, staff noted that a "special challenge of this project is to demonstrate the Museum's commitment to African-American audiences, and its desire to share its educational and recreation resources to the multi-cultural community."[7]

While Greenfield Village built on an already well-established African American history program, the indoor museum's collection was lacking. To extend the depiction of black history to the museum, the museum purchased the Montgomery, Alabama, bus that Rosa Parks was riding on December 1, 1955, when she refused to give up her seat in the "colored" section to a white passenger and was arrested, ultimately leading to the 1956 Supreme Court ruling that segregated transportation was unconstitutional. That part of the story, of course, is well known; what is less known, however, is what happened to the bus. It continued to operate until 1971, when it was bought by a Montgomery scrap dealer; in 2001 his heirs put the bus up for sale through an Internet-based auction house, MastroNet. The company verified the bus's historical authenticity by locating a scrapbook belonging to the former manager of the

Montgomery bus line. Adjacent to articles about the arrest of Parks, he had written the bus's number and the name "Blake"; James Blake was the driver who called the police that day. At the auction, the museum paid $492,000 for the bus and $24,000 for the scrapbook. Over the next two years, curators prepared an exhibit centering on the bus. Text panels chronicled Parks's early life, her participation in Alabama's civil rights movement, and her move to Detroit in 1957, where she worked as a receptionist and secretary for U.S. House member John Conyers until she retired in 1988.[8]

The restored bus was unveiled to great fanfare in 2003, but not all were convinced of its authenticity. While the museum's curators believed that the scrapbook proved that the bus was the one Rosa Parks rode, Ken Tilley, the photo archivist for the Alabama Department of Archives and History, remained unconvinced. "We've looked at the photographs," he said, "and you can't tell what bus it was." Interestingly, some visitors seem to have adopted Henry Ford's approach to the past, which was mostly agnostic about whether authentic objects were preferred over replicas. Willie Edwards, a fifty-four-year-old millwright from Detroit, said, "I don't care whether it's the right one. It's from that era. There's a lot of power in that bus."[9]

The bus continued to receive media attention throughout the early 2000s. When Parks died in Detroit in 2005, Michigan senator Carl Levin mentioned both the bus and Orville Hubbard in his remarks at her memorial service. Reminding those who had gathered to honor Parks of Hubbard's 1963 battle with Michigan's civil rights commission, he said, "We may never know for sure why after years of legal skirmishes, Mayor Hubbard dropped his court challenge and decided to comply with the civil rights commission's order. But I believe it was the forces of freedom that Rosa Parks helped unleash. . . . And it is a sweet victory . . . that the actual bus on which Rosa Parks made her stand is now in Dearborn." In a letter to the editor of the *Detroit Free Press,* Susan L. Hubbard, the mayor's granddaughter, wrote that Levin had "launched an attack on Dearborn, the Hubbard family, and the Henry Ford museum by suggesting that the city was a 'segregated' community." Levin's remarks and Hubbard's letter are clear evidence that Orville Hubbard's legacy continued to shape the metro area's present, and that for some, a bus whose history was tied most directly to the civil rights battles in the American south was a reminder of a local past that was not on display at the Henry Ford Museum.[10]

Restorations at Greenfield Village commenced in September 2002, shortly after staff began work on the Rosa Parks bus. The site closed for eight months while $15 million was spent on new roads, sewers, and sidewalks, as well as new communications and electrical systems. Christian Overland, the village's director, said that the changes would serve as the "foundation for the future": "It'll be easier for visitors to get around, and with these improvements we can hold more events and programs." At the same time, in response to a decline in attendance in 2001, nineteen staff positions were cut, a 6 percent reduction. Hamp noted that although the site had had a rough year, most cultural organizations around the country were suffering after the September 11 terrorist attacks; Americans were financially strapped and reluctant to travel.[11]

During the restoration, many alterations focused on the village landscape, and particularly on making it, in Hamp's words, "more amenable to visitors." Confusing or outdated signage was removed, and imprecise directions were replaced with clear markers. A new twenty-foot-tall wrought-iron entrance gate and brick columns topped with sculpted pineapples welcomed visitors, along with a new ticket booth and expanded parking. Once inside the gates, visitors encountered Josephine Ford Plaza, which featured an expanded souvenir store, sculptures, and a fountain. And near the Village Green they found a new restaurant called A Taste of History.[12]

Another aspect of the improvement program involved replacing the original dirt paths and asphalt walkways, which had been left in place since 1929 to create a historic ambience, with paved roads and sidewalks. Heating was added to several buildings as well, so that visitors were no longer forced to experience the same chilly interiors that earlier Americans had endured. Yet Overland argued that staff were committed to depicting a past that was "authentic, and as historically accurate as possible," and insisted, "We're not a simulated or fabricated experience. This is what it felt like to be living at a previous time in history."[13]

As Steven Hamp later summarized the renovation, "Lots of things were reoriented and the place was fundamentally reorganized." The process met with a few hiccups along the way, including "one of the coldest winters on record in Michigan." Work continued up until the last minute; when the site reopened in the spring of 2003, Hamp recalled, "our guys were throwing shovels over the fence as people entered. Like all museum openings, we went down to the wire." "I don't think any other outdoor museum has undertaken that kind of near-total restoration," he reflected, and for him the site is now "much more user-friendly and makes much more sense organizationally."[14]

Part of the reorganization involved the creation of a new map that called attention to what visitors would see throughout the village. Buildings and other exhibits were divided into themed sections and given a descriptive title. In the section called "Henry Ford's Model T," for example, visitors could take an eight-minute ride in an authentic Model T. The "Liberty Craftworks" section showcased a revamped gristmill, and "Edison at Work" encompassed all of the buildings paying homage to Edison. In the "Main Street" area, visitors could sit on benches in front of the Wright Brothers' Home and watch a short play based on the brothers' return to their Ohio bicycle shop after the successful flight at Kitty Hawk. "Working Farms" included the Henry Ford birthplace and the Firestone Farm, and "Porches and Parlors" featured other homes, including the Mattox House and the Hermitage Quarters. Finally, at "Railroad Junction" visitors were invited to take a trip around the village on a train.[15]

The new restaurant, A Taste of History, embodied the administration's desire to define the village as a history attraction. The nearby Eagle Tavern, built in 1831, focused on historic foodways, but at A Taste of History the line between past and present was more blurred. The cafeteria-style restaurant offered a mix of historic and contemporary fare. For example, the Hobo's Lunch—a peanut butter and jelly sandwich, goldfish crackers, an apple, and a cookie—was tied in a red bandana that hung on a stick. The packaging (if not the contents) invited children to play hobo as they ate their lunch. The lives of real hobos—homeless Americans who rode the rails in search of work during the Great Depression—were full of danger and misery, but the Hobo's Lunch encouraged children to associate hoboing with leisure and fun by ignoring a more difficult past.

In 2003, Greenfield Village and the Henry Ford Museum were renamed The Henry Ford, with the tagline "America's Greatest History Attraction." Patricia Mooradian, the site's chief operating officer, told a reporter, "There's been confusion about who we are. Locally, we get called the village, and nationally, people think we're an automobile museum." She noted that a survey taken before the change showed that visitors did not know about the many components of the site. According to Steven Hamp, the Smithsonian Institution, which included fifteen museums, and Disney World, which comprised the Epcot, Magic Kingdom, MGM Studios, and Animal Kingdom parks, pioneered the streamlined name approach. The new name also reflected a shifting interpretation of the site as poised between an educational museum and a theme park, and of its visitors as customers who wanted to be offered the best value. Wayne Hunt of the Pasadena-based Hunt Design Associates, who developed the new marketing strategy, argued that "as a place grows and offers more, it needs to explain itself in a simpler way," and that "The Henry Ford will get people to ask: 'What's that include?' "[16]

Hamp recognized that some found the new name and tagline controversial. "We needed a name to adequately describe the entire multi-venue experience and we came up with The Henry Ford," he said. He also recognized that the tagline "was sort of 'in your face' to some museum professionals." When an electronic billboard advertising The Henry Ford was placed on the freeway, the president of a major foundation called him and asked, "What the hell are you guys doing over there?" Hamp recalled that "some people thought that what we were doing was not the kind of thing that museums did at the time, but we thought it was," and added, "We were, actually, ahead of the curve." For him, "the title works because it captures the diversity of the place."[17]

Beginning in May 2004, The Henry Ford offered something new: the Ford Rouge Factory Tour. Public tours of the factory had ended in 1980, and now visitors clamored for a chance to see the famous—and still working, although on a much smaller scale—assembly lines. In May, two-thirds of the tickets had been sold through June, and a spokeswoman for the Detroit Metro Convention and Visitors Bureau reported that factory tours were the most frequent request from visitors from outside the metro area. The museum and the village were now directly linked to a living part of the metro area's history.[18]

The two-hour tour began with a fifteen-minute bus trip from the museum to the Rouge complex. The buses, covered with scenes from Diego Rivera's *Detroit Industry* series—painted between 1932 and 1933 for the Detroit Institute of Arts—suggested that visitors should imagine themselves in the past, when automotive workers and the manufacturing process were celebrated as art. The murals obscured the bus's windows, ensuring that visitors remained in the past once inside. Instead of viewing the present industrial landscape on their trip to the Rouge, visitors' attention was forced toward a small television screen, which offered a brief history of the Ford Motor Company and the famous Rouge factory.

Once at the Rouge, visitors viewed a gallery displaying Ford's classic cars. They then watched a short documentary film about the plant that briefly mentioned the "Battle of the Overpass," in 1937, when Ford's security force attacked peaceful demonstrators on the pedestrian bridge over Miller Road. The second film was described as "multisensory" and was titled *The Art of Manufacturing*. Projected on a seven-panel screen in a virtual reality theater, it showed how the Rouge became a central manufacturing site during World War II. After viewing the films, visitors were given a panoramic view of the Rouge from the observation deck above the Dearborn Truck Plant, followed by a walk along the mezzanine above the plant floor. Mark Pischea, the executive director of the Motor Cities–Automobile National Heritage Area, told a reporter, "We need to make sure we understand that this is our legacy. . . . This is the history of our grandparents that our children and their children will be studying." But the tour did not leave the automobile and mass production in the past. As visitors walked along the mezzanine, guides explained that the Rouge was being restored as an environmentally friendly building, combining the best of both auto industry technology and green production methods.[19]

The Rouge tour offered a unique opportunity for administrators to link the history on display to the past and present of the metro area. From the very beginning, however, when visitors were prevented from viewing the actual roads that took them there, they were encouraged to forget the troubled present of Detroit. Inside, the films and objects on display did little to ground the site in the metropolitan area, and the emphasis on green technology suggested a progress narrative that ignored the realities of the floundering automotive industry.

In 2005, Steven Hamp resigned his post and joined the Ford Motor Company as vice president and chief of staff to CEO William Clay Ford Jr. Patricia Mooradian, who had long served as chief operating officer, was appointed the first woman president of The Henry Ford. Hamp had recruited Mooradian in 1999 as the vice president of program and marketing. When she took the reins in 2005, efforts to reinvent the site had met with only limited success in terms of increasing visitors. Daily attendance was still down 15 percent from, the previous year. Layoffs reduced a staff of three hundred by 4 percent, and several vacant positions were left permanently unfilled. But Mooradian remained hopeful and was particularly enthusiastic about the site's special events such as "Holiday Nights" and the Halloween celebration. The new president said she would continue to add exhibitions and features with a mass appeal.[20] To attract more visitors, the Henry Ford participated in the state's "Pure Michigan" ad campaign. Launched in 2005, the campaign aimed to lure out-of-state tourists by highlighting places like Mackinaw Island and Greenfield Village. The choice of locations, along with the rhetoric of the ads, clearly worked to sever associations between Michigan and the popular images of urban blight that defined Detroit.[21]

The Henry Ford again received national attention when Mitt Romney announced his presidential campaign at the site in 2007. According to one pollster, Romney, who was far behind in the polls at the time, picked Michigan not only because his father had been governor of the state, but also because he needed to "reflect traditional Midwestern values." Romney used the opportunity to cast himself as a values candidate, and in his speech he asserted that the American family needed to be strengthened "with a mother and father in the life of every child." He also reminded voters of his family's association with the auto industry; his father, George Romney, headed American Motors before serving as Michigan's governor from 1963 to 1969.[22]

Mooradian continued to support efforts to add African American histories to the site. In 2011, The Henry Ford received the Emancipation Proclamation on loan from the National Archives to accompany their "Discovering the Civil War" exhibit. To encourage attendance, administrators waived the admission fee and opened the museum for thirty-six hours. On the first day, 4,100 people stood in line hoping for a glimpse of the document.[23]

In 2012, The Henry Ford hosted yet another presidential candidate, incumbent Barack Obama, who was in town for a fundraiser hosted by a wealthy local supporter. When President Obama arrived at The Henry Ford, he toured the museum and took a moment to view the Rosa Parks bus. "I just sat in there for a moment," he said, "and pondered the courage and tenacity that is part of our very recent history." That night, Obama spoke to six hundred guests who had paid up to $5,000 to attend the event, which included Motown music and a sculpture of the president on loan from the Charles H. Wright Museum of African American History in Detroit.[24]

As the use of the site by both Romney and Obama indicates, the objects and buildings on display in the museum and village were divergent enough that they could be harnessed to serve a variety of personal and political agendas. Alterations to the village during the Hamp and Mooradian administrations reinforced this varied use of the site by visitors and other institutions.

A New Dearborn

In 1997, Michael Guido, who was in his third term as Dearborn's mayor, continued to be a controversial figure in both the African American and Arab American communities. In December, NAACP leaders staged a much-publicized protest at a city-owned golf course after allegations by black employees that they had been mistreated. Black motorists also charged that Dearborn police stopped them unfairly, and black shoppers claimed that they remained unwelcome at the city's largest mall, Fairlane Town Center. Guido firmly denied charges that he and his administration were racist. "If I dislike someone," he told a reporter, "it's not because I'm a racist, it's because there's something about their character that I don't like." Guido also said that he felt he had done his part after the NAACP filed charges. His staff questioned golf-course employees and found no evidence of wrongdoing. An analysis of traffic tickets indicated that one quarter were issued to African Americans, a percentage he said was consistent with the number who drove through the city. The Reverend Wendell Anthony, president of the Detroit chapter of the NAACP, however, faulted Guido for not taking the charges seriously enough.[25]

Guido also continued to attack the city's Arab American population (by now 30 percent of Dearborn's 97,000 residents). In 1999, during a city council meeting, a resident of the largely Arab American south end and a member of the Concerned Residents of South Dearborn asked the mayor to explain what they perceived as his neglect of their community. Guido responded: "If your organization wanted to do something, you should work on trying to train the immigrants to this country on personal hygiene and habits of cleanliness." He defended the comment by arguing that it did not differ from what service agencies and government officials teach all immigrants. But Guido's attitude would change sharply in 2001, when he found himself running for a fifth term against an Arab American opponent, Abed Hammoud, an assistant Wayne

County prosecutor. By assiduously courting Arab American voters, Guido managed to win reelection with 79 percent of the vote, but he now clearly understood that the city's Arab American community was a powerful voting block.[26]

In 1999, Dearborn's Arab Community Center for Economic and Social Services (ACCESS), which was founded when the Arab American community fought against urban renewal in 1971, began discussing plans to build a museum devoted to representing Arab American history. In 2000 the group bought a boarded-up furniture store across from Dearborn's City Hall, and soon plans to tear down the store and build a museum were under way.[27]

ACCESS had used The Henry Ford to host several cultural events during the late 1990s, and Anan Ameri, an ACCESS member who would become the new museum's president, drew on the group's relationship with The Henry Ford as plans for the Arab American museum developed. Ameri recalled that after ACCESS bought the building, they told Steven Hamp that while they had a "vision" of what they wanted to build, they did not "really come from a museum background." Hamp "was very open and actually assembled a group of his staff in different fields such as education, design, and marketing and made that group available to us." Ameri and her staff met with the Ford team throughout the planning process, and as they gathered proposals for permanent exhibits they would get feedback from Ford staff that helped them decide "which ones were the best."[28]

Fundraising for the National Arab American Museum (AANM) began in February 2002, with the aim of raising $8 million for a 38,500-square-foot museum as well as a Youth and Family Center and Community Health Care and Research Center. Among the many donors was the Ford Motor Company, which contributed $2 million. When the museum opened in 2005, its permanent exhibit included sections on the arrival of Arabs in America, their achievements in the face of negative stereotyping, and famous Arab Americans in politics, the arts, and sports. In a review published in the *Journal of American History,* Raymond Silverman, a professor of art history at the University of Michigan, pondered the consequences of focusing on the national rather than the local history of Arab Americans at the museum. "One of the museum's messages is that Arab Americans are not all the same," he wrote. "In positioning the AANM as a *national* institution, ACCESS has, to a certain extent, diminished the museum's capacity to serve the local community." In some ways, the same could be said about The Henry Ford.[29]

The AANM's relationship with The Henry Ford continued after the museum's opening. Steven Hamp served on the AANM's board until 2008, when Patricia Mooradian was appointed to the executive committee of the museum's National Advisory Board. Ameri said that she often consulted with

Mooradian. "She comes from a marketing background," Ameri noted, "and she has been amazingly helpful." In general, she said, The Henry Ford's staff "have been good neighbors."[30]

The AANM and the political gains of Dearborn's Arab American community indicated that the city was no longer controlled by a predominantly white power structure. The new image of Dearborn as defined by diversity rather than racism may have encouraged local suburban residents of different races and ethnicities to visit Greenfield Village. In fact, by 2010 the suburbs all around Detroit were changing. William Frey of the Brookings Institution attributed the decline in Detroit's population, which had fallen 25 percent since 2000, not only to the collapse of the industry-based economy but also to the departure of many black residents to the suburbs. Coupled with a steady increase in programs, exhibits aimed at African American audiences, and the changing culture and politics of Dearborn, claims from former administrators such as Skramstad and Hamp that the Greenfield Village audience was more diverse by 2013 are likely true.[31]

The history of Greenfield Village exposes the complex process by which the past was assembled at one outdoor history museum. But the story also offers a starting point for broader conversations about the internal and external forces that shape representations of the past at museums. Identifying the contexts in which museums operate—from staff to visitors to national and local politics—gives us a clearer understanding of their histories.

Henry Ford used Greenfield Village to depict a selective version of the past, one that celebrated customs and values he feared were disappearing from the present. Ford likely hoped that visitors would embrace his veneration of farmers and inventors instead of politicians and military heroes, and he was not alone. Indeed, he was not the first or the last to preserve the material culture that defined the lives of ordinary people. Throughout the early twentieth century, preservationists, curators, and academics argued for versions of history that complemented Ford's. The general public was similarly enthralled by buildings and objects associated with Edison, the Wright Brothers, and small-town life. As we've seen, however, when the village opened to the public in 1933 a number of factors facilitated diverse visitor encounters.

After Ford's death, administrators responded to both new standards being set in the field of public history and, increasingly, to their visitors. To meet the demands of both, they shored up their interpretive programs, while at the same time expanding visitors' options for diversion. Encounters with the past at Greenfield Village continued to be personal, and visitors continued to view themselves as authorities, touting not their historical expertise but their agency as customers. When marketing teams identified a "typical visitor," administrators constricted collective encounters by focusing on attracting a specific kind of customer, one who sought a leisure experience, was untroubled by Dearborn's local politics, and used the past in ways very similar to Henry Ford.

When Harold Skramstad arrived in 1981, he ushered in a new age. New educational goals and financial solvency became priorities, in some cases despite complaints from longtime patrons. Visitors were presented with a more diverse and inclusive representation of American history, particularly through the addition of the African American Family Life and Culture program. Skramstad and his staff also embraced the village's location in the Detroit metro area by engaging in a number of efforts to build a productive relationship with the city's black community and appeal to locally based audiences.

During the 1990s, administrators continued to work to attract a more diverse visitor population and created venues more explicitly aimed at entertaining audiences. Both Hamp and Mooradian maintained the African American Family Life and Culture program at the village and expanded exhibits on African American history in the museum. Additions such as the IMAX theater in the museum and the Taste of History Restaurant in the village suggested that administrators believed one way to attract new visitors was to expand the site's attractions. Today, Greenfield Village continues to mix history and entertainment. Administrators and visitors have clearly embraced the new tagline: "America's Greatest History Attraction." The educational experience and the leisure experience occur simultaneously. On a single afternoon in 2011, for example, one group of visitors were using the village as a wedding venue while others toured the nearby Hermitage Slave Quarters (fig. 19).

Of all the pasts represented at Greenfield Village, only a few nod to the Detroit metro area, which is somewhat surprising given the widespread interest in the history of the city and its suburbs. Countless media stories have chronicled Detroit's rise and fall, explaining why and how the Arsenal of Democracy has become, according to *Forbes* magazine, the most miserable city in America.[32] The statue of Orville Hubbard in front of Dearborn's city hall and Senator Levin's mention of him at Rosa Parks's memorial service in 2005 indicate that many locals have not forgotten the historical tensions between Dearborn and Detroit.

A number of factors make representing a local past at Greenfield Village challenging; as a total landscape, the village is an imagined place, making historical interpretations based on place difficult to develop. The site's physical resources most obviously discourage interpretations of Detroit and its suburbs, as the vast majority of buildings are not tied directly to the city. Further, many residents have called the media's portrayal of Detroit's troubled present unfair and unproductive; they might be reluctant to buy a ticket to see a

FIGURE 19. A wedding photo-shoot in the foreground while visitors tour the interior of the Hermitage slave quarters in the background. Photo by author, 2011.

historical representation that grapples with the city's decline.[33] The Friendship Concert held in 1986 showed, however, that when audiences called on a willing administration, Greenfield Village could be used as a space to reckon with the metro area's history of race relations.

Sustained efforts by Skramstad, Hamp, Mooradian, and their respective staffs to build relationships with Detroit's residents do suggest that audiences are far more diverse today than they were in the 1970s. A more diversified local visitor population, however, has not been followed by the installation of more buildings and exhibits representing the history of the greater Detroit area. In light of the role that visitors' views have played in administrative decisions, it seems likely that audiences have not requested them. Greenfield Village will continue to blend entertainment and history as long as visitors express a desire to consume such a past. As customers, visitors can shape the degree to which the histories they buy reaffirm a consensus past or challenge it, whether it is national or local in scope. At Greenfield Village, visitors have always played and will continue to play a critical role in helping conversations about history move beyond bunk.

Notes

Abbreviations

BFRC   Benson Ford Research Center, The Henry Ford, Dearborn, Mich.
EIR   Edison Institute Records, BFRC

Introduction

1. Geoffrey C. Upward, *A Home for Our Heritage: The Building and Growth of Greenfield Village and Henry Ford Museum, 1929–1979* (Dearborn, Mich.: The Henry Ford Museum Press, 1979), 59.

2. Ibid., 48, 59–60, 118.

3. See Steven Watts, *The People's Tycoon: Henry Ford and the American Century* (New York: Knopf, 2005), 5 (birth of Henry Ford), 65 (founding of Ford Motor Company), 128 (mass production of Model T), 178 (Five Dollar Day); and Upward, *A Home for Our Heritage,* 59–60.

4. Upward, *A Home for Our Heritage,* 59–60, 101–3; Wyn Wacchorst, *Thomas Alva Edison: An American Myth* (Cambridge: MIT Press, 1981), 167.

5. Upward, *A Home for Our Heritage,* 59–60, 76, 118.

6. For a discussion of Ford's Five Dollar Day, see Watts, *People's Tycoon,* 178–98. Thomas Sugrue, in *The Origins of the Urban Crisis: Race and Inequality in Postwar Detroit* (Princeton: Princeton University Press, 1996), argues that "the period from the 1940s to the 1960s set the stage for the fiscal, social, and economic crises that confront urban America today" (5). He identifies Dearborn under mayor Orville Hubbard's political machine as one of the white suburban communities that opposed public housing to maintain segregation (76–77). Sugrue's work shapes my discussion of how administrators and marketers worked to separate Greenfield Village from Detroit.

7. The present-day city of Dearborn, where Greenfield Village is located, was incorporated in 1929 when Dearborn annexed the city of Fordson, which in 1923 had been incorporated as Springwells and included both the former Greenfield Township, where Clara Ford was born, and Springwells Township, where Henry Ford was born. Dearborn Historical Museum, *It Wasn't Always Called Dearborn* (Dearborn, Mich.: City of Dearborn, 2012).

8. U.S. Census data from 1930 lists the population of Dearborn as 50,358. For an early history of the Rouge Factory see Watts, *People's Tycoon,* 280–95.

9. "Henry Ford Museum and Greenfield Village Corporate Name and Logo Chronology," vertical file, BFRC; Frank Provenzano, "New Name to Retool Image of Ford Museum and Village," *Detroit Free Press,* January 28, 2003; Upward, *A Home for Our Heritage,* 75–76.

10. See Upward, *A Home for Our Heritage,* 34–36 (Menlo Park), 114 (the Wright brothers' home and cycle shop), 28 (the general store), 43 (Logan County Courthouse), 45 (chapel construction), 85 (the cooper's shop), 107 (the Noah Webster home), and 105 (McGuffey birthplace).

11. Upward, *A Home for Our Heritage,* 111 (history of the Grimm Jewelry Store), 86 (history of the Bagley Avenue Shop).

12. James Prichards, "Census Data Shows Detroit Now Nation's Poorest City," Associated Press, August 31, 2005.

13. Charles B. Hosmer, *Preservation Comes of Age: From Williamsburg to the National Trust, 1926–1949* (Charlottesville: University Press of Virginia for the Preservation Press, 1981), 74–132.

14. Mike Wallace, "Visiting the Past: History Museums in the United States," in *Mickey Mouse History and Other Essays on American Memory* (Philadelphia: Temple University Press, 1996), 9–16, quot. on 13.

15. Diane Barthel, *Historic Preservation: Collective Memory and Historical Identity* (New Brunswick, N.J.: Rutgers University Press, 1996), 38–39. Steven Conn argues that Ford's Edison Institute marked the last of museums organized and built with the framework of an object-based epistemology in mind in his chapter "Objects and American History: The Museums of Henry Mercer and Henry Ford," in *Museums and American Intellectual Life, 1876–1926* (Chicago: University of Chicago Press, 1998), 151–91. I agree with Conn, but claim that Greenfield Village draws on other popular historical display techniques well established by the 1920s. For another brief treatment of Greenfield Village that places it in the larger context of living-history museums, see Warren Leon and Margaret Piatt, "Living-History Museums," in *History Museums in the United States: A Critical Assessment,* ed. Warren Leon and Roy Rosenzweig (Urbana: University of Illinois, 1989), 64–97.

16. David L. Lewis, *The Public Image of Henry Ford: An American Folk Hero and His Company* (Detroit: Wayne State University Press, 1976), 224–28; Howard P. Segal, *Recasting the Machine Age: Henry Ford's Village Industries* (Amherst: University of Massachusetts Press, 2005), 6, 28; Vincent Curcio, *Henry Ford* (Oxford: Oxford University Press, 2013), 165; Watts, *People's Tycoon,* 425–26. For discussions of Ford's views on history see Roger Burlingame, *Henry Ford* (New York: Knopf, 1954), 85, 95–96.

17. For reflections on how the politics of the present shape representations of the past at public history sites, see Pierre Nora, "Between Memory and History: Les Lieux de Mémoire," trans. Marc Roudebush, *Representations* no. 26 (Spring 1989): 7–24; David Lowenthal, *The Past Is a Foreign Country* (Cambridge: Cambridge University Press, 1985); Lowenthal, *Possessed by the Past: The Heritage Crusade and the Spoils of History* (New York: Free Press, 1996), xi; Eric Hobsbawm and Terence Ranger, eds., *The Invention of Tradition* (Cambridge: Cambridge University Press, 1992); Michael Kammen, *Mystic Chords of Memory: The Transformation of Tradition in American Culture* (New York: Vintage, 1991); Jay Anderson, *Time Machines: The World of Living History* (Nashville: American Association for State and Local History, 1984); David Glassberg, *Sense of History: The Place of the Past in American Life* (Amherst: University of Massachusetts Press, 2001); Edward T. Linenthal, *Preserving Memory: The Struggle to Create America's Holocaust Museum* (New York: Columbia University Press, 1995); and Edward T. Linenthal and Tom Engelhardt, eds., *History Wars: The Enola Gay and Other Battles for the American Past* (New York: Owl Books, 1996).

18. Lisa McGirr, *Suburban Warriors: The Origins of the New American Right* (Princeton: Princeton University Press, 2001); Matthew D. Lassiter, *The Silent Majority: Suburban*

Politics in the Sunbelt South (Princeton: Princeton University Press, 2006); Kevin M. Kruse, *White Flight and the Making of Modern Conservatism* (Princeton: Princeton University Press, 2005); Kevin M. Kruse and Thomas J. Sugrue, eds., *The New Suburban Histories* (Chicago: University of Chicago Press, 2006).

19. Kevin Boyle, *Arc of Justice: A Saga of Race, Civil Rights, and Murder in the Jazz Age* (New York: Holt, 2004). Boyle examines the case of Ossian Sweet to demonstrate how battles over housing defined the color line in Detroit as early as the 1920s. For a discussion of the 1943 and 1967 riots see Sugrue, *Origins of the Urban Crisis*, 17–31, 259.

20. For Orville Hubbard's terms as mayor see David L. Good, *Orvie: The Dictator of Dearborn: The Rise and Reign of Orville L. Hubbard* (Detroit: Wayne State University Press, 1989), 395–98. Studies of Dearborn's Arab population include Laurel D. Wigle and Sameer Y. Abraham, "Arab Nationalism in America: The Dearborn Arab Community," in *Immigrants and Migrants: The Detroit Ethnic Experience*, ed. David W. Hartman (Detroit: Wayne State University Press, 1974), 279–302; and Nabeel Abraham and Andrew Shryock, eds., *Arab Detroit: From Margin to Mainstream* (Detroit: Wayne State University Press, 2000).

21. Carl Becker, "Everyman His Own Historian" (address delivered in December 1931), *American Historical Review* 37, no. 2 (January 1932): 231–36, quot. on 234; Eric Foner, ed., *The New American History* (Philadelphia: Temple University Press, 1997), ix; Ellen Fitzpatrick, *History's Memory: Writing America's Past, 1880–1980* (Cambridge: Harvard University Press, 2002), 8.

22. Roy Rosenzweig and David Thelen, eds., *The Presence of the Past: Popular Uses of History in American Life* (New York: Columbia University Press, 1998); Glassberg, *Sense of History*, 209–10. Historians have not limited their queries to how contemporary Americans harness the past, however; see David Blight, *Race and Reunion: The Civil War in American Memory* (Cambridge: Harvard University Press, 2001), for a study of how reconciliationist, white supremacist, and emancipationist visions of the Civil War "collided and combined" in the fifty-year period following the end of the war. By scrutinizing popular literature, Memorial Day ceremonies, veterans' reunions and memoirs, monument construction, the development of "Lost Cause" culture, and political rhetoric, Blight documents the complex process through which the reconciliationist vision triumphed. Emily Rosenberg's *A Date Which Will Live: Pearl Harbor in American Memory* (Durham, N.C.: Duke University Press, 2003) investigates film, political policies, and commemorations to expose how contested cultural meanings attached to Pearl Harbor shaped the memory of this event over the course of five decades. Dydią DeLyser's *Ramona Memories: Tourism and the Shaping of Southern California* (Minneapolis: University of Minnesota Press, 2005) shows how the heroine of Helen Hunt Jackson's 1884 novel *Ramona* became the "most important woman in the history and geography of southern California" (188). Examining both how city boosters used *Ramona* to promote tourism and why so many tourists demanded the creation of attractions connected to the novel, DeLyser documents how *Ramona* tourism facilitated the invention of Southern California. These works serve as models for studying Greenfield Village's audiences.

23. Richard Handler and Eric Gable, *The New History in an Old Museum: Creating the Past at Colonial Williamsburg* (Durham, N.C.: Duke University Press, 1997); Cathy Stanton, *The Lowell Experiment: Public History in a Postindustrial Setting* (Amherst: University of Massachusetts Press, 2006).

24. George H. Hein, *Learning in the Museum* (London: Routledge, 1998), 42–45; Harris H. Shettel et al., *Strategies for Determining Exhibit Effectiveness*, report no. AIR E95 4/66-FR (Washington, D.C.: American Institutes for Research, 1968); Paulette M. McManus,

"Changes in Evaluative Attitudes to Visitors," *Journal of Museum Education* 21, no. 3 (Fall 1996): 3–5; Kenneth A. Yellis, "Museum Education," in *The Museum: A Reference Guide*, ed. Michael Steven Shapiro and Louis Ward Kemp (Westport, Conn.: Greenwood Press, 1990), 167–98.

25. Upward, *A Home for Our Heritage*, 95.

1. The Fording of American History

1. Steven Watts, *The People's Tycoon: Henry Ford and the American Century* (New York: Knopf, 2005), 280–85; David L. Lewis, *The Public Image of Henry Ford: An American Folk Hero and His Company* (Detroit: Wayne State University Press, 1976), 161; "Ford Rouge Factory Tour: History of the Rouge," The Henry Ford, 2005, www.thehenryford.org/rouge.

2. Watts, *People's Tycoon*, 406; Geoffrey C. Upward, *A Home for Our Heritage: The Building and Growth of Greenfield Village and Henry Ford Museum, 1929–1979* (Dearborn, Mich.: The Henry Ford Museum Press), 26, 177.

3. Lewis, *Public Image of Henry Ford*, 20, 41.

4. Watts, *People's Tycoon*, 178–82, 200–201; Vincent Curcio, *Henry Ford* (Oxford: Oxford University Press, 2013), 71–81.

5. Henry Ford, *My Life and Work* (Garden City, N.Y.: Garden City Publishing, 1922).

6. Watts, *People's Tycoon*, 3–19; Upward, *A Home for Our Heritage*, 5, 116.

7. Watts, *People's Tycoon*, 6–7; "Greenfield Village Interactive Map," The Henry Ford, 2013, www.thehenryford.org/village.

8. Etta B. Degering, *McGuffey: The Greatest Forgotten Man* (Hagerstown, Md.: Autumn Publishing, 2011), 17–18, 64, 113–15.

9. Angela Sorby, *Schoolroom Poets: Childhood, Performance, and the Place of American Poetry, 1865–1917* (Lebanon, N.H.: University of New Hampshire Press, 2005), xxix–xxxiii; Watts, *People's Tycoon*, 10. William Holmes McGuffey compiled the first four readers, but his younger brother wrote the last two. John H. Westerhoff, *McGuffey and His Readers: Piety, Morality, and Education in Nineteenth Century America* (Nashville: Abington, 1978), 70.

10. Watts, *People's Tycoon*, 8–11.

11. Dearborn Historical Museum, *It Wasn't Always Called Dearborn* (Dearborn, Mich.: City of Dearborn, 2012); Watts, *People's Tycoon*, 23–28; "Population of the 100 Largest Urban Places: 1880," Table 11, U.S. Bureau of the Census, www.census.gov.

12. Watts, *People's Tycoon*, 34–48; Curcio, *Henry Ford*, 20–21.

13. Allan Nevins, *Ford: The Times, the Man, the Company* (New York: Scribner, 1954), 135; Watts, *People's Tycoon*, 36.

14. Watts, *People's Tycoon*, 34–40. For a discussion of the colonial kitchen and the 1893 World's Fair see Rodris Roth, "The New England, or 'Olde Tyme,' Kitchen Exhibit at Nineteenth-Century Fairs," in *The Colonial Revival in America*, ed. Alan Axelrod (New York: Norton, 1985), 159–83. By the 1890s elite women in Deerfield had preserved several homes and opened their "common parlors" for tours. Residents such as Ellen Miller and Margaret Whiting founded the Society of Blue and White Needlework and used their parlors and bedrooms to display and sell colonial-inspired crafts; see Marla R. Miller and Anne Digan Lanning, "'Common Parlors': Women and the Recreation of Community Identity in Deerfield, Massachusetts, 1870–1920," *Gender & History* 6, no. 3 (November 1994): 435–55; Edward N. Kaufman, "The Architectural Museum: From World's Fair to Restoration Village," in *Museum Studies: An Anthology of Contexts*, ed. Bettina Messias Carbonell

(Oxford: Blackwell, 2004), 221; Melinda Young, "The Beginnings of the Period Room," in Axelrod, *The Colonial Revival in America*, 231. Seth Bruggeman's *Here, George Washington Was Born: Memory, Material Culture, and the Public History of a National Monument* (Athens: University of Georgia Press, 2008) offers an excellent summary of the period room's growing popularity (56). For example, in 1896 Charles Wilcomb opened a colonial period room in San Francisco, and in 1907 George Francis Dow created a series of period rooms and hired women dressed in costume to serve as docents at the Peabody Essex Institute in Salem, Massachusetts. In many ways, Ford was simply following a tradition of preserving colonial architecture and objects long established by other lay preservationists; see Patricia West, *Domesticating History: The Political Origins of America's House Museums* (Washington, D.C.: Smithsonian Institution Press, 1999), 42; and Katherine C. Grier, *Culture and Comfort: Parlor Making and Middle-Class Identity, 1850–1930* (Washington, D.C.: Smithsonian Books, 1988), 53–55.

15. Watts, *People's Tycoon*, 41–45.

16. Lewis, *Public Image of Henry Ford*, 17. All quotations in this paragraph are from Watts, *People's Tycoon*, 58–62.

17. Watts, *People's Tycoon*, 64–82 (work on the 999 race car), 84–100 (Ford's relationship with Malcolmson).

18. Ibid., 86–90, 123.

19. Ibid., 135–41.

20. For a discussion of nativism and efforts to restrict immigration, see Roger Daniels, *Guarding the Golden Door: American Immigration Policy and Immigrants since 1882* (New York: Hill & Wang, 2004); Andrew Gyory, *Closing the Gate: Race, Politics, and the Chinese Exclusion Act* (Chapel Hill: University of North Carolina Press, 1998); and John Higham, *Strangers in the Land: Patterns of American Nativism, 1860–1925* (New Brunswick, N.J.: Rutgers University Press, 1973).

21. U.S. Department of Commerce, Bureau of the Census, *Statistics of Population, 1890* (Washington, D.C.: Government Printing Office, 1891).

22. Neil Baldwin, *Henry Ford and the Jews: The Mass Production of Hate* (New York: Public Affairs, 2001), 27–35.

23. Ibid., 27–30; Watts, *People's Tycoon*, 206–7. On the department's long and controversial history, see Watts, *People's Tycoon*, 199–224. The Sociological Department as it had been known in 1914 was disbanded in 1921; see Douglas Brinkley, *Wheels for the World: Henry Ford, His Company, and a Century of Progress* (New York: Penguin, 2003), 278. The department resumed more activities during World War II under the directorship of H. S. Ablewhite and was disbanded in 1948; see Brinkley, *Wheels for the World*, 279; and Ford R. Bryan, *Henry's Lieutenants* (Detroit: Wayne State University Press, 1993), 301.

24. Jonathan Schwartz, "Henry Ford's Melting Pot," in *Immigrants and Migrants: The Detroit Ethnic Experience*, ed. David W. Hartman (Detroit: Wayne State University Press, 1974), 252–59, esp. 256.

25. Baldwin, *Henry Ford and the Jews*, 42.

26. Ibid., 6–7.

27. Upward, *A Home for Our Heritage*, 3; Watts, *People's Tycoon*, 11. The author of the poem is apparently unknown.

28. Ford R. Bryan, *Clara: Mrs. Henry Ford* (Detroit: Wayne State University Press, 2001), 135.

29. Watts, *People's Tycoon*, 274; Curcio, *Henry Ford*, 133. On the paper's growth see Watts, *People's Tycoon*, 377–78; and Curcio, *Henry Ford*, 133–35.

30. Watts, *People's Tycoon,* 377–81, quot. on 381.

31. Quoted ibid., 425.

32. Henry Ford, "What Makes Immigration a Problem?," in *Ford Ideals: Being a Selection from "Mr. Ford's Own Page," in the Dearborn Independent* (Dearborn, Mich.: The Dearborn Publishing Company, 1922), 401–4, quot. on 404; Watts, *People's Tycoon,* 3–13.

33. Ford, *Ford Ideals,* 293, 154, 157.

34. Howard P. Segal, *Recasting the Machine Age: Henry Ford's Village Industries* (Amherst: University of Massachusetts Press, 2005), 19, 4, 6–7, quot. on 7. On Fordlandia see Greg Grandin, *Fordlandia: The Rise and Fall of Henry Ford's Forgotten Jungle City* (New York: Metropolitan Books, 2009).

35. Watts, *People's Tycoon,* 392; Baldwin, *Henry Ford and the Jews,* 209–10.

36. Quoted in "Ford Now Retracts Attacks on Jews," *New York Times,* July 8, 1927.

37. Watts, *People's Tycoon,* 397.

38. "Ford Is an Anarchist," *Chicago Tribune,* June 23, 1916; "Writer of Ford Editorial on Witness Stand," *Chicago Tribune,* July 1, 1919; for a summary of the trial see Watts, *People's Tycoon,* ix–x. Until 1940 it was not illegal to fire an employee for enlisting in the military. For the "History is more or less bunk" quote see Charles N. Wheeler, "Fight to Disarm His Life's Work, Henry Ford Vows," *Chicago Tribune,* May 25, 1916. Ford would go on to shorten the phrase to "History is bunk" in 1921: "History Is Bunk, Says Henry Ford," *New York Times,* October 29, 1921.

39. "Quick! A Barrel for Mr. Ford," *Chicago Tribune,* August 26, 1918.

40. Watts, *People's Tycoon,* 265–71. For reports of Ford's testimony see "The Grilling of Henry Ford," *Literary Digest,* August 9, 1919, 44–46; and "Henry Ford at Bay," *Forum,* August 1919, 129–44.

41. Upward, *A Home for Our Heritage,* 2–3.

42. James M. Lindgren, *Preserving Historic New England: Preservation, Progressivism, and the Remaking of Memory* (New York: Oxford University Press, 1995), 50–66; James Harvey Robinson, *The New History* (New York: Macmillan, 1912); Ellen Fitzpatrick, *History's Memory: Writing America's Past, 1880–1980* (Cambridge: Harvard University Press, 2002), 1–12, 51–97.

43. Upward, *A Home for Our Heritage,* 2–3.

44. West, *Domesticating History,* 90, 42. See also Lindgren, *Preserving Historic New England,* 50–66.

45. Watts, *People's Tycoon,* 405. Brittany Miller, in "A Mechanism of Museum-Building Philanthropy (1925–1970)" (MA thesis, Indiana University, 2010), does an excellent job of detailing how Ford's collecting process worked; see 118–19 for Taylor's biography. See also Briann G. Greenfield, *Out of the Attic: Inventing Antiques in Twentieth-Century New England* (Amherst: University of Massachusetts Press, 2009), for an extended discussion of how antiques were invented as aesthetic objects.

46. Ned Kaufman, *Place, Race, and Story: Essays on the Past and Future of Historic Preservation* (New York: Routledge, 2009), 220; Upward, *A Home for Our Heritage,* 2–3.

47. "Henry Ford Buys Famous Old Wayside," *New York Times,* July 11, 1923; Brooke D. Wortham, "Mythologies of an American Everyday Landscape: Henry Ford at the Wayside Inn" (PhD diss., Massachusetts Institute of Technology, 2006), 80–84. See also "Longfellow's Wayside Inn: A Non-Profit Massachusetts Historic Landmark," www.wayside.org.

48. Sorby, *Schoolroom Poets,* 2, 33–34.

49. "Ford to Learn Oldtime Dances to 'Fit' His Wayside Inn Home," *New York Times,* August 29, 1924; Watts, *People's Tycoon,* 383.

50. "Mine Host Ford Fiddles for Dance," *New York Times,* February 9, 1923; "Ford Reopens Wayside Inn to Public," *New York Times,* February 24, 1924; "$2.50 for a Ford Dinner," *New York Times,* March 8, 1924.

51. "Preserves Colonial Home," *New York Times,* May 24, 1924; "Ford Buys Two Early New England Homes to Rebuild Near Wayside Inn at Sudbury," *New York Times,* July 14, 1924.

52. Henry Ford and Mrs. Henry Ford, *The Story of Mary and Her Little Lamb* (1928; repr., Whitefish, Mont.: Kessinger, 2003); "Ford Buys 'Little Red School,'" *New York Times,* January 20, 1926; "Mary and Her Lamb Join the Immortals," *New York Times,* February 13, 1927; Michael Kammen, *Mystic Chords of Memory* (New York: Vintage, 1991), 344; "School Where Mary Took Lamb Will Reopen," *New York Times,* January 14, 1927; Wortham, "Mythologies of an American Everyday Landscape," 102–5.

53. Eunice Fuller Barnard, "Henry Ford Invents a School," *New York Times Magazine,* April 13, 1930, 1; "Ford Testing Ideas at Sudbury School," *New York Times,* March 10, 1932.

54. Upward, *A Home for Our Heritage,* 4, 37.

55. Gary Kulik, "Designing the Past: History-Museum Exhibitions from Peale to the Present," in *History Museums in the United States,* ed. Warren Leon and Roy Rosenzweig (Chicago: University of Illinois Press, 1989), 12–17.

56. Charles H. Richards, *The Industrial Museum* (New York: Macmillan, 1925), 1.

57. Jay Pridmore, *Inventive Genius: The History of the Museum of Science and Industry, Chicago* (Chicago: Museum Books, 1996).

58. Edward N. Kaufman, "The Architectural Museum: From World's Fair to Restoration Village," in Carbonell, *Museum Studies,* 279. Hazelius was inspired to preserve the past in 1872, when he went on holiday to the Swedish province of Dalecarlia and found that the quiet, pastoral landscape was in the full throes of industrialization. Hazelius collected costumes and implements he felt characterized the formerly agrarian culture and society of his beloved small town, and opened his seventy-five-acre museum in Stockholm. Guides dressed in period costume and performed traditional arts and crafts. While it is unknown whether Ford toured any of these museums, he may well have been aware of their existence.

59. "Henry Ford Asked to Buy Ancient Virginia Town," *Detroit Free Press,* August 31, 1924; Watts, *People's Tycoon,* 404; Hosmer, *Preservation Comes of Age,* 14–15. In fact, many city boosters turned to heritage tourism as an economic solution in the early twentieth century. For a very different story of how this process worked see Chris Wilson, *The Myth of Santa Fe: Creating a Modern Regional Tradition* (Albuquerque: University of New Mexico Press, 1997).

60. "Henry Ford Asked to Buy Ancient Virginia Town"; Watts, *People's Tycoon,* 404; Hosmer, *Preservation Comes of Age,* 14–15.

61. Watts, *People's Tycoon,* 401; Brinkley, *Wheels for the World,* 30, 324–25, 377–78; letter from Kenneth Chorley to Henry Ford, February 5, 1935, folder 959-Rock–Rocz, box 1823, accession no. 285, Henry Ford Office Papers, Ford Motor Company Records Collection, BFRC; see also Miller, "A Mechanism of American Museum-Building," 69.

62. Anders Greenspan, *Creating Colonial Williamsburg* (Washington, D.C.: Smithsonian Institute Press, 2002), 8–9, 40; Hosmer, *Preservation Comes of Age,* 12–31.

63. Hosmer notes in *Preservation Comes of Age* that "the Flynts might object to having their preservation-restoration described as an outdoor museum, but it seems clear that they did intend to use the village as a living community and an educational exhibit" (1219). See Miller, "A Mechanism of American Museum Building," 64, for information about Ginsberg & Levy, Inc.

64. Hosmer, *Preservation Comes of Age,* 109–20; Diane Barthel, *Historic Preservation: Collective Memory and Historical Identity* (New Brunswick, N.J.: Rutgers University Press, 1996), 39.

65. Hosmer, *Preservation Comes of Age,* 97–109. See also Nicholas Fox Weber, *The Clarks of Cooperstown: Their Sewing Machine Fortune, Their Great and Influential Art Collections, Their Forty-Year Feud* (New York: Knopf, 2007).

66. Hosmer, *Preservation Comes of Age,* 131–32.

2. A Permanent Pageant of America

1. Geoffrey C. Upward, *A Home for Our Heritage: The Building and Growth of Greenfield Village and Henry Ford Museum, 1929–1979* (Dearborn, Mich.: The Henry Ford Museum Press, 1979), 21–23, 25, 34–37.

2. Ibid., 33. In "Progress and Preservation: Representing History in Boston's Landscape of Urban Reform, 1820–1860," *New England Quarterly* 82, no. 2 (June 2009): 304–34, Whitney Martinko argues that by broadening the definition of what counts as historic preservation, we can trace its origins in the United States to the early nineteenth century. She contends that many believed that not only antique objects but also parts of buildings were relics that served as spiritual connections to the past.

3. Samuel Crowther, "Henry Ford's Village of Yesterday," *Ladies' Home Journal,* September 1928, 10.

4. Ford R. Bryan, *Henry's Lieutenants* (Detroit: Wayne State University Press, 1993), 81–87.

5. "The Reminiscences of Mr. Edward J. Cutler" (March 1952, based on interviews conducted in May and June 1951), Ford Motor Company Archives, Oral History Section, BFRC, 19.

6. Upward, *A Home for Our Heritage,* 50–51.

7. Ibid., 50–51.

8. Ibid., 51.

9. "Reminiscences of Mr. Edward J. Cutler," 27–28.

10. Upward, *A Home for Our Heritage,* 113; "One-Room School in Greenfield Village," www.thehenryford.org/education, 3.

11. Crowther, "Henry Ford's Village of Yesterday," 10–11, 116, 118; Upward, *A Home for Our Heritage,* 48, 114.

12. Joseph S. Wood, *The New England Village* (Baltimore: Johns Hopkins University Press, 1997), 151. For a discussion of the New England village as a cultural construction see David Glassberg, *Sense of History: The Place of the Past in American Life* (Amherst: University of Massachusetts Press, 2001), 129–64.

13. Martinko, "Progress and Preservation."

14. Upward, *A Home for Our Heritage,* 28–29.

15. "Reminiscences of Mr. Edward J. Cutler," 60–61; Steven Watts, *The People's Tycoon: Henry Ford and the American Century* (New York: Knopf, 2005), 322.

16. David L. Lewis, *The Public Image of Henry Ford: An American Folk Hero and His Company* (Detroit: Wayne State University Press, 1976), 242–46.

17. Upward, *A Home for Our Heritage,* 39, 44, 43.

18. Ibid., 78.

19. Ibid., 42, 105; for the dates that Ford attended the Miller School and its construction in Greenfield Village, see "One-Room School in Greenfield Village," 3.

20. Upward, *A Home for Our Heritage,* 77; "Fred Black Oral History Final Copy," folder

8, accession no. 65, BFRC, 65. For the breakdown of Greenfield Village School students see "Family Analysis of Greenfield Village Schools, September, 1960," box 3, accession no. 138, EIR.

21. Eva O'Neal Twork, *Henry Ford and Benjamin B. Lovett: The Dancing Billionaire and the Dancing Master* (Detroit: Harlo Press, 1982), 25–26 (quot.), 127, 66.

22. E. Lucille Webster, *An Autobiography of a One-Room School Teacher: Scotch Settlement School of Henry Ford's Greenfield Village* (Dearborn, Mich.: E. Lucille Webster, 1978), 67–69, quot. on 68.

23. Ibid., 91.

24. Ibid., 75; Upward, *A Home for Our Heritage*, 81, 97–98.

25. Webster, *Autobiography*, 91.

26. Upward, *A Home for Our Heritage*, 78.

27. Webster, *Autobiography*, 77–91.

28. Mike Wallace, "Visiting the Past: History Museums in the United States," in *Mickey Mouse History and Other Essays on American Memory* (Philadelphia: Temple University Press, 1996), 13. Wallace argues that by the 1920s "Ford had become a most atypical capitalist. Ford Motor, though gigantic, was still a family firm. He hated the newer forms of organization and the initiation of competition through models and colors instituted by Alfred P. Sloan at General Motors. He also despised financiers and considered Chrysler a plot by Wall Street bankers to destroy him" (13). Ford also critiqued the modern industrial corporation, and in this he was not alone. While some, like Diego Rivera, were using the modern factory to inspire celebrations of industrial workers, other artists, writers, and politicians used the same imagery to critique corporations. As Alan Brinkley has shown, individuals with dramatically divergent politics, such as Huey Long and Father Charles Coughlin, argued that the "most troubling feature of modern industrial society . . . was the steady erosion of the individual's ability to control his own destiny. Large faceless institutions; wealthy, insulated men; vast networks of national and international influence: all were exercising power and controlling wealth that more properly belonged in the hands of ordinary citizens." Brinkley, *Voices of Protest: Huey Long, Father Coughlin, and the Great Depression* (New York: Vintage, 1983), 144.

29. Watts, *People's Tycoon*, 431.

30. Upward, *A Home for Our Heritage*, 85, 115–116.

31. Watts, *People's Tycoon*, 444–45; Maurice Sugar, *The Ford Hunger March* (Berkeley: Meiklejohn Civil Liberties Institute, 1980), 31, 40–45, 67–70.

32. David L. Lewis, *The Public Image of Henry Ford: An American Folk Hero and His Company* (Detroit: Wayne State University Press, 1976), 250–66.

33. Upward, *A Home for Our Heritage*, 109, 81.

34. Ibid., 82–83.

35. Jonathan Schwartz, "Henry Ford's Melting Pot," in *Immigrants and Migrants: The Detroit Ethnic Experience*, ed. David W. Hartman (Detroit: Wayne State University Press, 1974), 256.

36. Jane S. Smith, *The Garden of Invention: Luther Burbank and the Business of Breeding Plants* (New York: Penguin, 2010), 1–13; Upward, *A Home for Our Heritage*, 111; "Reminiscences of Mr. Edward J. Cutler," 81.

37. Seth Bruggeman, "Introduction: Locating the Birthplace in American Public Memory," in *Born in the U.S.A.: Birth, Commemoration, and American Public Memory*, ed. Bruggeman (Amherst: University of Massachusetts Press, 2012), 9, 11.

38. Elizabeth Anne Martin, *Detroit and the Great Migration, 1916–1929* (Ann Arbor: Bentley Historical Library, University of Michigan, 1993), available at http://bentley.umich.edu.

39. Kevin Boyle, *Arc of Justice: A Saga of Race, Civil Rights, and Murder in the Jazz Age* (New York: Holt, 2004), 1–11.

40. Beth Tomkins Bates, *The Making of Black Detroit in the Age of Henry Ford* (Chapel Hill: University of North Carolina Press, 2012), 2–3, 253–54; Thomas Sugrue, *The Origins of the Urban Crisis: Race and Inequality in Postwar Detroit* (Princeton: Princeton University Press, 1996), 25. For discussions of Ford's racial policies and views see also Lloyd H. Bailer, "The Negro Automobile Worker," *Journal of Political Economy* 51, no. 5 (October 1943): 416; and Watts, *People's Tycoon*, 489–91.

41. Bates, *Making of Black Detroit*, 145; Amy Maria Kenyon, *Dreaming Suburbia: Detroit and the Production of Postwar Space and Culture* (Detroit: Wayne State University Press, 2004), 131–35.

42. Bates, *Making of Black Detroit*, 156.

43. For a discussion of how neighborhood associations used housing to maintain the color line in Detroit see Boyle, *Arc of Justice*, 1–11; Watts, *People's Tycoon*, 131–35; and Kenyon, *Dreaming Suburbia*, 135.

44. Ford's fascination with Foster led him to purchase the house, which was located in Lawrenceville, Pennsylvania, but its association with Foster was dubious at best. Foster's biographer John Tasker Howard told Ford that elderly residents had misled Ford's agents; while Foster's father had owned the home, there was no evidence that Stephen Foster ever lived there. After two well-publicized trips to Lawrenceville, Ford announced that the home was Foster's. In 1935 it was added to Greenfield Village, with seventy of Foster's descendants in attendance. But one year later one of Foster's niece's, Evelyn Foster Morneweck, published a pamphlet titled *The Birthplace of Stephen C. Foster as Recorded by His Father, Mother and Brother, and Other Contemporary Authorities,* charging Ford with disparaging her uncle's memory by presenting the public with false information. In 1939, Ford gave the producer Darryl F. Zanuck permission to use images of the home for *Suwanee River,* a movie about Foster's life. When Zanuck's colleagues discovered that the home's historical authenticity was questionable, however, they decided not to use it. Finally, after Ford's death, Greenfield Village trustees hired a professional historian, Milo M. Quaife, to verify the home's authenticity. Quaife found that Foster's actual birthplace was torn down in 1865, and after 1953 the home was referred to as the Stephen C. Foster Memorial; today it is called the Sounds of American Gallery. See David L. Lewis, *The Public Image of Henry Ford: An American Folk Hero and His Company* (Detroit: Wayne State University Press, 1976), 279.

45. Ken Emerson, *Doo-Dah! Steven Foster and the Rise of American Popular Culture* (New York: Simon & Schuster, 1997), 1–16.

46. Ibid., 257–58.

47. Upward, *A Home for Our Heritage,* 112.

48. Gary Kremer, *George Washington Carver: In His Own Words* (Columbia: University of Missouri Press, 1983), 1–38, 40-43.

49. Quentin R. Skrabec Jr., *The Green Vision of Henry Ford and George Washington Carver: Two Collaborators in the Cause of Clean Industry* (Jefferson, N.C.: McFarland, 2013), 154.

50. For a discussion of Carver's biography and how those with divergent politics used him as a symbol, see McMurry, *George Washington Carver.*

51. Skrabec Jr., *The Green Vision of Henry Ford and George Washington Carver,* 167–68; Kremer, *George Washington Carver,* 3; Patricia West, *Domesticating History: The Political Origins of America's House Museums* (Washington, D.C.: Smithsonian Books, 1999), 136–

43. The Carver farm is now the George Washington Carver National Monument. Although the cabin where Carver was born was destroyed around 1880, a foundation outline constructed by park staff marks the approximate site.

52. Upward, *A Home for Our Heritage*, 112; Ford Bryan, "A Prized Friendship: Henry Ford and George Washington Carver," and vertical file, "G. W. Carver," file 2, both in BFRC; Skrabec, *The Green Vision*, 168.

53. "Greenfield Village Map, 1947," THF109472, box 1, accession no. 21, EIR. It's unclear why Ford asked the governors of every state to donate wood for the paneling, other than that he thought it was interesting and unique, and that his friend Carver would appreciate it, perhaps because of his interest in the natural world.

54. Upward, *A Home for Our Heritage*, 112–13.

55. West, *Domesticating History*, 136–57.

56. "Reminiscences of Mr. Edward J. Cutler," 159.

57. William T. Martin, "Search for Place of McGuffey's Birth," *New York Times*, January 5, 1930; "Ford to Buy Birthplace of McGuffey," *New York Times*, January 9, 1934; Upward, *A Home for Our Heritage*, 77.

58. Fred Howard, *Wilbur and Orville: A Biography of the Wright Brothers* (New York: Ballantine, 1998), 1–12.

59. "Ford Buys Birthplace of Wrights' First Plane," *New York Times*, July 4, 1936; "Biographical Note," 4, Finding Aid for Wright Brothers Collection, 1867–2006, accession no. 1623, BFRC. Wilbur Wright had died in 1912.

60. "Reminiscences of Mr. Edward J. Cutler," 79.

61. "Wrights' Plane in London Again Sought for America," *New York Times*, March 9, 1930.

62. "Reminiscences of Mr. Edward J. Cutler," 78; Upward, *A Home for Our Heritage*, 114.

63. Quoted in "Shrine to Wrights Dedicated by Ford," *New York Times*, April 17, 1938.

64. "Fred Black Oral History," box 6, folder 8, accession no. 65, BFRC, 32–34; Upward, *A Home for Our Heritage*, 3, 8, 108.

65. "Reminiscences of Mr. Edward J. Cutler," 63.

66. Upward, *A Home for Our Heritage*, 176; Upward includes an organizational chart from 1934 (96).

67. Watts, *People's Tycoon*, 333–36; Upward, *A Home for Our Heritage*, 96; "Reminiscences of Mr. Edward J. Cutler," 122.

68. Upward, *A Home for Our Heritage*, 96.

69. Ibid., 24–25.

70. "Fred Black Oral History," 33.

71. "Reminiscences of Mr. Edward J. Cutler," 123, 142–43.

72. Upward, *A Home for Our Heritage*, 89, 94; "Edison Institute Museum and Village Pamphlet," box 1, accession no. 116, EIR.

73. Upward, *A Home for Our Heritage*, 76–77.

74. Ibid., 76.

75. "Edison Institute Annual Report: 1939," box 1, accession no. 110, EIR.

76. Upward, *A Home for Our Heritage*, 93; "Edison Institute Annual Report: 1939." For more on the Sandwich Glass Plant, see "Sandwich Glass Plant Affidavit, n.d.," and "Greenfield Village Sandwich Glass Plant History," both accession no. 186, EIR.

77. Upward, *A Home for Our Heritage*, 176; "Finding Aid for Ford Fair Lane Office Record Series, 1895–1951," 4, accession nos. 284 and 844, BFRC.

78. Upward, *A Home for Our Heritage*, 118; Watts, *People's Tycoon*, 524–27, quot. on 526.

79. "Reminiscences of Mr. Edward J. Cutler," 164–65; Upward, *A Home for Our Heritage*, 127.

80. "Reminiscences of Mr. Edward J. Cutler," 166.

81. Lewis, *The Public Image of Henry Ford*, 472–73, quot. on 472.

3. The Public's Village

1. Geoffrey C. Upward, *A Home for Our Heritage: The Building and Growth of Greenfield Village and Henry Ford Museum, 1929–1979* (Dearborn, Mich.: The Henry Ford Museum Press, 1979), 76; Samuel Crowther, "Henry Ford's Village of Yesterday," *Ladies' Home Journal*, September 1928, 10; Eunice Fuller Barnard, "Ford Builds a Unique Museum," *New York Times Magazine*, April 5, 1931, 3.

2. Thomas Sugrue, *The Origins of the Urban Crisis: Race and Inequality in Postwar Detroit* (Princeton: Princeton University Press, 1996), 27.

3. "Detroit Is Dynamite," *Life*, August 17, 1942, 15; Sugrue, *Origins of the Urban Crisis*. Sugrue writes that "the 1940s and 1950s seemed to many a moment of hope, a time of opportunity to reverse the trends toward racial segregation and discrimination of the previous quarter-century" (55).

4. "Ford Rouge Factory Tour: History of the Rouge," The Henry Ford, 2005, www.the-henryford.org/rouge; "Population of the 100 Largest Urban Places: 1930," www.census.gov.

5. Nabeel Abraham and Andrew Shryock, "On Margins and Mainstreams," in *Arab Detroit: From Margin to Mainstream*, ed. Abraham and Shryock (Detroit: Wayne State University Press, 2000), 19.

6. Jonathan Schwartz, "Henry Ford's Melting Pot," in *Immigrants and Migrants: The Detroit Ethnic Experience*, ed. David W. Hartman (Detroit: Wayne State University Press, 1974), 256; Thomas A. Klug, "Labor Market Politics in Detroit: The Curious Case of the 'Spolansky Act' of 1931," *Michigan Historical Review* 14, no. 1 (Spring 1988): 6; Campbell Gibson and Kay Jung, "Table 23: Michigan—Race and Hispanic Origin for Selected Large Cities and Other Places: Earliest Census to 1990," U.S. Census Bureau, 2005; Abraham and Shryock, "On Margins and Mainstreams," 19; Sameer Y. Abraham, Nabeel Abraham, and Barbara Aswad, "The Southend: An Arab Muslim Working-Class Community," in *Arabs in the New World: Studies on Arab-American Communities*, ed. Sameer Y. Abraham and Nabeel Abraham (Detroit: Wayne State University Press, 1983), 164–81. On the economic diversity of Detroit's suburbs, and specifically Dearborn, see Oliver Zunz, *The Changing Face of Inequality: Urbanization, Industrial Development, and Immigrants in Detroit, 1880–1920* (Chicago: University of Chicago Press, 1982), 354–59.

7. "A Talk by William A. Simonds before the Society of Automotive Engineers at the Dearborn Inn ca. 1937," Guide Reference Manuals, box 3, accession no. 141, EIR.

8. Upward, *A Home for Our Heritage*, 76, 177; advertising in 1930s issues of *Detroit Free Press*; Writers' Program of the Work Projects Administration, *Michigan: A Guide to the Wolverine State* (New York: Oxford University Press, 1941), 210; "Henry Ford Museum and Greenfield Village Calendar Year Attendance Totals," box 1, accession no. 235, EIR.

9. "The Edison Institute Museum and Village," pamphlet, 1947.

10. The interpretive thrust of the tour scripts written between 1929 and 1947 does not demonstrate a significant change in terms of the interpretation at the buildings. See "Guide Reference Manuals Records: 1929–1980," accession no. 141, EIR.

11. "Greenfield Village Tour: 1945," box 8, accession no. 141, EIR. Unless otherwise noted, further quotations and descriptions are taken from this document.

12. Upward, *A Home for Our Heritage,* 112.

13. The phrase "pluck and luck" comes from Horatio Alger's *Luck and Pluck; or, John Oakley's Inheritance* (1869), and "rags to respectability" comes from Alger's *Ragged Dick* (1868). Ford had a personal definition of self-made manhood, but he certainly tapped into a broader American narrative and sometimes myth. Scholarly treatments of the history of self-made manhood as rhetoric and myth that shaped American politics and culture are numerous; a useful analysis of the literature can be found in Jeffrey Decker, *Made in America: Self-Styled Success from Horatio Alger to Oprah Winfrey* (Minneapolis: University of Minnesota Press, 1996).

14. On John Brainard Chapman see "One-Room School in Greenfield Village," www.thehenryford.org/education.

15. In 1982 the Magill Jewelry Store would be reinterpreted as Mrs. Cohen's Millinery. See Nancy Villa Bryk, "Mrs. D. Cohen's Millinery Comes to Greenfield Village," *The Herald,* vol. 73 (1982), accession no. 186, Magill Jewelry Store, box 1, clippings folder, EIR.

16. Scholars have long identified the links between myths about self-made manhood and women's roles. For specific examples see Gail Bederman, *Manliness and Civilization: A Cultural History of Gender and Race in the United States, 1880–1917* (Chicago: University of Chicago Press, 1996); Rotundo, *American Manhood;* and Patricia West, *Domesticating History: The Political Origins of America's House Museums* (Washington, D.C.: Smithsonian Institution Press, 1999).

17. Wyn Wacchorst, *Thomas Alva Edison: An American Myth* (Cambridge: MIT Press, 1981), 6, 205.

18. Gilbert King, "Charles Proteus Steinmetz, the Wizard of Schenectady," Past Imperfect (*Smithsonian Magazine* blog), August 16, 2011, http://blogs.smithsonianmag.com/history.

19. See James Tobin, "Robert Frost in Ann Arbor," *Michigan Today,* June 10, 2010.

20. On the construction of the Sir John Bennett Jewelry Store see Upward, *A Home for Our Heritage,* 85.

21. Ford R. Bryan, *Clara: Mrs. Henry Ford* (Detroit: Wayne State University Press, 2001), 213–15.

22. "Greenfield Village Tour: 1941," and "Guide Reference Manuals 1929–1980," box 2, accession no. 141, EIR; "Logan County Court House; Slave Huts; Town Hall; ca. 1937," folder 11, box 1, accession no. 141, EIR.

23. In 1981 staff would find that W. W. Taylor, who secured the building in 1928, called it a "Hearse House," and that Edward C. Cutler had stated that the hearse house was turned into a firehouse as soon as it arrived in the village because an actual firehouse from New England would have been too tall. In a 2003 report, Robert Casey, curator of transportation at The Henry Ford, noted that Taylor bought the hearse storage shed but that he "did not do much research on the history of the building . . . because Ford planned to house an antique fire engine in the building." Deluge Fire House, "History," accession no. 186, EIR.

24. See also Upward, *A Home for Our Heritage,* 33, 93.

25. George Brown Goode, *The Principles of Museum Administration* (York: Coultas & Volans, 1895); Benjamin Ives Gilman, *Museum Ideals of Purpose and Method* (Cambridge, Mass.: Riverside Press, 1918); Edward Robinson, *The Behavior of the Museum Visitor* (Washington, D.C.: American Association of Museums, 1928); Arthur W. Melton, *Problems of Installation in Museums of Art* (Washington, D.C.: American Association of Museums, 1935). See also Kenneth A. Yellis, "Museum Education," in *The Museum: A Reference Guide,* ed. Michael Steven Shapiro and Louis Ward Kemp (Westport, Conn.: Greenwood Press, 1990), 167–98.

26. Upward, *A Home for Our Heritage,* 77–78; "Greenfield Village Journal 1934–1946," boxes 1–2, accession no. 105, EIR. Journal entries cited below by date refer to these volumes; there are eleven in all, one for each of the years between 1934 and 1937 (box 1) and 1938 and 1946 (box 2).

27. 1930 U.S. Federal Census and U.S. School Yearbooks online collection, both at ancestry.com. Jerome Wilford's occupation is listed as "Guide" in the Dearborn, Michigan, *City Directory* for 1934, 188.

28. 1930 U.S. Federal Census, U.S. City Directories, 1821–1989, and U.S. School Yearbooks online collections, ancestry.com; "Donald M. Currie" (obituary), *Daily Tribune* (Royal Oak, Mich.), October 15, 2006.

29. 1930 U.S. Federal Census, U.S. City Directories, 1821–1989, and U.S. School Yearbooks online collections, ancestry.com.

30. Journal entries, July 7, 1934, and July 10, 1934.

31. David W. Blight makes a similar point in *Race and Reunion: The Civil War in American Memory* (Cambridge: Belknap Press of Harvard University Press, 2001); he writes that "during the Civil War the reminiscence industry as a whole (in print media and in veterans' posts) promoted a kind of *democratization* of memory" (179).

32. Journal entry, June 18, 1934.

33. John Kelly, "Lincoln's Chair at Ford's Theatre Took Winding Journey to Michigan," *Washington Post,* November 13, 2010; journal entries, August 7, 1934, and June 29, 1936.

34. Journal entries, June 21, 1936, July 8, 1940, and June 20, 1943.

35. Journal entry, June 19, 1934.

36. Journal entries, July 7, 1934, and March 26, 1936.

37. Journal entries, July 27, 1934, and August 20, 1934.

38. Journal entries, August 22, 1934, September 9, 1940, and June 25, 1936.

39. Journal entries, June 27, 1936, and September 5, 1936.

40. Journal entries, June 29, 1936, July 10, 1941, and November 10, 1941.

41. Journal entries, August 27, 1937, and January 24, 1940.

42. Journal entries, November 29–December 5, 1942, August 5, 1942, and August 13, 1942.

43. Ray Batchelor, *Henry Ford: Mass Production, Modernism, and Design* (Manchester: Manchester University Press, 1994), 142.

44. Carl Becker, "Everyman His Own Historian," *American Historical Association* 37, no. 2 (January 1932): 231–36. Becker's address, originally delivered to the American Historical Association in December 1931, suggested a new kind of historical inquiry recognizing the highly subjective and relativistic role the historian played. Becker's challenge opened the door not just for historians, but for all humanities scholars, by broadening definitions of evidence and of who was worthy of historical study. As historians' interest in everyday life grew, they would find that the sources they now needed were preserved in museums, historic houses, and the homes of antiquers. Indeed, many Americans had retained the material culture that documented their family experiences long before Becker announced the relevance of everyday life to the historical profession.

4. Searching for an Identity

1. Geoffrey C. Upward, *A Home for Our Heritage: The Building and Growth of Greenfield Village and Henry Ford Museum, 1929–1979* (Dearborn, Mich.: The Henry Ford Museum Press, 1979), 123–25.

2. Ibid., 123–25; "Biography, Hayward Ablewhite," Ford biographical file, folder A, BFRC.

3. Upward, *A Home for Our Heritage,* 123–36; Ford R. Bryan, *Clara: Mrs. Henry Ford* (Dearborn, Mich.: Ford Books, 2001), 305.

4. Upward, *A Home for Our Heritage,* 24–25, 123–27; for Campsall's, Cameron's, and Simonds's biographies see Ford R. Bryan, *Henry's Lieutenants* (Detroit: Wayne State University Press, 1993), 58–65, 53–57, 242–49.

5. Upward, *A Home for Our Heritage,* 124.

6. Ibid., 176; "A. K. Mills, Director of Edison Institute," *New York Times,* September 13, 1954; "Finding Aid for Mills and Nevins and Hill Series, 1948–1977 (Bulk 1950–1964)," accession no. 506, EIR, 4; "Biography/Clippings: A. K. Mills," Ford Biographical Vertical File, folder Me–Mi, BFRC.

7. Patricia West, *Domesticating History: The Political Origins of America's House Museums* (Washington, D.C.: Smithsonian Institution Press, 1999), 129–36.

8. Mike Wallace, "Preserving the Past: A History of Historic Preservation in the United States," in *Mickey Mouse History and Other Essays on American Memory* (Philadelphia: Temple University Press, 1996), 177–222.

9. Anders Greenspan, *Creating Colonial Williamsburg* (Washington, D.C.: Smithsonian Institute Press, 2002), 91, 111–12.

10. Samuel Chamberlain and Henry N. Flynt, *Frontier of Freedom: The Soul and Substance of America Portrayed in One Extraordinary Village, Old Deerfield, Massachusetts* (New York: Hastings House, 1957), 1.

11. Steven Lubar and Kathleen M. Kendrick, *Legacies: Collecting America's History at the Smithsonian* (Washington, D.C.: Smithsonian Institution Press, 2001). For essays reflecting on the state of industrial history museums at the turn of the millennium, see Steven Lubar and Steven Cutcliffe, eds., "New Perspectives on Industrial History Museums," special issue, *The Public Historian* 22, no. 3 (Summer 2000).

12. Richard Handler and Eric Gable, *The New History in an Old Museum: Creating the Past at Colonial Williamsburg* (Durham, N.C.: Duke University Press, 1997), 3–27.

13. Greenspan, *Creating Colonial Williamsburg,* 149. For a discussion of the expansion of African American history museums, see James Oliver Horton and Spencer R. Crew, "Afro Americans and Museums: Towards a Policy of Inclusion," in *History Museums in the United States,* ed. Warren Leon and Roy Rosenzweig (Chicago: University of Illinois Press, 1989), 215–36.

14. Mike Wallace, "Visiting the Past: History Museums in the United States," in *Mickey Mouse History and Other Essay,* 3–32; Greenspan, *Creating Colonial Williamsburg,* 60–147.

15. "Allston Boyer, Developer of Resorts, Dies at 60," *Daytona Beach Morning Journal,* August 12, 1972.

16. Allston Boyer, "Curriculum Report," box 1, accession no. 88, EIR, 1–3.

17. Ibid., 10. According to Edward Cutler, during Henry Ford's presidency some of the staff did live in some of the village homes, Smith's Creek Station, the Sarah Jordan Boarding House, and the Clinton Inn. "The Reminiscences of Mr. Edward J. Cutler" (March 1952, based on interviews conducted in May and June 1951), Ford Motor Company Archives, Oral History Section, BFRC, vol. 2, 136–37.

18. For Brown's professional background see Karen Haywood, "Head Start Founder Back to Basics," *Free-Lance Star* (Fredericksburg, Va.), June 17, 1991.

19. Holmes Brown, "Greenfield Village—Ford Museum Tour," box 1, accession no. 88, EIR, 1–5.

20. Ibid., 7.

21. Upward, *A Home for Our Heritage*, 123–24.

22. Ibid., 142-43.

23. Russell and Corinne Earnest, "Dr. Donald A. Shelley and Richard S. Machmer Remembered," *Maine Antique Digest*, July 2006, www.maineantiquedigest.com; "Dr. Donald Shelley, Ex-Museum Official," *Reading (Pa.) Eagle*, April 20, 2006.

24. Upward, *A Home for Our Heritage*, 102, 137–38, 146–48.

25. Ibid., 142–43.

26. Ibid., 123–24, 127; "Caddy, Frank," Ford Archives Vertical File, BFRC.

27. Upward, *A Home for Our Heritage*, 156.

28. George E. Hein, "Museum Education," in *A Companion to Museum Studies*, ed. Sharon Macdonald (Oxford: Wiley-Blackwell, 2011), 340–352; Erik Christiansen, *Channeling the Past: Politicizing History in Postwar America* (Madison: University of Wisconsin Press, 2013), 189. Hein writes that "the United States was long recognized as the leader in developing the educational role of museums," beginning in the nineteenth century, although "the actual educational work was carried out in a haphazard and unsatisfactory manner" and was "subject to the same constraints that limited the formal education sector" (341). It wasn't until after World War II that museum education began to mature into an "acknowledged profession." Although many institutions preferred to use the term "interpretation" rather than "education," because "education" had "acquired such negative connotations for museum educators—implying obligatory, formal, fact-laden information transfer" (340), education clearly drove the establishment of specialized programs and departments at museums after 1945.

29. "Plans and Progress," box 1, accession no. 140, EIR, 1–2.

30. Upward, *A Home for Our Heritage*, 139.

31. "Edison Institute Staff Biographies," box 3, accession no. 57, EIR.

32. "Annual Report: 1961–1962," and "Annual Report: 1963–1964," both in box 2, accession no. 110, EIR. Subsequent annual reports cited in this chapter carry the same accession number.

33. Upward, *A Home for Our Heritage*, 125, 151; for data on the number of schoolchildren who visited annually, see "Annual Reports, 1954–1964," box 1; "Annual Report, 1977–1978," box 2; and "Edison Institute School System, Records 1927–1970," accession no. 138, BFRC.

34. "Organization Charts 1950–1980," box 1, accession no. 265, EIR.

35. "Annual Report: 1961–1962," box 2; "Annual Report: 1963–1964," box 2.

36. For more on the history of the automotive industry see Thomas Sugrue, *The Origins of the Urban Crisis: Race and Inequality in Postwar Detroit* (Princeton: Princeton University Press, 1996).

37. "Annual Report: 1961–1962"; "Annual Report: 1963–1964." Note that annual reports for the years 1965–1976 are missing from the Edison Institute records.

38. "Annual Report: 1962–1963"; Upward, *A Home for Our Heritage*, 141.

39. Upward, *A Home for Our Heritage*, 140–41.

40. Ibid., 153–60.

41. "Annual Report: 1977," box 2.

42. Sugrue, *Origins of the Urban Crisis*, 258, 126, 229; *Report of the National Advisory Commission on Civil Disorders* (Washington, D.C.: GPO, 1968), 22.

43. David L. Good, *Orvie: The Dictator of Dearborn: The Rise and Reign of Orville L. Hubbard* (Detroit: Wayne State University Press, 1989), 31; for Dearborn population see Table 14, *1980 Census of Population and Housing*, www.census.gov; Campbell Gibson and Kay Jung, "Table 23: Michigan—Race and Hispanic Origin for Selected Large Cities and Other Places: Earliest Census to 1990," U.S. Census Bureau, 2005.

44. Good, *Orvie,* 156–58.

45. Ibid., 157.

46. Ibid., 160.

47. Ibid., 157–60.

48. William Serrin, "Mayor Hubbard Gives Dearborn What It Wants—And Then Some," *New York Times,* January 12, 1969.

49. Sugrue, *Origins of the Urban Crisis,* 131–32.

50. Good, *Orvie,* 32, 309; "Rights Compliance Solved in Dearborn," *New York Times,* July 31, 1965.

51. Sugrue, *Origins of the Urban Crisis,* 259; for Hubbard's response see Good, *Orvie,* 320.

52. Serrin, "Mayor Hubbard Gives Dearborn What It Wants."

53. Good, *Orvie,* 330.

54. Ibid., 341–42; "ACCESS: A Brief History," www.accesscommunity.org; Karen Rignall, "Building an Arab-American Community in Dearborn," *Journal of the International Institute* 5, no. 1 (Fall 1997), http://quod.lib.umich.edu/j/jii/; Sameer Y. Abraham, Nabeel Abraham, and Barbara Aswad, "The Southend: An Arab Muslim Working-Class Community," in *Arabs in the New World: Studies on Arab-American Communities,* ed. Sameer Y. Abraham and Nabeel Abraham (Detroit: Wayne State University Press, 1983), 164–81.

55. Good, *Orvie,* 338.

56. Ibid., 339–40.

57. *Milliken v. Bradley,* 418 U.S. 717 (1974); Good, *Orvie,* 357–72.

58. Letter to Mr. William T. McGraw, director of Michigan Tourist Council, "Public Relations Miscellaneous Correspondence, 1965–1967," box 2, accession no. 57, EIR.

59. Photographs of visitors are located in "Special Events: Country Fair 1951–1966," box 3; "Special Events: Let Freedom Ring, 1964, 1966, 1968–69," box 5; "Special Events: Turkey Shoot, 1955, 1956–57," box 6, all in accession no. 1929, EIR.

60. See Andrea Burns, From *Storefront to Monument: Tracing the Public History of the Black Museum Movement* (Amherst: University of Massachusetts Press, 2013), chap. 1.

61. "Organized Afro History Topics at Hillger School," *Michigan Chronicle,* May 4, 1968; S. A. Greg, "Afro-American History Class Introduced at U-D," *Michigan Chronicle,* February 24, 1968; "Negro History Week Now an Obsolete Device," *Michigan Chronicle,* February 17, 1968; "Thomas A. Edison Cleared Way for 'A Century of Progress,'" *Michigan Chronicle,* February 24, 1968.

62. "Action Line," *Detroit Free Press,* September 26, 1968.

63. Letter from Robert Dawson, box 34, accession no. 235, EIR.

64. "Bicentennial Year Travel Intentions," December 4, 1975, box 9, accession no. 143, EIR, 17, 14.

65. "Tapping the Tourist and Convention Market: A Proposal to the T&C Committee Dearborn Chamber of Commerce," box 35, accession no. 235, EIR, 1.

5. Visitors Respond

1. "Visitor Survey: August 1954," box 1, accession no. 57, EIR.

2. George H. Hein, *Learning in the Museum* (London: Routledge, 1998), 54, 42–45; Kenneth A. Yellis, "Museum Education," in *The Museum: A Reference Guide,* ed. Michael Steven Shapiro and Louis Ward Kemp (Westport, Conn.: Greenwood Press, 1990), 175–76; Paulette M. McManus, "Frames of Reference: Changes in Evaluative Attitudes to Visitors," *Journal of Museum Education* 21, no. 3 (Fall 1996): 3; Robert T. Bower, *The People's Capitalism*

Exhibit: A Study of Reactions of Foreign Visitors to the Washington Preview (Washington, D.C.: Bureau of Social Science Research, 1956); Alvin Goins and George B. Griffenhagen, "Psychological Studies of Museum Visitors and Exhibits at the U.S. National Museum," *The Museologist* no. 67 (1958): 6–10; William Cooley and Terrence Piper, "Study of the West African Art Exhibit of the Milwaukee Public Museum and Its Visitors," in *The Museum Visitor: Selected Essays and Surveys of Visitor Reaction to Exhibits in the Milwaukee Public Museum,* ed. Stephan F. de Borhegyi and Irene A. Hanson (Milwaukee: Milwaukee Public Museum, 1968). Despite the increased interest in museum visitors at both private and government-funded museums, during the 1960s and 1970s national-level data about visitor behavior remained elusive. For example, census abstracts reported the number of Americans who attended museums during the 1960s and 1970s, but did not include specifics such as the income level or race of museum visitors. U.S. Census Bureau, *Statistical Abstract of the United States: 1970* (Washington, D.C.: GPO, 1970), 206; U.S. Census Bureau, *Statistical Abstract of the United States: 1980* (Washington, D.C.: GPO, 1980), 248.

3. Rosanne Butler, director of archives and records at Colonial Williamsburg, e-mail to author, March 13, 2013.

4. Laura E. Abing, "Old Sturbridge Village: An Institutional History of a Cultural Artifact" (PhD diss., Marquette University, 1997), 144–46; Tom Kelleher, chief historian and curator of mechanical arts at Old Sturbridge Village, e-mail to author, March 6, 2013.

5. Abing, "Old Sturbridge Village," 144–46; Kelleher, e-mail to author.

6. Lizabeth Cohen, *A Consumers' Republic: The Politics of Mass Consumption in Postwar America* (New York: Vintage, 2004), 309.

7. Ibid., 8; Marguerite Shaffer, *See America First: Tourism and National Identity, 1880–1940* (Washington, D.C.: Smithsonian Institution Press, 2001), 316.

8. "Annual Report: 1977," box 2, accession no. 110, EIR.

9. Douglas Brinkley, *Wheels for the World: Henry Ford, His Company, and a Century of Progress* (New York: Penguin, 2003), 656–58; "Annual Report: 1977."

10. Brewer Associates Incorporated, "A Decade of Marketing Activities at The Edison Institute," box 69, accession no. 235, EIR.

11. Percentages were calculated from the answer to a question about which site visitors attended. "Summer Visitor Survey," 1969–1975, boxes 23–33, accession no. 235, EIR. Subsequent visitor surveys cited in this chapter carry the same accession number.

12. The percentage was calculated from the answer to the question "Is this your first visit to the Village?" "Summer Visitor Survey," 1969–1977, boxes 23–43.

13. Percentages were calculated from the answer to the question "How many hours did you travel to get here?" "Summer Visitor Survey," 1975–1977, boxes 33–57; Brewer Associates, "A Decade of Marketing Activities," 7–9, quot. on 9.

14. Brewer Associates, "A Decade of Marketing Activities," 40.

15. Ibid., 6.

16. *Household Money Income in 1976 and Selected Social and Economic Characteristics of Households* (Washington, D.C.: GPO, 1978). Percentages calculated from "Summer Visitor Survey, 1976," box 38.

17. Percentages calculated from surveyors' analysis of responses to the question "Head of family's occupation." "Summer Visitor Survey," 1969–1971, boxes 23–28.

18. Erik Christiansen, *Channeling the Past: Politicizing History in Postwar America* (Madison: University of Wisconsin Press, 2013), 206–7; Midwest Research Institute, "The Williamsburg Visitor of 1975," November 12, 1975, Report Files, Colonial Williamsburg Foundation Archives, Williamsburg, Virginia.

19. Percentages were calculated from questions about which section of the village visitors liked the most and which ones they liked the least; the phrasing of this question varied over the years. "Summer Visitor Survey," 1969–1977, boxes 23–57.

20. See, for example, Greg Castillo, *Cold War on the Home Front: The Soft Power of Midcentury Design* (Minneapolis: University of Minnesota Press, 2010). For more on the symbolic meaning of the home see Elaine Tyler May, *Homeward Bound: American Families in the Cold War Era* (New York: Basic Books, 2008). For a discussion of property values, the New Right, and the civil rights movements see Lisa McGirr, *Suburban Warriors: The Origins of the New American Right* (Princeton: Princeton University Press, 2001); Kevin M. Kruse, *White Flight and the Making of Modern Conservatism* (Princeton: Princeton University Press, 2005); Matthew D. Lassiter, *The Silent Majority: Suburban Politics in the Sunbelt South* (Princeton: Princeton University Press, 2006); and Kevin M. Kruse and Thomas J. Sugrue, eds., *The New Suburban Histories* (Chicago: University of Chicago Press, 2006).

21. To analyze the content of the comments, I first reviewed the 1969 summer survey, looking for recurring words that suggested categories, and I arrived at the seven broad categories I mention in the text. I then used those categories to code the comments included in the other nine summer surveys. As might be expected, many comments fell into more than one category, and figure 15 reflects these overlaps. For example, a 1972 visitor wrote: "Village is well kept is in a class with Williamsburg, VA. Also pull thru parking for cars with trailers and overnight campers." This comment was coded for both leisure and appearance. The percentage of each category was stable between 1969 and 1978; consequently, I aggregated the data for each year into one measure.

22. "Visitor Survey 1976 Spring, 1976 Summer, 1977 Spring, 1977 Summer, and 1977 Fall," box 43; "Visitor Survey, 1978 Spring, 1978 Winter, 1979 Spring, and 1979 Winter," box 45.

23. "Visitor Survey, Summer 1971: Visitor Card Survey Comments: (Con) up to and including July 21, 1971," box 28, 2.

24. Admission prices for the Detroit Zoo from author's phone conversation with Detroit Zoo Public Relations department, December 27, 2012; for Greenfield Village prices see "Admission Policy, 1960, 1966–79," box 1, accession no. 203, EIR.

25. Shaffer, *See America First,* 320.

26. "Visitor Survey, Summer, 1969," box 23; "Visitor Survey, Summer, 1976, August 2–8: Pro Comments," box 38.

27. "Visitor Survey, Summer 1969, Favorable Comments," box 34; "Visitor Survey, Summer 1969, Unfavorable Comments," box 34; "Visitor Survey, Summer, 1972," box 27.

28. "Visitor Survey, Summer 1975, Comments received May 28–June 6," box 33, 1; "Visitor Survey, Summer 1976, Aug. 2–8: Con Comments," box 38, 1; "Visitor Survey, Summer, 1973, Con survey comments July 30–August 3, 1973," box 28, 3.

29. Visitor Survey, Summer, 1973 (July 30–August 3 receive dates) Pro Comments," box 28, 1; "Visitor Survey, Summer, 1973: Con Comments, July 16 thru July 20, 1973," box 28, 22; "Visitor Survey, Summer, 1973, Con survey comments July 30–August 3, 1973," box 28, 3; Visitor Survey, Summer 1977 Received week of Aug. 22," box 57.

30. Visitor Survey, Summer, 1969," box 23, 22; "Visitor Survey, Summer, 1971: Visitor Survey Card Comments (Con) for period July 19 through July 25," box 28, 2; "Visitor Survey, Summer, 1973 (July 30–August 3 receive dates) Pro Comments," box 28, 1.

31. "Visitor Survey, Summer 1977 Received week of Aug. 22," box 57; "Visitor Survey, Summer 1973," box 28, 1.

32. "Visitor Survey, Summer 1977: Week of Aug. 22 Con Comments," box 57, 1; "Visitor Survey, Summer 1971," box 28, 3; "Visitor Survey, Summer 1971," box 28, 3.

33. "Visitor Survey, Summer 1969, Unfavorable Comments," box 34; "Visitor Survey, Summer 1971," box 28, 1; "Visitor Survey, Summer 1977, Con Comments," box 43.

34. "Visitor Survey, Summer 1969, Unfavorable Comments," box 34; "Visitor Survey, Summer, 1973 August 6–10," box 28, 2; "Visitor Survey, Summer 1975, Received August 8–29, Con Comments," box 33, 1. For a discussion of Detroit's economy in the 1970s see Heather Thompson, *Whose Detroit? Politics, Labor, and Race in a Modern American City* (Ithaca: Cornell University Press, 2001).

35. "Visitor Survey, Summer, 1973, July 23–27," box 28, 2; "Visitor Survey, Summer 1975, Constructive Criticisms," box 33.

36. "Visitor Survey, Summer 1971 (Pro) for period of July 19 through July 25," box 28; "Visitor Survey, Summer 1975, Constructive Criticisms," box 33; "Visitor Survey, Summer 1978," box 47.

37. "Visitor Survey, Summer 1975: Comments Received July 26–August 8: Pro Comments," box 33, 1; "Visitor Survey, Summer, 1971: Visitor Survey Card Comments (Con) for the period of July 13 through July 19, 1971," box 28, 1; "Visitor Survey, Summer 1975, Rec. July 25–August 7," box 43; "Visitor Survey, Summer, 1973, July 23–27," box 28, 4.

38. "Visitor Survey, Summer 1972," box 27, 19; "Visitor Survey, Summer 1976, Aug. 2–8: Constructive Criticism," box 38, 1; "Visitor Survey, Summer, 1973, August 13–17," box 23, 3; "Visitor Survey, Summer 1977, Con Comments," box 43.

39. Cohen, *Consumer's Republic*, 309.

6. The New History at an Old Village

1. Larry Lankton, "Something Old, Something New: The Reexhibition of the Henry Ford Museum's Hall of Technology," *Technology and Culture* 21, no. 4 (October 1980): 595, 612.

2. James S. Wamsley, "Harold K. Skramstad, Jr.," box 63, accession no. 235, EIR, 3–4; Harold K. Skramstad, telephone interview by author, February 14, 2013.

3. Eric Foner, introduction to *The New American History*, ed. Foner (Philadelphia: Temple University Press, 1997), ix; Ellen Fitzpatrick, *History's Memory: Writing America's Past, 1880–1980* (Cambridge: Harvard University Press, 2002), 1–12, 51–97.

4. Anders Greenspan, *Creating Colonial Williamsburg* (Washington, D.C.: Smithsonian Institute Press, 2002), 154–55.

5. Ibid., 231.

6. James Davison Hunter, *Culture Wars: The Struggle to Define America* (New York: Basic Books, 1991), 34; Boorstin and Stevens quoted in Bryan Wolfe, "How the West Was Hung, Or, When I Hear the Word 'Culture' I Take Out My Checkbook," *American Quarterly* 44, no. 3 (September 1992), 418–38, quot. on 430. This paragraph and the one that follows appeared in slightly different form in my essay "New Right, New History, Common Ground: Populism and the Past," in *The 1980s: A Critical and Transitional Decade*, ed. Kimberly R. Moffitt and Duncan A. Campbell (Lanham, Md.: Lexington Books, 2011), 162.

7. Quoted in Michael Janofsky, "Mock Auction of Slaves: Education or Outrage," *New York Times*, October 8, 1994.

8. "Tears and Protest at Mock Slave Sale," *New York Times*, October 11, 1994.

9. Janofsky, "Mock Auction of Slaves"; see also Greenspan, *Creating Colonial Williamsburg*, 148.

10. Charles K. Hyde, "'The Automobile in American Life': An Exhibit at Henry Ford Museum, Dearborn, Michigan," *Technology and Culture* 30, no. 1 (January 1989): 105;

Roddy Ray, "Museum, Village Get a $1 Million Challenge," *Detroit Free Press,* December 17, 1984.

11. Skramstad interview.

12. Ibid.; "Curriculum Committee Report, 1981," box 1, accession no. 88, 19–24, and "Organizational Chart: 1980–1985," box 1, accession no. 265, EIR.

13. "Curriculum Committee Report," 64. The following discussion draws on Swigger, "New Right, New History," 170–76.

14. "Curriculum Committee Report," 24.

15. Ibid., 25.

16. Ibid., 24.

17. Ibid., 43, 46–48.

18. Ibid., 52.

19. Ibid., 60–61.

20. Skramstad interview; Wamsley, "Harold K. Skramstad, Jr.," 7.

21. Wamsley, "Harold K. Skramstad, Jr.," 6.

22. "Greenfield Village Map: 1983," box 2, accession no. 21, EIR.

23. Martin Agency, "Henry Ford Museum and Greenfield Village 1983 Marketing and Communications Program," box 79, accession no. 235, EIR, 2–3.

24. Ibid., 15.

25. Ibid., 3.

26. Ray, "Museum, Village Get a $1 Million Challenge."

27. John Guinn, "Greenfield Village Recreates the Era of Tent Chautauquas," *Detroit Free Press,* May 6, 1984.

28. Maryanne George, "Firestone Family Farm Joins Greenfield Village," *Detroit Free Press,* June 30, 1985.

29. Ibid.; John M. Staudenmaier, "The Giant Wakens: Revising Henry Ford's History Book," *Technology and Culture* 29, no. 1 (January 1988): 121.

30. Candace T. Matelic, "Method, Concept, and Professional Exchange," *Journal of Museum Education: Roundtable Reports* 10, no. 3 (Summer 1985): 14; Staudenmaier, "The Giant Wakens," 121–22.

31. Roger Chesley, "Transported House Gives Plantation Life Setting," *Detroit Free Press,* August 12, 1988.

32. Ibid.

33. See "Guide Reference Manuals Records: 1929–1980," accession no. 141, EIR.

34. Staudenmaier, "The Giant Wakens," 118–21.

35. "People," *Jet Magazine,* February 17, 1992, 20; Skramstad interview.

36. G. Donald Adams, "Using Research to Guide the Development and Marketing of an African-American Exhibit," *Visitor Studies: Theory, Research, and Practice* 5, no. 1 (1993): 136–42, quot. on 137.

37. Skramstad interview.

38. "People," 20; Adams, "Using Research to Guide Development," 139.

39. All quotations and summaries in this and the following two paragraphs are from Adams, "Using Research to Guide Development," 140–41.

40. Sabrina Walters, "Exhibits at Greenfield Village Focus on 19th-Century Blacks," *Detroit Free Press,* August 9, 1991. For corrections to this article see "Getting It Straight," *Detroit Free Press,* August 10, 1991.

41. "Evaluating the Interpretive Program Presented at Hermitage Slave Houses and

Mattox House: Comments from Members of the Transition Team," accession no. 186, EIR, 6–7, 37, 45, 55.

42. Ibid.; Walters, "Exhibits at Greenfield Village." See also "Edward J. Cutler Interviews 1955–1956," accession no. 167, EIR. Cutler recounts that the Mattox house needed extensive rehabilitation because it was so unstable upon arrival.

43. "Mattox House On-Site Manual," BFRC, 15.

44. "Evaluating the Interpretive Program," 7.

45. Quoted ibid., 7.

46. "Mattox House On-Site Manual," 15.

47. Robert Musial, "Greenfield Village's Renovated Store Brings Past to Life," *Detroit Free Press,* April 21, 1994.

48. Ibid.

49. "Evaluating the Interpretive Program," 1–2.

50. Ibid., 107–19, quot. in appendix C.

51. Ibid., 125–27.

52. Ibid., 134.

53. Isabel Wilkerson, "After Four Terms, Us versus Them Still Plays in Detroit," *New York Times,* September 17, 1984; Bill McAllister, "Detroit's 'Hostile Suburbs,'" *Washington Post,* December 4, 1986.

54. "Blacks Renew a Boycott in Suburb of Detroit," *New York Times,* December 25, 1985; James Barron, "Parks New Racial Issue in Dearborn," *New York Times,* January 19, 1986; Adams, "Using Research to Guide Development," 137.

55. Skramstad interview.

56. Wylie Gerdes, "Dearborn Parks Talks in Works," *Detroit Free Press,* January 8, 1986; Skramstad interview.

57. Wylie Gerdes, "Dearborn Ends Parks Ban Talks," *Detroit Free Press,* February, 26 1986.

58. Judy Diebolt, "Dearborn Attorney Calls Past Irrelevant to Trial on Parks," *Detroit Free Press,* June 24, 1986.

59. Brenda J. Gilchrist, "Judge Voids Non-Resident Ordinance," *Detroit Free Press,* September 30, 1986.

60. "Friendship Concert Folder," box 17, accession no. 254, EIR.

61. Ibid.; Skramstad interview.

62. Wylie Gerdes, "Dearborn Trying to Accentuate the Positive," *Detroit Free Press,* November 27, 1986.

63. See Dennis Niemiec, "Dearborn Image of Controversy," *Detroit Free Press,* April, 4 1989.

64. Reynolds Farley, Sheldon Danziger, and Harry J. Holzer, *Detroit Divided* (New York: Russell Sage Foundation, 2000), 136.

65. Kathleen Moore, "The Motown Sound: The Music and the Story," *Curator* 38, no. 4 (December 1995): 275–80.

66. Skramstad interview.

67. Quoted in Beth Krodel, "People's Choice: Blacks and Arabs Have Called Him a Racist, but Dearborn's Mayor Remains a Political Juggernaut," *Detroit Free Press,* March 31, 1997.

7. From History Museum to History Attraction

1. Quoted in Jim Finkelstein, "New Brass at Ford Museum," *Detroit News,* June 28, 1996; Harold Skramstad, "An Agenda for Museums in the Twenty-first Century," in *Reinvent-*

ing the Museum: Historical and Contemporary Perspectives on the Paradigm Shift, ed. Gail Anderson (Lanham, Md.: AltaMira Press, 2004), 118–32, quot. on 131–32. Originally published as "An Agenda for American Museums in the Twenty-first Century," *Daedalus* no. 128 (Summer 1999): 109–28.

2. Steven Hamp, telephone interview by author, March 16, 2013.

3. Ibid.; Joy Hakansan Colby, "Steven K. Hamp: He Preserves the Past with a Vision for the Future," *Detroit Free Press,* April 23, 2000.

4. Robert Ankeny, "Ford Backs High-Tech High School," *Automotive News,* April 22, 1996; Hamp interview.

5. David Lyman, "Improvements Will Make Henry Ford Museum a Cooler Place to Visit," *Detroit Free Press,* April 15, 1998.

6. All quotations in this and the next paragraph are from David Lyman, "Museum Modernizing the Past," *Detroit Free Press,* November 15, 1999.

7. Sylvia Rector, "Cuisine Is a Nod to the Past," *Detroit Free Press,* February 9, 2000; Desiree Cooper, "Group Keeps Black Troops' History Alive," *Detroit Free Press,* July 31, 2003; "The Henry Ford 2000 Annual Report," box 38, accession no. 241, EIR; "Detroit 300: Partner Programs Application," box 50, accession no. 241, EIR.

8. James Pasternak, "A Bus Ride to Civil Rights' Ground Zero," *National Post* (Toronto), March 1, 2002. The original lot description from the MastroNet auction, which includes a detailed account of bus's later history and the authentication process, is available at www. legendaryauctions.com/LotDetail.aspx?inventoryid=16379.

9. Francis X. Donnelly and Oralandar Brand-Williams, "Rosa Parks Shares Day with Symbol of Movement," *Detroit News,* February, 2, 2003.

10. "Remarks of Senator Carl Levin at the Rosa Parks Memorial Service in Detroit, Michigan," November 2, 2005, www.levin.senate.gov/newsroom; "From Our Readers: Senator Levin Wrong about Dearborn, Hubbard," *Detroit Free Press,* November 11, 2005.

11. Frank Provenzano, "Greenfield Village to Shut for Major Changes," *Detroit Free Press,* June 14, 2002; Frank Provenzano, "Greenfield Village Jobs Cut—Restructuring Is Response to Decline in Attendance," *Detroit Free Press,* January 9, 2002. In 2001 the village reported an attendance figure of approximately 1.36 million, a 17 percent decrease from the previous year.

12. Hamp interview; Frank Provenzano, "The Future of History," *Detroit Free Press,* June 8, 2003.

13. Provenzano, "The Future of History."

14. Hamp interview.

15. Provenzano, "The Future of History."

16. Frank Provenzano, "New Name to Retool Image of Detroit-Area Ford Museum, Village," *Detroit Free Press,* January 28, 2003.

17. Hamp interview.

18. Chris Vander Doelen, "Ford Tour Is Detroit's Hottest Ticket," *Prince George (B.C.) Citizen,* May 6, 2004; Frank Provenzano, "Rouge Tour Opens to Sellout Crowd," *Detroit Free Press,* May 3, 2004. As of 2103 the tours are still being offered in substantially the same form.

19. Provenzano, "Rouge Tour Opens to Sellout Crowd."

20. Provenzano, "The Future of History."

21. Rick Hampson, "Seeking Tourists, States Try to Recast Their Image," *USA Today,* August 9, 2010.

22. Gary Heinlein, "Native Son Romney Targets 'Values Vote,'" *Detroit News,* February 14, 2007.

23. Josh Katzenstein, "Symbol of Freedom on Display in Michigan," *Detroit News,* June 21, 2011.

24. Guy Adams, "Obama Travels Back in Time on the Bus Where Rosa Parks Made History," *The Independent* (London), April 20, 2012.

25. Beth Krodel, "People's Choice: Blacks and Arabs Have Called Him a Racist, but Dearborn's Mayor Remains a Political Juggernaut," *Detroit Free Press,* March 31, 1997.

26. U.S. Census Bureau, "The Arab Population: 2000," 8, www.census.gov; Niraj Warikoo, "Sept. 11 May Have Left an Imprint on Mayoral Contest in Dearborn—Some See Ethnicity as Factor in Race," *Detroit Free Press,* October 31, 2001; Niraj Warikoo, "Guido Is Re-Elected Mayor—His Arab American Rival Drew National Media's Attention," *Detroit Free Press,* November 7, 2001.

27. Anan Ameri, telephone interview by author, May 7, 2013.

28. Ibid.; see also "New Detroit Cultural Forum: ACCESS / Henry Ford Museum and Greenfield Village Collaboration," box 35, accession no. 241, EIR; "Ethnic Detroit in the 21st Century: Who We Are and Where We're Going," box 41, accession no. 241, EIR.

29. David Shepardson, "Arab-American Museum Lands $2 Million Ford Gift," *Detroit News,* February 13, 2002; Karen Bouffard, "Arab-Americans Build National Museum," *Detroit News,* September 25, 2003; Edward Rothstein, "A Mosaic of Arab Culture at Home in America," *New York Times,* October 24, 2005; Raymond Silverman, "Arab American National Museum," *Journal of American History* 93, no. 3 (December 2006): 821–25.

30. Ameri interview; Fay Saad, e-mail to author, May 7, 2013; "National Advisory Board," Arab American Museum, www.arabamericanmuseum.org.

31. Katherine Q. Seelye, "Detroit Is Being Drained of Its Population and Hope," *International Herald Tribune,* March 24, 2011; Harold K. Skramstad, telephone interview by author, February 14, 2013; Hamp interview.

32. Kurt Badenhausen, "Detroit Tops 2013 List of America's Most Miserable Cities," February 21, 2013, www.forbes.com.

33. Thalia Mavros's short documentary *Detroit Lives* (Palladium Boots, 2010) shows the frustration many residents feel about unbalanced media coverage of the city. The film's interviews suggest that residents who are critical of the media's focus on Detroit's problems might also react unfavorably to historical representations that emphasize the city's economic troubles or its history of racial tension. The film is available online at www .palladiumboots.com.

Index

JESSIE SWIGGER earned a PhD in American studies from the University of Texas at Austin. She is currently an assistant professor at Western Carolina University, where she teaches courses in public history and urban history.